Assessing Information Security

Strategies, tactics, logic and framework

Assessing Information Security

Strategies, tactics, logic and framework

A VLADIMIROV
K GAVRILENKO
A MICHAJLOWSKI

IT Governance Publishing

IT Governance Publishing
IT Governance Limited
Unit 3, Clive Court
Bartholomew's Walk
Cambridgeshire Business Park
Ely
Cambridgeshire
CB7 4EH
United Kingdom

www.itgovernance.co.uk

First published in the United Kingdom in 2010
by IT Governance Publishing.

ISBN 978-1-84928-035-8

'He who is willing and able to take the initiative to exploit variety, rapidity, and harmony – as the basis to create as well as adapt to the more indistinct – more irregular – quicker changes of rhythm and pattern, yet shape the focus and direction of effort – survives and dominates.'

Colonel John Boyd

PREFACE

Assessing Information Security is a book about the philosophy, strategy and tactics of soliciting, managing and conducting information security audits of all flavours. It is often controversial and is written to be so. When we throw criticism at others, we expect to be criticised ourselves. It contains a lot of what you can rightfully label as 'common sense'. However, this 'common sense' is frequently ignored or overlooked, leading to disastrous consequences. Thus, it must be reiterated and reinforced, sometimes from an unexpected angle or viewpoint. On the other hand, there is hope that some of the statements and issues presented in this book, will at least be challenging and thought-provoking. When compiling various references and assembling the content, the general feeling was 'How did we miss it before?' or 'How could anyone fail to mention or formulate that?'. Such impressions can be contagious.

We don't aim to provide an A to Z, step-by-step guide, on how to perform information security assessments. It would contradict the whole spirit of this work and fail the test of time. This is not a technical manual, compliance guideline, or security policies and procedures checklist. If you are looking for one, you should search elsewhere, preferably online or in the specialised periodic press. Nowadays, the tempo is exceedingly fast. For instance, if someone wants to write a tome on hands-on hacking and counter-hacking (as we did in the past with *Wi-Foo* and *Hacking Exposed Cisco Networks*), the chances are that when the book hits the shelves, many issues, methods and techniques it describes, will already be obsolete. Today we tend to view such approach as arguably counterproductive. What we are trying to accomplish instead, is to provide a fluid framework for developing an astute 'information security mind', capable of rapid adaptation to evolving technologies, markets, regulations, laws, etc. To do so, we appeal to our observations and experience as an information security auditing team and the infinitely larger volume of applicable wisdom produced and accumulated by others. There is a fable about the evolution of a musician who said 'Me' at the age of 20, 'Me and Mozart' when turning 30, 'Mozart and Me' when approaching their 40s and, eventually, 'Mozart' at 50.[1] It appears that we have reached the 'Mozart and Me' stage and will inevitably proceed to the final conclusion of this cycle. The reflections of relevant great minds of past and present clearly point at the necessity of a synthetic interdisciplinary approach. Transcending the boundaries of the specialised IT security auditing field becomes inevitable. A solid understanding of the overall information security paradigms is called for. Therefore, we sincerely hope that this book might become an entertaining read for all information security adepts, whether coming from a corporate, managerial, governmental, technical or academic background.

[1] Apparently, it is based on a real historical quote attributed to Gounod: '*When I was very young, I used to say 'I'; later on, I said 'I and Mozart'; then 'Mozart and I'. Now I say 'Mozart'*.

ABOUT THE AUTHORS

Dr. Andrew A. Vladimirov, CCNP, CCDP, CISSP, CWNA, TIA Linux+, is a security researcher with a wide scope of expertise, ranging from network security and applied cryptography, to the relevant aspects of bioinformatics and neural networking. He published his first scientific paper at the age of 13 and is one of the co-founders of Arhont Ltd, one of the leading information security consultancies in the UK. Andrew has an extensive background in performing information security assessments, ranging from external and internal penetration tests, to configuration, security policies, processes and procedures reviews. He has also participated in creating and implementing ISMS and secure architecture designs for large companies, assisted corporations with meeting ISO27001, FSA Annex 2 and other compliance demands, and took part in numerous forensic investigations. Andrew has published a variety of security advisories and papers, authored a chapter on wireless security in *Network Security: The Complete Reference,* McGraw-Hill/Osborne, and is a co-author of *Wi-Foo: The Secrets of Wireless Hacking*, Addison Wesley (2004) and *Hacking Exposed: Cisco Networks,* McGraw-Hill/Osborne (2006). On the basis of these publications and his relevant practical experience, he has composed and read tailored public and private training courses on the subjects of internal security audits, information security strategies, and wireless offence and defence. Andrew is supportive of both open source and full disclosure movements. He is a graduate of King's College London and the University of Bristol.

About the Authors

Konstantin V. Gavrilenko (London, UK) has more than 15 years' experience in IT and security, and together with his co-authors, is a co-founder of Arhont Ltd. Konstantin's writing draws primarily from his real-world knowledge and experience in security consultancy and infrastructure hardening, for a vast range of clients. He is open-minded and enthusiastic about research, where his main areas of interest lie in information security in general and, more specifically, in networking and wireless. He is proud to say that he is an active supporter of open source solutions and ideology, public disclosure included. Konstantin has published a variety of advisories uncovering new software vulnerabilities, alongside essays on assessment types and methodologies, articles on other information security-related topics, and is a co-author of the bestselling *Wi-Foo: The Secrets of Wireless Hacking*, Addison Wesley (2004) and *Hacking Exposed: Cisco Networks*, McGraw-Hill/Osborne (2006). He holds a first class BSc Honours degree in Management Science from DeMontfort University and an MSc in Management from Lancaster University.

Andriej A. Michajlowski (London, UK) first became enticed by UNIX flavours back in high school times. He cultivated and expanded his knowledge into the networking aspects of information technology, while obtaining his bachelor's degree from the University of Kent at Canterbury. Soon he was engrossed in network security and penetration testing of various wireless and wired devices and systems. On accomplishing his MBA, he co-founded information security company, Arhont Ltd, participated in security research, published articles and advisories, and greatly contributed to the overall success of the Arhont team. Andriej's technical particularities include user and device authentication mechanisms, database and directory services, wireless networking and application security, and systems integration. He has participated in compliance consulting at many financial and legal sector organisations, and has extensive experience in performing internal and external information security assessments. Andriej has also co-authored *Wi-Foo: The Secrets of Wireless Hacking*, Addison Wesley (2004) and *Hacking Exposed: Cisco Networks*, McGraw-Hill/Osborne (2006).

CONTENTS

INTRODUCTION

'We can't just look at our own personal experiences or use the same mental recipes over and over again; we've got to look at other disciplines and activities and relate or connect them to what we know from our experiences and the strategic world we live in. If we can do this we will be able to surface new repertoires and (hopefully) develop a Fingerspitzengefühl[2] *for folding our adversaries back inside themselves, morally-mentally-physically – so that they can neither appreciate nor cope with what's happening – without suffering the same fate ourselves.'*

Colonel John Boyd

A thorough treatise dedicated to various aspects of information security auditing must cover why and what kind of assessments have to be performed, subject to a particular situation. It is expected to elaborate by whom, when, how, and in which specific sequence, they should be executed. It ought to address how to present the audit results in the most palatable manner and which corrective actions these findings might trigger. However, all we have just listed are mere technicalities. If you concentrate on them too much, without applying a sufficient level of abstraction, you are risking missing something of a much greater importance: their logical, and even philosophical, backbone.

---

[2] This German term literally means 'fingertip feeling', and is synonymous with the English expression of 'keeping your finger on the pulse', while emphasising intuition.

You will fall into a trap of adhering to rigid 'if-then-else' mechanical instructions. These can easily become outdated and flawed, even by a subtle change in the operating environment. A smart opponent can outwit them by utilising non-conventional ways. Until the new appropriate schemes are generated, usually by someone else and late, you are lost.

In contrast, if you have a firm holistic grasp of the whole picture and understand what we may rightfully call 'the philosophy of information security', you can easily adjust to any change 'on the fly'. Even more, you can shape the change yourself, and become its primary engine and source. This means that you will be able to dictate the rules of the game, and it is others that would have to adapt. Or, to put it plainly, 'submit'. The 'bird's eye view' idiom is misleading: an eagle hovering high in the clouds can spot a tiny mouse lurking in thick grass and nosedive in no time. This is a good analogy of what we have alluded to as a 'sufficient level of abstraction', coupled with a rapid and precise act.

Unfortunately, when we scoured for what others have said about 'the philosophy of information security' and its implications towards security assessments in specialised texts, we got strongly disenchanted. We stumbled across multiple security management sources presenting solely managerial, technical displaying purely technological, and legal offering exclusively legal perspectives. The existing information security standards are presented as an infallible verity that contains everything a security specialist might need. There are multiple occasions of transient, specific or narrowly technical statements passed as grand philosophical truths. Tactical discourses are presented as strategic paradigms. Endless arguments about information security being a process, approach, system, a state of mind or even a lifestyle are rampant. Generalisations like 'be paranoid' or 'everything is vulnerable' are omnipresent. We are not implying that these are somehow incorrect. They have their time, place, value and significance. However, they do not form a coherent integral framework that can be easily adapted to a variety of relevant situations, in both theory and practice.

We have also turned to other disciplines for guidance. For instance, we have looked at modern mathematical chaos and game theories. Both are fine examples of applicable 'coherent integral frameworks' that offer useful insights. However, it was the philosophy of war and its core principles that truly hit the 'nail on the head'. This is hardly surprising. When writing *Wi-Foo*, we employed numerous quotes from ancient Chinese military masterminds, as epigraphs for the majority of chapters. Being highly reusable and appropriate, some of these epigraphs are repeated in this book. At that time, we found a high suitability of statements written more than 2,000 years ago, to what is still considered a cutting edge technology of today, at the very least amusing. They also provided a needed symbolic martial arts link. In this work, the assertions, opinions, estimations and judgements of master strategists of all times are not just some fancy spice up citations and epigraphs, they form its *fluid backbone*. They are the 'Mozart' part of 'Mozart and I'.

Apart from the noted completeness, coherence, all-around applicability, systematic nature and apt abstraction, we are fond of taking advantage of the philosophy of war, for the following reasons:

- Focus on conflict and its polarity.

- Realism and utilitarianism.
- Simplicity and clarity of statements.
- Clear distinction between strategy and tactics.
- Taking into account a wide selection of variables.
- Reusable terminology.
- Multidisciplinary approach.

As a matter of fact, the contextual replacement of 'war' or its synonyms by 'information security' or 'information security assessment', in many excerpts of military classics, naturally produces shrewd observations. Practise this technique on the infamous '*Everything is very simple in war, but the simplest thing is difficult*' saying, of Carl von Clausewitz and see where it might lead your thoughts. Then, perform this simple exercise every time you encounter a martial classic citation in this book.

Of course, applying philosophy and the strategy of war to other disciplines is not news. In particular, this was extensively (and, perhaps, excessively) done in business management. We have encountered a linguistic opinion stating that 'Sūn Zǐ Bīng Fǎ', traditionally translated as 'Sun Tzu Art of War', actually means 'Sun Tzu Competitive Strategies'. The Boston Consulting Group *Clausewitz on Strategy* book affirms: '*As perplexing as this may appear at first for a work on warfare, Clausewitz speaks loudly and clearly to the modern business executive who is inclined to listen. He does not, of course, speak the language of today's audience. He does better: He speaks the executive's mind*'. This is one of the reasons why we make a sustained heavy use of his thoughts throughout this work. Note, that Clausewitz himself did compare business and military conflict: '*It would be better, instead of comparing it with any art, to liken it to business, which is also a conflict of human interests and activities; and it is still more like state policy, which again, on its part, may be looked upon as a kind of business on a great scale*'.

Nonetheless, this approach has met with sharp and objective criticism. The spearhead of critics is that business, after all, is not war. It is more akin to politics and diplomacy. A company is not an army detachment. Its chief executive officer is not a general. But perhaps the mightiest blow comes from the modern game theory. From its point of view, the majority of situations in business and commerce can be described as 'non-zero-sum games'. That is, they are co-operative. They involve complex relationships between different sides, with net gain or loss. There is a mutual benefit, even from some forms of intercourse with direct competitors, and we are not at other information security companies' throats. We have met their professionals during various industry conferences and informal gatherings and have exchanged ideas and shared research. We have also had many beers together! This is good for the industry, thus it eventually benefits us all.

However, consider the following suppositions:

- *Information security is a form of warfare.*
- *In essence, it has plentiful similarities with counter-intelligence and counter-insurgency efforts.*

The latter is one of the cornerstone ideas actively elucidated in this book. Note, that more than a decade ago, RAND researchers, John Arquilla and David Ronfeldt, coined a term 'netwar', to distinguish 'an emergent form of low intensity conflict, crime, and activism' waged, employing 'decentralised and flexible network structures'. They also proposed the somewhat ill-fated term 'cyberwar', which is constantly abused and misunderstood by the media and general public.

Returning to the game theory:

- *Applied information security is a zero-sum or strictly competitive game.*

Co-operating with a cybercriminal does not make any more sense than collaborating with a burglar who broke into your house. One can, and should learn a lot from security incidents, but this is not co-operation. Collaboration with criminals is a crime *per se*. Co-operation with the enemy is treason. According to Clausewitz, '*the principle of polarity is only valid when it can be conceived in one and the same thing, where the positive and its opposite the negative, completely destroy each other. In a battle both sides strive to conquer; that is true polarity, for the victory of the one side destroys that of the other*'. Thus, we conclude that the philosophy and strategy of war is fully applicable to the field of information security in theory and practice.

Where does this bring us? Let's formulate some basic founding principles.

- *Information security is the science and art of protecting data.*

It is not merely a system, process, approach, service, and set of methods, mindset and so forth. It is much more. We will discuss the perceived 'science versus art' dichotomy at the end of the very last chapter of this book.

- *IT security is the science and art of protecting data in electronic format.*

IT security is a sub-discipline of general information security. Protecting data in electronic format inevitably includes defending all systems, media and communication channels that carry it. It will also affect all people that have, or can potentially have, access to this data and resources.

- *Information security assessments are a practical way of improving the information security state.*

They can and should be more than only evaluating the risks, or verifying compliance to security policies, or finding and consequently eliminating tangible security gaps. This is the main subject of our study.

Further interesting clarifications can be gathered from the so-called teleology of conflict. Anatol Rapoport was a renowned mathematician with major contributions to game theory and cybernetics. In his foreword to a (much criticised) Penguin edition of Carl von Clausewitz's opus magnum *On War*, Prof. Rapoport has suggested three main teleological concepts of warfare:

- *Eschatological*
- *Political*
- *Cataclysmic.*

In Rapoport's own words, '*metaphorically, in political philosophy war is compared to a game of strategy (like chess); in eschatological philosophy, to a mission or the dénouement of a drama; in cataclysmic philosophy, to a fire or an epidemic*'.

From the information security specialist's standpoint, we find the eschatological approach as nearly irrelevant. It has played a grand role in the history of mankind, primarily due to its immense propaganda value and power. Examples of classical 'eschatological conflicts' include crusades, jihads, Communist 'final worldwide revolution', Nazi 'domination of the master race' and American 'Manifest Destiny'. The instances which are more close to this particular discourse are the so-called 'war on drugs', 'war on guns' or 'war on knife crime', sometimes declared by law enforcement bodies. Being realists, we understand that in the foreseeable future there will be junkies, dealers, shootings and stabbings, unless some unthinkable miracle happens. In a similar manner, you may announce and promote the epic 'war on cybercrime', 'war on SPAM', or 'war on Web applications insecurities'. It may motivate some people to do something about these issues, but that is the best you can hope to achieve by such an act.

The political concept of warfare is the one we find to be the most pragmatic, fruitful and efficient. In relation to applied information security, it is advocated throughout this entire work. As such, it can be rightfully dubbed as 'Neo-Clausewitzian'. This is particularly evident in Chapter 2 of this book, dedicated to directing and shaping effects that policies, governance and compliance have on information security assessments. Note, that the political approach is always heavily at play when security budget considerations are discussed.

Unfortunately, many security professionals consciously or instinctively adhere to what can amount to a cataclysmic concept of information security. This outlook seems to be common among both management and 'techs'. It is reflected in viewing security as a mere part of business continuity, disaster recovery and prevention, or even service availability. It is often expressed by the defeatist 'c'est la vie statements', such as 'everything can and would be hacked anyway' or 'we can do our best, but sensitive data will still leak out'. It appeals on the grounds of realism, along the line that 'the pessimist is a well-informed optimist'. *However, we scorn this way of thinking as fundamentally, strategically flawed.*

The cataclysmic approach to information security reduces initiative, decreases morale, and promotes a passive defensive response, if not paralysis of action. By succumbing to it, one may even start accepting security incidents as something close to a divine wrath that can only be (partially) softened by countermeasures and insured against. *Experienced security auditors should be able to determine whether the cataclysmic doctrine dominates the company's or organisation's information security paradigm, and deliver appropriate warnings and explanations.*

Comparing a natural disaster or unfortunate accident to a premeditated malice is senseless. Even if the end effects are the same, both preventive and reactive responses will have to differ. Assessing the related risks and predicting their impact will be distinct. To summarise:

- *There are passive and active security incidents.*

Accidentally losing a memory stick or portable computer with sensitive data is a common instance of the former. Deliberate unauthorised access is an example of the latter. This can be compared to non-combat and combat-related losses in the military.

- *Passive security incidents happen due to error.*
- *Active security incidents happen due to the combination of error and a hostile act.*

Nearly all successful attacks involve some mistake on the defender's side. Infectious disease happens when virulence of the microbe and lack of immunity of the infected host are superimposed.

- *Passive security incidents can pave a way for their active counterparts.*

An accidental access control flaw or sensitive information leak are likely to be deliberately abused later. It is better to be prepared for the worst.

- *Security assessments must evaluate probabilities and the potential impacts of passive and active security incidents.*

While different in nature, both present significant risks that should be reduced. Besides, see the previous point.

- *To assess the likelihood of passive security incidents it is usually sufficient to analyse controls, their implementations and enforcement.*

In the example of accidental loss of data on a portable carrier, it is generally enough to verify that:

1 Correct security policies that prohibit the use of portable storage media in the company or organisation are present.
2 All users are aware of them and have agreed in a written form.
3 The policies are reinforced by appropriate technical means, such as specialised software blocking use of all USB ports.
4 The enforcing software is present on all corporate systems that contain, or may contain, sensitive data. It is correctly installed, configured, maintained and documented.

Alternatively, the prohibition of use can be substituted by employing strong cryptography.

However,

- *To assess the probability and impact of active security incidents, a more aggressive and all-encompassing path must be taken.*

In the specific example above, we will have to add the fifth point: verify that the USB port blocking software cannot be circumvented. If this is possible, than it becomes necessary to discover how much effort and skill such a hack would require from a potential attacker. And then the sixth point – check whether other mobile storage media that does not rely on USB ports can be, and is used, to carry information. If encryption is employed, strength of ciphers, keys and its actual implementation must be analysed. Again, how much skill, effort and time the attacker has to expend to break it, needs to be estimated. In a nutshell, all these additional security auditing means are a form of penetration testing which is always active and intrusive intervention.

Thus, we have finally arrived at a crucial statement of unequalled, unsurpassed gravity:

- *Prevention and mitigation of any hostile information security act always involves the clash of human wills.*

Which is, essentially, a specially adapted version of:

- '*All war supposes human weakness, and against that it is directed*' (Clausewitz).

While this is common sense ('guns don't kill people, people kill people'), in information security it is strongly obscured and obfuscated by technology, bureaucracy and lack of abstraction. Even when you are dealing with a 'purely technical' threat, such as viruses and worms, you are not battling an inanimate piece of code. It is nothing else than yours and your allies will, against the will of malicious software creators and deliberate users. If you are a technical specialist, just add skill to will. If you are an IT manager or a CISO, that skill is managing or directing the technical team. For some, this may sound unsettling. Still, disgruntled employees, cybercriminals, vandals, industrial spies or political activists are all flesh and bone. Unless your name is John Connor and the year is 2027, you are not engaged in some chimeric stand-off against swarms of hostile machines.

There are information security consultants that would assume a discussion of 'social engineering' any time 'the human factor' is mentioned. The implications we are looking at in this book are of a much broader scope. In this context, social engineering is one of the highly important technicalities. If Clausewitz meant anything like it when he wrote about war being aimed at human weakness, he would have written about the penetration of enemy ranks by spies. It was the closest equivalent of social engineering at his times. What the master strategist did have in mind is that:

- '*The activity in war is never directed solely against matter, it is always at the same time directed against the intelligent force which gives life to this matter, and to separate the two from each other is impossible.*'
- '*If we desire to defeat the enemy, we must proportion our efforts to his powers of resistance. This is expressed by the product of two factors which cannot be separated, namely, the sum of available means, and the strength of the will.*'

Note, that the energy in the excerpt is directed at 'matter' and 'intelligent force' 'at the same time', as they are fully indivisible. The significance of the 'material side' (resources, documentation, technology) is by no means denigrated. Instead, the balance between 'human' and 'material' factors is underlined. *In the event of any security incident, both will be simultaneously affected as they are inseparable. Therefore, both have to be synchronously audited, analysed, measured and protected so that all available means of defence are employed, yet you do not overreact.*

You may still ask 'what the 19th Century military strategist could know about the role and contributive proportions of such things in modern times?'. Collate his words with the following extract from the current US MCDP (Marine Corps Doctrinal Publication) 1 *Warfighting*: '*No degree of technological development or scientific calculation will diminish the human dimension in war. Any doctrine which attempts to reduce warfare to ratios of forces, weapons, and equipment neglects the impact of the human will on the conduct of war and is therefore inherently flawed*'.

Based on multiple observations, we have developed our own little model of the 'clash of wills' in typical information security conflicts. We call it 'the FUD game'. FUD is a common abbreviation standing for Fear, Uncertainty and Doubt. FUD undermines will.

The rules of the 'FUD game' are simple: the attackers are trying to maximise FUD of defenders while diminishing their own and vice versa. The first to increase the opponent's FUD above the breakpoint of their will, gains the upper hand. A typical 'defender FUD' can be described as:

- *Fear* of being successfully compromised and held personally responsible for negligence and blunder.

- *Uncertainty* regarding how, where, and when the effective blow will occur.
- *Doubt* in one's abilities to prevent the breach.

A typical 'attacker FUD' encompasses:

- *Fear* of being discovered, caught and persecuted.
- *Uncertainty* regarding defender knowledge, skill and means.
- *Doubt* in one's ability to disengage without leaving a give-away trace.

The situation is asymmetric. In the real world, the Uncertainty element tends to favour the attacking side. Fear, though, often reinforces competent defenders: in the case of defeat the (legal) repercussions for attackers are far more severe. The defending side has another important advantage: there is no actual draw. Repelling the opponents and simply avoiding the breach counts as the defender's victory. *The key factors for winning the FUD game appear to be resolve, initiative, good observation and orientation, foresight, cunning and swiftness. Chance also plays its role. Other factors are subordinate, providing that neither side has enormous superiority in technological prowess.*

With this observation we shall complete this hopefully provocative preamble that sets logical and philosophic grounds for the principal work.

CHAPTER 1: INFORMATION SECURITY AUDITING AND STRATEGY

'We should base our decisions on awareness rather than on mechanical habit. That is, we act on a keen appreciation for the essential factors that make each situation unique instead of from conditioned response.'

MCDP 1 *Warfighting*

Rephrasing Clausewitz, to produce a workable scheme for information security assessments, is one of the tasks that are inherently simple, yet the simplest thing is difficult to implement. It is simple because the underlining logic is clear. It can be formulated in a minute. Here it comes from the (independent) auditor's viewpoint:

- Find out about goals and conditions of the assessment.
- Plan the appropriate actions.
- Select the corresponding methodologies and tools.
- Check and test everything you can within the limits of budget, requirements, time and means.
- Pull the results together.
- Measure and analyse risks.
- Consider realistic remedies.
- Generate an impressive report.
- Work with the client on any follow-up acts if needed.

A mirror version of this scheme, as seen from the auditee perspective, is also easy to generate. It will have to be more strategic in nature. The auditor receives goals and directions, but it is the management of the auditee that formulates and sets them. It must also select suitable auditors for the task and a qualified manager to oversee the process. At the end of the day, for the auditors, the assessment is often a separate assignment within a limited time span. For the auditee, it is an element of some larger long-term security programme. Or, at least, it should be.

Wing Tsun is an effective and increasingly popular Chinese martial art. Bruce Lee has derived his Jeet Kune Do from it. There are only eight principles in Wing Tsun. Some even reduce them to four: forward pressure, sticking to the opponent, using the opponent's strength, and centreline control. Reading and comprehending these fundamentals 1,000 times will not make you a formidable fighter. That would require many years of intense practice. Still, there is no guarantee that you will win every single fight. Even in cases where the governing principles do not have to be built into resisting and inert (physical, organisational, corporate) body by dedicated sustained effort, things are not straightforward. For example, knowing the major winning strategies would not instantly make you a chess grandmaster and chess is but an ancient board game with immutable rules.

Unlike chess, in the field of modern information security, there are no defined winning strategies which are accepted by everyone. This leads to two extremes. One is reducing everything to specialised schematics, detailed local standards, checklists and guidelines, and ad-hoc 'technical' countermeasures and safeguards. Correspondingly, the auditors would be asked to test and analyse them. This reduces information security and its assessments to nothing more than craft. The other extreme is exactly the opposite. Personal experience, judgement and professional intuition are proclaimed as infinitely superior to all other ways, usually viewed as too conservative and formal. Detailed planning is often disregarded. This attitude is common amongst many security auditors. However, even fine arts have certain rules, and chaotic systems are mathematically deterministic while looking random at the first sight.

We do not believe that a healthy balance between these extremes cannot be reached. Neither do we think that there are no general strategies, principles and philosophies that can increase the effectiveness of information security audits and streamline them, while preserving necessary adaptability, diversity, creativity and initiative. After all, military science has researched and employed such fundamentals for centuries. Is sustaining and assessing the information security of a company or organisation of any size, more complex than waging a modern interstate combat? Some theoretical groundwork for a potentially productive approach to this issue was already laid in the introduction, and a few broad principles were formulated. But prior to proceeding further with this ambitious exercise, we need to address that annoying 'why' question.

To do or not to do?

'Military action is inauspicious – it is only considered important because it is a matter of life and death, and there is the possibility that it may be taken up lightly.'

Li Quan.

There are many sound theoretical and logical reasons why information security assessments must be performed which come from both managerial and technical perspectives. The majority of them can be summarised as 'if things are not regularly verified, analysed and improved by specialists they would go wrong and eventually collapse'. More often than not, in the real world these reasons are simply ignored.

Companies or organisations that do subscribe for professional security auditing usually do it because:

1 Compliance and regulations demand it.

Today the PCI Security Standards Council seems to be the most successful at that. FISMA and HIPAA in the US and FSA in the UK definitely deserve some credit.

2 A security incident has happened.

One that's been caned is worth two that haven't, for sure. At least some of the security audits we have performed in the past were follow-ups to computer forensics.

3 There is someone with high security awareness and understanding amid the executives who lobbies it through.

This usually applies to specialised hi-tech companies or government agencies.

4 The company or organisation is a lucrative target for cybercriminals or malcontents and knows it.

This is commonly complemented by points 1 and 2. Aspiring to 3 is warmly recommended.

5 There is an internal security auditing team in the company anyway.

They should be kept busy to justify their salaries.

Other, less common causes can drive such a decision too. For example, we ran (internal) IT security assessments for companies where the IT management head had just changed. The new IT director wanted to 'clean the house', get a better grasp of what is going on and, no doubt, show the bosses that his predecessor was incompetent. We have also performed independent security reviews of novel pre-production appliances and software for their vendors.

The mindsets of ignorance

Overall, it is more educating and informative to analyse the reasons explaining why companies and organisations do not perform any information security assessments. If they have a turnover of six digits or more, we can safely bet that these reasons are within the manager's skulls no matter what they might say about the budget. There are three most common 'mindsets of ignorance':

1 The 'it will never happen to us' mindset.

We will not tell hair-raising stories about wile cybercriminals and sly insiders in return. This is constantly done by today's media – just visit any major news site. With his metaphor of knights and dragons, Ira Winkler has already examined the security media hype very well – consult his *Zen and the Art of Information Security* book if interested. What we will note, nonetheless, is that 'it' always befalls those to whom 'it will never happen to' because they are not prepared. Consider it to be our modest contribution to Murphy's laws. By the way, 'but it has never happened to us and we are in business for many years' should be translated as 'we don't have an effective monitoring system set up and maintained, and audit trails are not our strongest point'.

Another variety of this tune people frequently whistle to is 'our data (systems, networks) are not interesting for any assailants-to-be'. First of all, one has to be in the attacker's shoes to know what is intriguing for such person and what isn't. Then, how would the assailants guess that 'it is not interesting' until they gain access to it? And if it is truly the case, why to waste time and effort spent on gaining this access while it can be used for other amusing things? Such as hacking into 'more interesting' systems to hide their tracks and preserve resources at your expense. Or sending SPAM. Or distributing 'wares and pr0n'. Or else. Besides, many attacks are simply opportunistic and indiscriminate, like spraying bullets in the dark.

2 The 'shiny box with flashing lights' mindset.

The 'it will never happen to us' is a major overall information security issue. The 'shiny box with flashing lights' mindset is more pertinent to information security assessments. It is human nature to associate security with something palpable, like walls, doors, locks, safes and barbed wire. Vendors actively exploit this perception for profit. Buy this appliance and you will become secure. Buy that software and you will become compliant. To stay secure and compliant, however, you need a whole complex of interrelated measures, many of which are not technical or cannot be solved by technology. Remember the discussion of 'human' and 'matter' factors in the Introduction. Guns alone never win wars, and even on a purely technical level, the safeguard must be properly positioned, configured, maintained and usually interconnected with other relevant systems and applications. Adversaries should not be able to bypass it by either a frontal or lateral attack. To ensure that all of this is done right and eliminate inevitable errors, timely IT security audits are a must. Otherwise, there is a good chance that you have simply wasted your cash on that precious intrusion prevention system, content filter or firewall.

3 The 'we are glad to accept this risk' mindset.

This attitude is typical for people who are able to see through the media and general public hype. As a result, they adapt the 'devil is not so black as he is painted' view. However, sanity tells that you cannot reduce, retain or transfer risks without a prior professional risk evaluation. Which brings us back to the topic of security assessments.

Are there any companies or organisations that actually do not need any information security audits at all? At the very minimum, such an entity would have to:

- Stay away from personal and other sensitive data, like customer databases and trade secrets.
- Thoroughly vet and fully trust all its employees, partners and guests.
- Be disconnected from the Internet and other untrusted networks.

We have never encountered such a corporate or governmental body in the real world.

On monetary contemplations

'Benefit and harm are interdependent, so the enlightened always consider them.'

Ho Yanxi

The budget is the main restricting factor in performing information security assessments. Even during a financial crisis, no highly skilled professional auditor wishes to toil for pennies. At the same time, selling security assessments is a raw spot of all companies that offer these valuable services.

Information security audits are intangible. We have already discussed the 'shiny box with flashing lights' mindset and its outcome. Even those who understand the need of performing the assessments often purchase 'the shiny box' first and only then ask the auditors to test it. This is potential financial loss. The assessors may or may not recommend getting the 'box' in the first place. They could advise you to get a somewhat different solution or position 'the box' at the bottom of the risk treatment priority list. They may suggest that a cheaper 'box' will suffice. In any case, if you have decided to seek professional advice (which is a necessary outcome of any proper security audit), get it first and then put it to good use.

To make the situation worse, practical end results of information security audits are usually 'negative'. By negative we mean that auspicious security assessments do not make easily recognisable good things happen. They stop the bad ones from unexpectedly popping up. In the words of ancient Chinese strategist Ho Yanxi, '*when trouble is solved before it forms, who calls that clever*?' Many published sources have stated that subscribing to regular security assessments is akin to getting an insurance policy. However, paying for something not to occur is not even an insurance premium. It is more like charges for in-depth private medical examinations. You do not undergo them to increase your direct income, and the procedures can be rather costly. However, they are 'a matter of life and death' that 'may be taken up lightly' by many.

Thus, from the financial standpoint, information security audits (and security in general) are viewed as a necessary evil. Psychologically, everyone wants to save on this evil and convince themselves that it isn't so necessary, after all. Information security is traditionally valued only in terms of reducing loss, and practically never as a profit generating factor. To aggravate the issue, significant parts of this loss are, again, intangible. Have a look at the costs of IT failure as stated in the ITIL V3 'Service Design'. In accordance to this widely accepted set of best practices for IT service management, the tangible costs can include:

- *Lost user productivity*
- *Lost IT staff productivity*
- *Lost revenue*
- *Overtime payments*
- *Wasted goods and materials*
- *Imposed fines or penalty payments.*

The intangible costs can comprise:

- *Loss of customers*
- *Loss of customer goodwill (customer dissatisfaction)*
- *Loss of business opportunity (to sell, gain new customers and revenue, etc.)*
- *Damage to business reputation*
- *Loss of confidence in IT service provider*
- *Damage to staff morale.*

Regarding the second category, ITIL V3 states that '*it is important not simply to dismiss the intangible costs (and the potential consequences) on the grounds that they may be difficult to measure*'.

To emphasise, the damages listed above are assumed to result from accidental failure, disaster or seldom lapse. In the case of a directed and planned act of hostile intelligent force they would be naturally magnified. Additional legal and investigative expenses are likely to be incurred. External public perception of the events would also be unfavourably different. Everyone is sympathetic to victims of a genuine cataclysm. In our highly competitive world, this is not so when *avoidable* trouble is deliberately caused by fellow humans. *Vae Victis* – '*Woe to the vanquished!*' There is at least one bank that none of the authors would use because it has suffered far too many security incidents that led to sizeable losses. This is not misfortune: every bank is getting regularly attacked by cybercriminals and other fraudsters, but the outcome is different. This is negligence.

Examine another curious observation we have made: if the act is deliberate, tangible and intangible losses tend to be more interconnected and amplify each other to a larger extent. According to Clausewitz, '*it is chiefly the moral force which is shaken by defeat, and if the number of trophies reaped by the enemy mounts up to an unusual height, then the lost combat becomes a rout*'. Making things worse, the disclosed security incidents often attract more assailants. The bad guys start viewing the victim company or organisation as a soft target and step in alike marauders.

Is it possible to consider information security as a potential source of profit? ITIL V3 'Service Strategy' explicitly names security as the essential element of warranty. The other key elements are availability, continuity and capacity. Note, that all three are dependent, or at least can be heavily influenced, by their security counterpart. Indeed, from the security specialist's perspective, availability is the 'A' in the infamous CIA triad. '*Warranties in general – continues the ITIL – are part of the value proposition that influences customers to buy*'. Nowadays, utility alone would not suffice.

This, no doubt, can be effectively exploited in marketing and advertisement. There are a great deal of services and products that come from different vendors, yet their utility is essentially the same. As everyone is catching up with the general technological side, the difference in security can provide the margin needed to overcome competition. At the same time, such a difference may not be very difficult to achieve. We have effectively partnered and regularly worked with IT integration and maintenance companies. Our assistance has allowed them to offer customers discounted security audits and other security services as part of a complete service package.

Of course, using information security as a selling point to achieve service and product warranty, superior to that of your competitors, carries its share of risks. It must be done with caution, since detrimental effects of any security blunder in case of such commercial proposition would be magnified. The balance of expenditure on the security element of the offer, which can easily grow to an unacceptable level, must be constantly checked against the additional profits gained. However, this approach is by no means impossible. It only takes some initiative, confidence and solid skills:

- *Therefore armed struggle is considered profitable, and armed struggle is considered dangerous (Sun Tzu).*
- *For the skilled it is profitable, for the unskilled it is dangerous (Cao Cao).*

Thus we conclude this brief discussion of 'whys' in respect to finance and choice and can safely turn back to more philosophical strategic matters.

The fundamentals

'War is only a part of political intercourse, therefore by no means an independent thing in itself. ***It has certainly a grammar of its own, but its logic is not peculiar to itself.****'*

Carl von Clausewitz

By definition, this is the most vital section of this book. Comprehending and putting the rest of the material to good practice depends on gaining a firm understanding of the fundamental principles. A lot of them are pure logic and common sense. Nevertheless, until the maxim is clearly formulated, its meaning and use will remain beneath the surface. That is, in the realm of intuition.

We have already expressed some of the basic postulates in the Introduction. To rehearse the most relevant ones:

- *Information security is a science and the art of protecting data.*
- *IT security is the science and art of protecting data in electronic format.*
- *Information security assessments are a practical way of improving the information security state.*
- *Security assessments must evaluate probabilities and potential impacts of passive and active security incidents.*
- *To assess the likelihood of passive security incidents it is usually sufficient to analyse controls, their implementations and enforcement.*
- *To assess the probability and impact of active security incidents a more aggressive and all-encompassing path must be taken.*

- *'Human' and 'material' information security elements have to be synchronously audited, analysed and measured.*

Like the scheme in the beginning of this chapter, these principles are sufficiently general to be applied to any security assessment, in any given situation. When we have looked at information security auditing from the 'bird's eye' perspective, trying to dissociate ourselves from narrow technological and procedural aspects, 20 such principles have surfaced. Let us list and analyse them in brief.

1 *Information security assessment is an act of corporate or organisational politics.*

This is a pure Clausewitzian statement that goes well with his infamous '*war is not merely a political act, but also a real political instrument, a continuation of political commerce, a carrying out of the same by other means*' quote. At the end of the day, it is the politics and strategic goals of a company or organisation that leastwise determine:

- Whether an audit will be undertaken.
- When and by whom it is going to be done.
- Its overall scope and type.
- How it will be managed on the auditee side.
- Which actual follow-up reactions will be performed.

This reflects the planning of large-scale security programmes by the auditee management, of which security assessments should be the integral parts.

2 Information security assessment is always shaped by political, administrative, technical and human 'terrain'.

Having strategic and political aims at its roots, the character and performance of information security assessments will be inevitably influenced by the auditee policies, operations and procedures, technology, relationships and personal traits of the people involved, etc. This is similar to effects terrain, environmental conditions, channels of communication, quality and quantity of troops and their armaments, etc. have on any battle.

3 Information security assessment must shape information security systems of its target.

Any action is reciprocal and triggers reaction. The absence of a tangible response is a type of reaction too. Even if the security assessment did not identify any gaps, it should still trigger (or prevent) change.

4 Information security assessment is never complete.

This can be compared with '*the result in war is never absolute*' (Clausewitz). Neither, in accordance to the strategy classic, it has to be: '*but this object of war in the abstract, this final means of attaining the political object in which all others are combined, the disarming the enemy, is by no means general in reality, is not a condition necessary to peace, and therefore can in no wise be set up in theory as a law*'. There is always something else to check, test, verify and analyse. You cannot discover all the existing flaws. You cannot 'disarm the enemy' by foreseeing and preventing every opportunity for hostile acts. Some security auditors are devoted perfectionists, but this perfectionism must be controlled to bear fruit. The approach based on prioritisation of risks is the key. Some actions can be placed at the bottom of the priority list and postponed for later. Which brings us to the commonly repeated maxim that ....

5 *Information security assessment must be a part of a continuous process.*

The environment changes. What was secure yesterday is not so today. What was sufficient to become compliant a month ago may be unsatisfactory now. Standards alter. Technology constantly moves forward and can introduce significant correctives. The audit methods evolve. Besides, as stated when examining the previous principle, the next audit can accomplish what the previous did not. On any hand, it is clearly required to verify both completeness and correctness of any follow-up reaction to its predecessor. Information security auditing is a powerful *way of monitoring the information security state*. A stand-alone assessment completely misses this point.

6 *Information security assessment should maintain a proper balance between tempo and depth.*

As often, the art is in doing as much as you can in as little time as you have. Because the conditions change, a protracted audit can end up with findings of its beginning becoming obsolete or irrelevant when the end is reached. All critical vulnerabilities and gaps should be promptly analysed and reported – '*each minute ahead of the enemy is an advantage*' (Gen. Blumentritt). However, hurrying up and missing important discoveries are another highly unpleasant extreme.

7 *Information security assessment must always exceed its **perceived** scope.*

This principle can be easily misunderstood. It does not mean that you have to go after more targets than were assigned by the audit agreement. What it implies is that information security of a company or organisation is a complex interconnected system. You cannot analyse a single component of this system without somehow contemplating the rest. Recall the introductory fundamental on 'material' and 'human' factors being simultaneously attacked or evaluated. For instance, the perceived scope of an external penetration test is verifying the security state of a network perimeter. At the first sight, this task is purely technical, being concentrated on any exposed services and perimeter safeguards. Nevertheless, in the process of testing all related policies and procedures, as well as management, qualifications and skills of the responsible personnel are inevitably checked. This must be accounted for when synthesising and analysing the test results. Indeed, '*war is never an isolated act*' (Clausewitz).

8 *Information security assessment always targets corporate or organisational ISMS.*

ISMS is the glue that ties and holds together different components of the entity's information security. It doesn't matter which particular technical, operational, policy or human elements are assessed, the auditors should always encounter and hit that glue. If at some point they don't, it should be counted as a discovered security gap.

9 *Information security assessment should aspire to establish the roots of all discovered vulnerabilities, weaknesses and gaps.*

Security flaws do not condense from utter nothingness. If their root causes are not properly addressed, the flaws reappear and proliferate, no matter how hard you are trying to remove them one by one. Close one gap and another gap opens. Finding a real source of a problem is an abstract *analytic* and *synthetic* task that requires both experience and holistic judgement. It can lurk anywhere, at any level. The true cause of what appears to be a solely technical issue could be operational or human. In the case of, for example, miscommunication the why of a perceivably human-centric vulnerability can be technical. A gap in security policies can be the origin of any related downstream shortcomings. One issue can have multiple roots. One source can create numerous issues.

10 Information security assessment should aspire to discover strategic problems through tactical means.

Strategic blunders are the worst. They have the highest negative impact and usually require tremendous corrective efforts. Yet, they are commonly obscured by a cloud of details on lower, 'tactical' planes. When searching for the real source of uncovered problems, try to look as high and as sweeping as you can. Metaphorically speaking, an astute security auditor should strive to be able to look at one drop of water and understand the ocean. For example, major shortfalls in high level information security management and yawning gaps in security policies, can sometimes be revealed by scanning networks and systems, or performing social engineering tests.

11 Information security assessment must be endorsed, controlled and debriefed at the top.

This is an extension of the much discussed 'top-down' approach in information security management. It will have its share of heavy scrutiny in the next chapter. In regard to security assessments, numerous issues the auditors might uncover are likely to require attention and intervention of the top management. Such matters are usually strategic, operational or human, but might be centred at technology if large costs or high risks are involved. At the end of the day, the key decisions concerning security audits and their outcome would be either taken, or at least vetted, at the entity's top. '*Experience in general also teaches us that notwithstanding the multifarious branches and scientific character of military art in the present day, still the leading outlines of a war are always determined by the cabinet, that is, if we would use technical language, by a political not a military functionary*' (Clausewitz).

12 Information security assessment should be understood and appreciated at the bottom.

It should not be viewed as an unpleasant distraction negatively interfering with the auditee personnel duties. In particular, the audit must not create the impression of being an oppressive instrument of the managing apparatus. Life is harsh, and at times discovered offenders are fired or disciplined because of the assessment findings. In our practice, there were cases in which what started as a casual internal IT security audit, ended up with computer forensics and legal repercussions. However, firing, reprimanding and otherwise scourging employees, is not some specific goal of information security assessments. The auditors should endeavour to win sympathies and gain assistance of the auditee staff, by presenting themselves as friendly advisers and handy troubleshooters. They must never be smug or boss others around. Active obstruction and resistance of the auditee personnel at whatever level, can easily ruin any security assessment. It has to be carefully avoided.

13 Information security assessment must produce transferrable results.

Where necessary, the auditors as a team should be able to speak the language of operational, asset and risk management, technology, human resources, compliance and even finance. Possible implications of the assessment results to all these areas should be reviewed and appropriately presented. They should be understood top, bottom, left and right.

14 Information security assessment must decrease the friction of the auditee.

Friction is a term we have borrowed from military science. Generally, the 'friction of war' refers to the effects of uncertainty, looseness, suspense and chance. The MCDP 1 *Warfighting* has a great description of what one can rightfully call internal friction: '*Friction may be self-induced, caused by such factors as lack of a clearly defined goal, lack of coordination, unclear or complicated plans, complex task organisations or command relationships, or complicated technologies. While we should attempt to minimise self-induced friction, the greater requirement is to fight effectively despite the existence of friction*'. All we need to do to apply this description to corporate or organisational information security is replace 'to fight' with 'to operate'. Figure 1 depicts factors that typically contribute to internal friction within a company.

Figure 1: Typical elements of internal friction

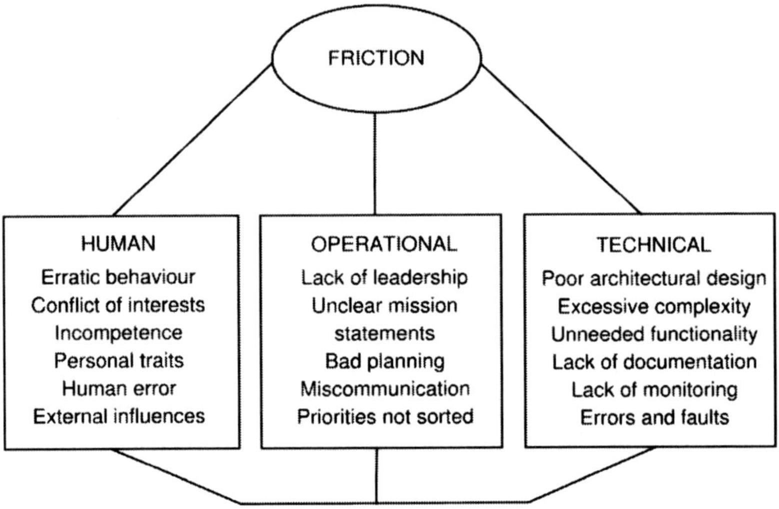

Note, that these factors are interconnected and might potentiate each other to a general detrimental result. By finding and eliminating various flaws and gaps, a thorough information security assessment and its follow-up can reduce internal friction and diminish FUD, at least within its sphere of immediate application.

15 Information security assessment should promote security awareness and initiative.

Another useful military term closely related to friction is 'fog of war'. 'Fog of war' refers to the unknown and concealed. It seeks to capture the uncertainty regarding your own capability, the potential adversary capability and adversary intent. From the IT security viewpoint, the Internet is covered with a thick 'fog of war'. There is a certain amount of this fog clouding your systems and networks, your ISMS, your employees. By dispelling it and increasing security awareness, information security audits curtail friction and FUD. Clarity, knowing more, and understanding what to do, stimulates initiative.

16 Information security assessment always operates with probabilities.

Information security audits are a highly practical and effective way of evaluating security risks. Even when the vulnerability is clearly defined, the risk it presents would always be 'fuzzy'. To measure this risk in a specific real-life situation, the auditors will need to weight and gauge numerous variables, some of which are ambiguous or not fully known. Due to the inevitable effects of friction, it is typically senseless to express risks in some absolute 'all-or-nothing' values. Besides, it is not possible to predict the adversary acts with absolute certainty. Thus, any analysis of the estimated attack scenarios can only state which scenarios are more likely to occur, and why.

17 Information security assessment is mainly a proactive countermeasure.

Sometimes, security incidents trigger information security assessments which provide a level of support to forensic investigations. Once we performed a penetration test that uncovered the vulnerability through which the attackers got in, and which could not be discovered by usual forensic methods alone. Nevertheless, security audits are casually done to prevent incidents, and not to react to them. As such, they deprive potential attackers of opportunities and initiative. '*If you can always remember danger when you are secure and remember chaos in times of order, watch out for danger and chaos while they are still formless and prevent them before they happen, this is the best of all*' (Ho Yanxi).

18 Information security assessment must be impartial.

This is one of the major reasons why the majority of information security audits are outsourced to third parties. It is more difficult to ensure neutrality of the internal auditor team. However, the auditee should watch out for any suspicious involvement of the third party consultants with their personnel and, especially, competitors. It also pays to have vendor-independent security auditors that would not aggressively push through any specific services or products of other companies for a commission. In such a case, they would be tempted to twist the assessment conclusions and recommendations to present the solution they promote in a favourable light. You hire the auditors to assess and analyse, not to advertise!

19 Information security assessment must be dissociated from the checked system.

By 'impartiality', we mean not taking any parts. By 'dissociation' – *not being a part oneself.* This is often an issue with the in-house auditor team. Outside the scope of its immediate tasks, it should be kept as isolated from its customary targets as possible. One of the evident reasons why this ought to be so, is avoiding development of any interfering mutual relations between the auditors and the audited. But there is more to it than meets the eye and this is an issue of *dissociation, not impartiality*.

The infamous Gödel's second incompleteness theorem can be stated as follows: *For any formal effectively generated theory T including basic arithmetical truths and also certain truths about formal provability, T includes a statement of its own consistency if and only if T is inconsistent*. Gödel has proved that the internal consistency of a system can never be proven except by employing reasoning which is not expressible within the system itself. Thus, you cannot determine the consistency (or inconsistency) of a system from within and have to be free of its constrains. *The in-house auditors should think and operate as if they were an independent third party*. But there is an even broader application of this reasoning. The best way to disassociate oneself from the auditee mindset and acquire clear external range of vision and perspective is wholly, unreservedly think like the adversaries: '*We should try to "get inside" the enemy's thought processes and see the enemy as he sees himself so that we can set him up for defeat. It is essential that we understand the enemy on his own terms. We should not assume that every enemy thinks as we do, fights as we do, or has the same values or objectives*' (MCDP 1 *Warfighting*).

20 Information security assessment results must be strictly confidential.

What could be a better gift to a foe than a document describing in detail which security gaps your company or organisation has and how to exploit them? That adversary can be internal. Life goes on. Love can turn to hate, happiness to dissatisfaction. A member of staff who is trustworthy today can become totally disgruntled tomorrow. The fewer people who have access to any information that demonstrates your potential weaknesses, the better. As Bruce Schneier emphatically pointed out, 'probably the safest thing you can do with the (security audit) report, after you read it, is shred it'.

On aggressive defence

'Because we typically think of the defence as waiting for the enemy to strike, we often associate the defence with response rather than initiative. This is not necessarily true. We do not necessarily assume the defensive only out of weakness.'

MCDP 1 *Warfighting*

Countering active security incidents is the most interesting part of it all. After all, it involves the clash of wills. Add skills, knowledge and understanding to the concoction, and you will get the whole picture. If one is able to fend off determined, deliberate, planned attacks, reducing the number of passive security incidents and diminishing their impact should be a cakewalk.

Great military minds have pondered the subject of offence versus defence for millennia. It appears that eventually they have worked out an admissible and respectable theoretical framework that addresses the issue in a variety of situations. In the field of information security we see nothing of a kind. At its best, there are disparate glimpses of what can be the fabric of such an endeavour. For example, security specialists often hum 'the best defence is offence' mantra. Fine. But what exactly does it imply in practice? Are we supposed to hack the hackers? Or publish private gossips about nosey disaffected employees on Facebook before they do the same to you or your enterprise? This doesn't make much sense.

An information security professional is engaged in a form of continuous warfare which is defensive by its very nature. The aim of this 'combat' is not to give an inch of the protected 'territory' (data, systems, resources) to the adversaries. The latter come of all breeds and can be positioned both outside (the 'invaders') or inside (the 'infiltrators' or 'insurgents'). Information security audits are an important way of this engagement. They should not be under- or overestimated.

Based on what we could learn from the military masterminds, there are three *interrelated* key strategies of successful defence:

- *Build up strong multilayered resistance*
- *Readily adapt to the opponents*
- *Compel the enemy to follow your rules of the game.*

The optimal defensive strategy adapted to a given situation should effectively combine the elements of all three.

Defence in-depth

The first strategy seems to be very straightforward. Beef up your defences on many existing levels while involving policy, operational, human, legal and technical elements. Such levels will have their sub-levels nested within. Try out a simple exercise. Count in your mind the points required for a proper echeloned defence of a large network. We estimate that at least the following are absolutely necessary:

1 Redundant load-balanced connections to multiple ISPs.
2 Fortified network perimeter.
3 Secure separation of internal networks.
4 Protection of traffic streams and infrastructure protocols.
5 Protection of all separate systems, including servers, workstations, mobile computers and various network appliances.

6 Secure redundant 24/7 monitoring and logging applied to everything listed above.
7 Trained technical personnel who are up to task.
8 Capable security management.
9 Appropriate vendor support contracts, SLAs and NDAs.
10 Security policies, procedures, guidelines, inventories, network schemes and technical manuals covering all aspects of above (including change control, incident response, etc.).

How many points did you come up with? What was missing? Are these security elements also missed within a real network infrastructure of your company or organisation?

Not understanding and servicing such hierarchical structures in a befitting way, usually leads to a major strategic fault we call a 'Maginot Line mentality'. As Clausewitz pointed out a century before the actual Maginot Line was built, '*if you entrench yourself behind strong fortifications, you compel the enemy to seek a solution elsewhere*'. The unblessed fortification line had 'On ne passe pas' ('they shall not pass') engraved in it. And they did not. Erich von Manstein outflanked the line through the Ardennes.

Some information security specialists still view what they protect as some kind of a medieval fortress with walls, ditches, watchtowers and sentinels at the gates. This is evidently a manifestation of the 'Maginot Line mentality'. The real borders of the 'fortress' are blurred, nebulous, fluid and continuously fluctuate.

We would rather call it an '*information security zone*':

- *An information security zone is everywhere your sensitive data and systems are. This is the 'territory' you need to defend. It continuously expands and contracts.*

You have telecommuters – it expands to their homes. You have employees with company laptops on business trips – it expands anywhere they go, including planes, hotels, taxies, cafés or all other places you can (or cannot) imagine. Any time, the laptops can be attacked via (wired or wireless) hacking and plain old theft. The employees can be attacked via social engineering, blackmail, bribery and so on. Growing popularity of Cloud Computing and Software-as-a-Service (SaaS) makes further enormous contributions towards reshaping information security zones of subscribers to these services, their partners and customers. They might increase *friction* by orders of magnitude. The cloud and fog of war go hand in hand.

In the introductory part we have noted that the experienced security auditor should be able to recognise and condemn the prevalent 'cataclysmic approach' of the auditee. 'Maginot Line mentality' is another strategic blunder of a similar scale that the auditors should be looking for. It is vital to understand that information security 'Maginot Line' can be created nearly anywhere. On a technical side, the most common occasion is the network perimeter. However, some may, for example, put all eggs into the basket of applied cryptography. Have you ever heard somcthing along the 'we don't care whether our data are lost, they won't be able to decrypt it anyway' line? Keystroke loggers and social engineering are just two of the many approaches the assailants can adopt to 'outflank' encryption and avoid 'frontal' brute force attacks. There could be security policy, operational or human resources 'Maginot Lines'. A third party hosting, cloud, SaaS or security services providers (ironically, including suppliers of information security audits!) can become one. Be vigilant and watch for its obvious signs.

Adapting to adversaries

The two remaining 'dynamic' or 'adaptational' strategies of defence are similar in their dependence on:

- *Knowing the enemy*
- *Maintaining the tempo*
- *Initiative.*

For them, timely information security audits play a truly pivotal role. We shall briefly examine this role here.

The 'adapt to the adversary' approach is by no means new. Nearly two and a half thousand years ago Sun Tzu has exalted it saying that '*the ability to gain victory by changing and adapting according to the opponent is called genius*'. He has also underlined that such adaptation must be creative and continuous: '*Therefore victory in war is not repetitious, but adapts its form endlessly*'. In the Introduction we stated that:

- *To assess the probability and impact of active security incidents a more aggressive and all-encompassing path must be taken.*

Such a path signifies that a robust security assessment should simultaneously analyse the auditee defences and potential assailant's capabilities. From the defender viewpoint it can be worded as '*assess yourself and your opponents*' (Ho Yanxi). Other relevant discourses of

Chinese strategy sages sometimes quoted by information security experts are:

- *So it is said that if you know others and know yourself, you will not be imperilled in a hundred battles; if you do not know others but know yourself, you will win one and lose one; if you do not know others and do not know yourself, you will be imperilled in every single battle (Sun Tzu).*
- *When you know yourself, this means guarding your energy and waiting. This is why knowing defence but not offence means half victory and half defeat (Zhang Yu).*

'Half victory and half defeat' is not what we aspire to. Recall that the 'fog of war' reflects '*the uncertainty regarding your own capability, the potential adversary capability and adversary intent*'. Thus, it has to be removed not only from your own, but also from the opponent's capabilities and designs. To do so, the auditors must thoroughly research the means of different attacker species, using all sources of information at their disposal, as well as their own experience and imagination. Then the established offensive means should be applied to test the auditee information security at different levels and points, and without causing unacceptable disruption or damage.

Technical penetration testing or social engineering specialists will now predictably say that this is exactly what they do. But the scope of applying this logic can be more broad. Just as we split all security incidents into active and passive, we can describe all information security assessments in exactly the same way:

- *A passive information security assessment is based upon verification against prefabricated checklists.*

- *An active information security assessment is based upon vigorously searching for vulnerabilities and gaps employing all relevant knowledge, experience, creativity and insight.*

One can be highly imaginative, dynamic and resourceful when analysing security policies, procedures or any other pertinent documentation. On the other hand, a penetration test or a social engineering check can be reduced to an application of a limited set of 'canned' cookbook gimmickry. This is saving time at the expense of depth. It has its place under the sun.

It should be emphasised, that both passive and active assessment classes are effective, proactive ways to discover and analyse risks. It is only the scope of risks that differs. So, you should not disdain the passive approach. While it certainly does not look artistic, it is much easier to calibrate and standardise. It is very useful at establishing information security baselines (in military terms – 'lines of retreat'). It can extend the breadth of an audit by checking more targets in a given period of time. To stress it again, the passive approach can also reduce that period, and getting ahead of the opponents is vital. What it won't do is help to prevent sophisticated and determined attacks centred around the element of surprise. Thus, you have to gauge the probability of such a threat prior to selecting the passive or active option.

Compelling adversaries to adapt

The third strategy of aggressive defence – forcing the opposition to adapt, or accept your rules of the game – certainly requires application of the active approach.

Historically, this is also the latest strategy. During the time of Sun Tzu, skilful adaptation to your foe was sufficient to be a strategy genius, although he did state that '*those skilled in war bring the enemy to the field of battle and are not brought there by him*'. Nevertheless, even Clausewitz wrote that '*while on the defensive, our forces cannot at the same time be directed on other objects; they can only be employed to defeat the intentions of the enemy.*' Nothing is said about shaping these intentions in a needed direction. This is not so nowadays.

Revisit the introductory thought, that information security practices have plentiful logical and strategic similarities to counter-intelligence and counter-insurgency efforts. USAF Colonel John Boyd (1927-1997), whose observations and thoughts we have already employed on multiple occasions, starting from the epigraph to the whole book, is considered by some to be a 'modern day Sun Tzu'. Being a jet fighter pilot, he was deeply exposed to high-tech, high speed manoeuvrable combat action. Besides, John Boyd took an active part in developing F-16 and F/A-18 Hornet fighter planes. His ideas heavily influenced the MCDP 1 *Warfighting* – another frequently quoted source of inspiration for this work. Colonel John Boyd vigorously contemplated on modern counter-blitz and counter-guerrilla action. We find his conclusions to be highly applicable to today's information security 'combat'. Below, some of them shall be meditated upon.

- *Blitz and guerrillas, by operating in a directed, yet more indistinct, more irregular, and quicker manner, operate inside their adversaries' observation-orientation-decision-action loops or get inside their mind-time-space as basis to penetrate the moral-mental-physical being of their adversaries in order to pull them apart, and bring*

> *about their collapse. Such amorphous, lethal, and unpredictable activity by blitz and guerrillas make them appear awesome and unstoppable which altogether produce uncertainty, doubt, mistrust, confusion, disorder, fear, panic.*

Replace 'blitz and guerrillas' by 'malicious hackers and cybercriminals' and you will see the main reasons for their apparent success (and for the accompanying media hype). Also, remember the 'FUD game'. This is how they win it. Of course, the offenders rarely want your entire collapse, although this is possible in the cases of revenge or politically motivated attacks. The observation-orientation-decision-action (OODA) loops (Figure 2) introduced by Colonel Boyd, reflect the following stages of any complete interaction process that involves decision making:

1 *Reconnaissance and data gathering (observation).*
2 *Analysis and synthesis of gathered data (orientation).*
3 *Determining the course of action (decision).*
4 *Physical, technical, managerial and other forms of implementing the decision in practice (action).*

Figure 2: The OODA loop

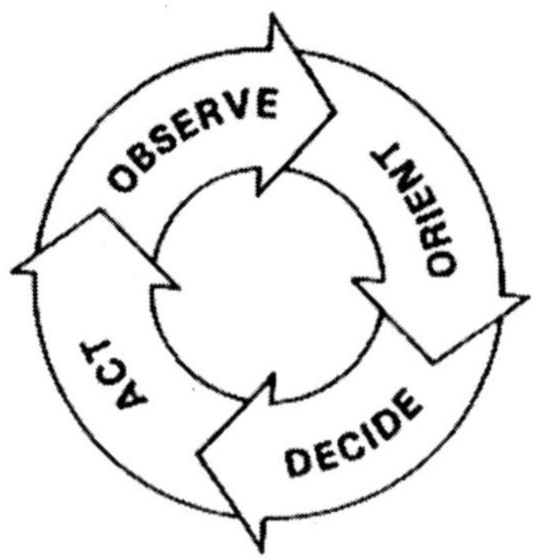

We will make extensive use of the OODA loop concept in the upcoming chapters of this book.

So, which suggestions did John Boyd provide to counter the foregoing threats?

- *In dealing with uncertainty, adaptability seems to be the right counterweight. The counterweight to 'uncertainty' cannot be 'certainty'.*

The applications of this principle to information security auditing were already discussed in the Fundamentals section, when we elaborated on the inherent incompleteness of security audits, etc. It will resurface elsewhere. Remove just enough fog of war to enable sufficiently effective observation. Throw just enough fog of war at the adversaries to make them confused and blur their vision.

- *To shape and adapt to change one cannot be passive; instead one must take the initiative.*

Active information security assessments require higher initiative. Aggressive defence is go-aheadedness, instead of 'cataclysmic doctrine' biding for a security accident to 'happen', so that something can be done about it afterwards.

- *Idea of fast transients suggests that, in order to win, we should operate at a faster tempo or rhythm than our adversaries – or, better yet, get inside adversary's observation-orientation-decision-action time cycle or loop.*

If information security auditors are more resolute, vigorous and knowledgeable than the attackers, and the assessment follow-up reactions do not lag, this is certainly possible.

- *The ability to operate at a faster tempo or rhythm than an adversary enables one to fold an adversary back inside himself so that he can neither appreciate nor keep-up with what's going on. He will become disoriented or confused.*

This amounts to winning the 'FUD game' and completely thwarting the attack. Disoriented attackers also turn into soft targets for punishment via disciplinary and law enforcement acts.

- *Spontaneous, synthetic/creative, and flowing action/counteraction operation, rather than a step-by-step, analytical/logical, and discrete move/counter-move game.*

Plain and simple, this is the pattern of information security that a company or organisation must follow. This is what the ISMS should promote and is how an effective information security assessment must be executed.

There could be multiple specific applications of these principles in various spheres of practical information security. On a technical side, by uncovering vulnerabilities and designing whole new methods of attack before the adversaries do, security researchers frequently overrun the opposition, effectively getting inside their OODA loops. Needless to say, many novel ways of attack are discovered in the process of performing security audits. Rapid inclusion of new heuristics (not simply signatures!) into intrusion prevention and anti-malware products might also allow you to get ahead of numerous attackers. When organisational and technical measures converge to create an effective monitoring and logging system, punitive action against in-house offenders can be taken before they do any actual harm. They can now get caught red-handed with ease. This means the attackers will be forced to react instead of the company or organisation reacting to them. Social engineering can be met with counter-social engineering, and the possibilities for sting operations are endless. We did social engineer assailants in the past to find out their future plans and targets, and determine their present capabilities and skills.

To summarise, blitz can be successfully met with counter-blitz and guerrilla-like tactics can decimate guerrillas. These are the key lessons from Colonel Boyd's strategic research. Contemplate it with utmost thoughtfulness, and you will find out how it might apply to your particular situation and assigned information security tasks.

On counteroffensive

'We conclude that there exists no clear division between the offence and defence. Our theory of war should not attempt to impose one artificially. The offence and defence exist simultaneously as necessary components of each other, and the transition from one to the other is fluid and continuous.'

MCDP 1 *Warfighting*

The discourse of the previous section automatically brings the question of whether it is possible to counterattack. This topic was speculated about by many information security professionals, again without producing any definite results. Military strategy actively contemplates and uses counter attacking even in the most bluntly defensive standoffs:

- *The ultimate aim of defensive war can never be an absolute negation, as we have observed before. Even for the weakest there must be some point in which the enemy may be made to feel, and which may be threatened (Clausewitz).*

- *A rapid, powerful transition to the attack – the glinting sword of vengeance – is the most brilliant moment of the defence. Anyone who does not think of it from the very beginning, or rather, anyone who does not include it within the concept of defence, will never understand the superiority of defence (Clausewitz).*

Note the key point in the second excerpt: *the capability of counterattack must be included within the system of defence for it to be truly superior*.

The main ways of bludgeoning in-house attackers are disciplinary and, sometimes, legal. Remember, that at least two thirds of serious information security incidents are internal, and are caused by disgruntled employees, and clashes of corporate or organisational politics. The main way to sledge-hammer external offenders is via law enforcement agencies, although you can sue the offenders or smear them by an effective media and word-of-mouth campaign. All these situational possibilities are fully, entirely dependent on your information security defences. Which, to remind, are policy, operational, technical and human, and should be regularly verified and improved employing appropriate security audits.

Let us review the classic example of a specific 'technical' countermeasure – the logs. To be taken seriously by law enforcement agencies' representatives, or accepted as a secondary, or hearsay evidence in a Court of Law, a set of defined conditions must be met:

1 There must be appropriate security policies covering audit trails in the company or organisation.

2. There must be a suitably qualified person responsible for maintaining and reviewing the logs.
3. Logs must be reviewed regularly.
4. The integrity of logs must be well-protected.
5. Logs must be correctly time stamped.

To meet these objectives effectively, logging should be centralised. Having redundant centralised log servers helps and having reliable and secure back-up of logs helps a lot. When an internal information security audit is performed, all these elements should be thoroughly verified. The absence or a flaw in any of them can easily make logging a useless time-consuming exercise, especially from a legal viewpoint.

This 'technicality' brings us to some important general conclusions:

- *Information security assessments must verify incident prevention/response capabilities and procedures of the auditee.*

In more specific terms:

- *Information security assessments should identify loopholes that can allow offenders to erase their tracks and get away.*

As you can see from the example above, such loopholes can be (surprise!) policy, technical, procedural and human. If you try to present as valid evidence any audit trails which are not a part of a continuous and documented process, but were specifically collected to react to a single security incident, the court won't take them.

The offenders have strategic gaps that can be and are successfully exploited. At the time of writing, the TJX case is still making big waves on the news. TJX hackers managed to get in – a battle won. Then they managed to retrieve the money – a decisive battle won. A great deal of cybercriminals fall exactly at this stage, if they are not part of a well-developed international crime organisation, with established channels of money laundering. Remember how Sumitomo bank hackers failed. Even so, in the end 'Maksik', 'Segvec' and at least some of their accomplices got caught. A decisive battle lost, and for these TJX hackers it nullifies the results of all battles previously won. Even if they did manage to stash some of the stolen cash somewhere, they are not likely to enjoy it. Not in a few decades, anyway.

One of the basic teachings of Sun Tzu is that you have to hit the adversaries where they do not defend. Thus, legal enforcement and disciplinary means are very efficient against the majority of offenders who are strongly technically inclined. They seldom understand and pay attention to procedures, laws, financial controls and the way in which law enforcement agencies operate. By concentrating on technology only, one also becomes highly vulnerable to social engineering. On the other hand, for a great deal of internal wrongdoers, technology is the Achilles' heel. They think that no one is watching. They think that if they have copied confidential data no one will spot it or prove it. They think that if they have deleted a file, or even formatted the whole hard drive, it cannot be restored. And so on. We have helped to bust such offenders many times. While you may think that this discussion has deviated from this book's theme into the realm of computer forensics, consider the following statement:

- *Information security assessments should be able to identify suspicious behaviour and signs of malevolent acts.*

This is similar to financial audits uncovering fraud, such as salami slicing. Information security assessments can, and sometimes will, trigger forensics. While the statement above appears to be mainly applicable to internal audits, experience shows that this is not always so.

The above discussion is centred on legal, enforcement and disciplinary paths of counteroffence. But can you counterattack technically? There is (or at least there was) a curious appliance or two that were advertised as 'active defence' safeguards. That is, they launched denial of service (DoS) attacks against assailants. This is a very bad idea. The obvious problem is that hackers can easily fake someone else's address to force such an appliance to attack it. Envision a situation in which two such devices belonging to different entities are tricked into playing a 'DoS ping-pong', one against the other. Besides, from the auditor's point, how does one run a security scan of a network border device that tries to knock you offline? Thus, if anyone offers you such an idea of active defence in any shape or form, stay away. The fog of war that clouds the Internet makes it entirely infeasible.

On the other hand, in applied wireless security, the coverage zone of your network is somewhat limited and, at least, can be reasonably monitored. If its security system is properly configured, all legitimate users must be authenticated. Thus, knocking off unauthorised users and misconfigured devices makes certain sense and can be applied. Nevertheless, when performing wireless security audits, on several occasions we have effectively tricked such systems into smiting rightful devices and users. What could be the lesson?

- *Information security assessments should verify that countermeasures are not excessive and cannot be the source of problems themselves.*

Recall the eternal 'difficult password problem'. If the passwords are too long, too complex, or are changed too often, users forget them or write them down.

On the conditions of success

'...on the defensive, there is no great gain to be won except by a great stake.'

Carl von Clausewitz

To conclude this chapter, we would like to say a few words on what should be considered as a successful defence. The end results of auspicious information security actions are:

1 *Preventing passive security incidents.*
2 *Preventing and repelling attacks.*
3 *Humiliating and apprehending offenders.*

Point one is about attention, awareness and appropriate controls. The other two points are a resolution of the 'clash of wills'. As Clausewitz has specified, '*mere endurance would not be fighting: and the defensive is an activity by which so much of the enemy's power must be destroyed, that he must give up his object*'. In information security, we are not fighting some brutal war of attrition. The 'enemy power' that 'must be destroyed' is, above all, the power of their will, their desire to launch, or resolve to carry on with the attack, or perform any other malicious acts.

One of the major compliments a technical attacker can deliver is 'this network (or system) is boring'. Boredom is the sister of unwillingness. Note the 'will' in the latter word. Unwillingness signifies unpreparedness, thus telling that you are better prepared than your opponents. From their point of view, a 'boring' system or network is one that does not have easily discoverable and exploitable gaps. This is only possible if a prior audit has identified all such gaps and the follow-up reaction has led to their complete elimination. Security by default is a myth. Insecurity by default is far more close to reality.

Sun Tzu stated, that '*in the case of those who are skilled in attack, their opponents do not know where to defend. In the case of those skilled in defence, their opponents do not know where to attack*'. Thus, the conditions of victory in terms of attack and defence are:

- *You know where (and how) to defend.*
- *The adversary does not even know where (and how) to begin.*

In relation to information security auditing, it signifies that the previous audits have properly identified and verified all these 'where's' and 'how's', and the latest audit was, well, unbelievingly boring. This, of course, applies to all major areas of our *information security zone*: policy, operational, technical and human. The auditee has reached the state in which, in the words of Sun Tzu, '*even if the opponents are numerous, they can be made not to fight*'. Now they have to maintain this state, '*be orderly within, and watch for gaps and slack*'. (Mei Yaochen)

CHAPTER 2: SECURITY AUDITING, GOVERNANCE, POLICIES AND COMPLIANCE

'... in strategy everything is very simple, but not on that account very easy.'

Carl von Clausewitz

In the previous chapter, we emphasised that the most dangerous flaws, are the flaws of security strategy. We have also discussed a few examples of such flaws. Strategic failures generate chain reactions of secondary and collateral shortcomings, many of which eventually become exploitable vulnerabilities – technical, operational and human. This is common sense that applies to numerous fields of expertise:

- *When your strategy is deep and far reaching, then what you gain by your calculations is much, so you can win before you even fight. When your strategic thinking is shallow and near-sighted, then what you gain by your calculations is little, so you lose before you do battle. Much strategy prevails over little strategy, so those with no strategy cannot but be defeated* (Zhang Yu).

We have also underlined that information security assessments should aspire to identify these strategic flaws, by cutting through the dusky thicket of details and assembling the whole picture of the auditee security state. Thus, the progress of hands-on audits is usually moving in the 'bottom-top' direction, from software applications, systems, networks, people, processes and documents, to the governance of the whole information security structure. The organisation and maintenance of this structure, as any

CISSP exam prep guide will stress, must be flowing in the opposite direction. After all, '*the one who figures on victory at headquarters before even doing the battle is the one who has the most strategic factors on his side*' (Sun Tzu). But is everything as straightforward as both textbooks and sages of the past tell?

On evaluating the top-down approach

'The subordination of the political point of view to the military would be contrary to common sense, for policy has declared the war; it is the intelligent faculty, war is only the instrument, and not the reverse. The subordination of the military point of view to the political is, therefore, the only thing which is possible.'

Carl von Clausewitz

A thorough information security assessment should seek to verify that:

- The top management of the auditee cares about information security of its company or organisation, instead of adopting a *laissez-faire* attitude.
- It is reasonably aware of *major overall* security issues and risks the company or organisation is facing.
- There is a good level of bidirectional communication and mutual understanding between the board and the manager responsible for corporate or organisational information security (usually the CISO).
- General information security strategies and programmes do exist, are documented and *followed through.*

One of the most obvious things to check is whether the information security policies include appropriate clauses on senior management support and are endorsed and signed by a representative of the board. When writing security policies for our clients we casually align them with the ISO27001:2005 standard. The same applies to our domestic set of policies. The ISO27001:2005 template suggests that the opening chapter of any compliant security policy should be dedicated to information security organisation and include a section on senior management support. This is how this section may typically look like:

- <section number> **Senior Management Support** *<insert company name> Information Security Policy is fully endorsed and supported by the company's Board of Directors.*
- *This Information Security Policy becomes effective immediately after it has been approved and signed by <insert Senior Management representative position>.*
- *The Senior Management has a direct responsibility for maintaining the Information Security Policy and providing advice and guidance on its implementation.*
- *<insert the representative position> shall be the principal Senior Management contact and representative overlooking corporate Information Security Policy matters.*
- *All <insert company name> Managers are directly responsible for implementing this Information Security Policy within their business areas, departments and teams, and for policies adherence by their staff.*
- *The Information Security Policy review procedure shall be endorsed and supported by <insert company name> Senior Management, and signed-off by the company <insert senior manager position> prior to initiation.*
- *<insert company name> Senior Management shall ensure a proper level of inter-departmental*

> *collaboration in relation to the Information Security Policy compliance and support throughout the company.*

So, always check that the auditee security policy contains similar opening statements (easy!) and they are adhered to in practice (difficult!).

A mistake that is sometimes made is picking on the auditee management regarding various operational, technical, physical and human resources information security details. The auditors might do it out of arrogance to demonstrate their prowess in a beloved specific field of knowledge. However, this is not the senior, or even specialised manager's job, and not knowing about many of these things is not their fault. The CIO, or even the CTO, can be highly regarded in the company. They can be on the Board of Directors, as commonly happens with high-tech IT-centred enterprises. They could also be information security gurus, but obviously don't have to be. The CISOs are often expected to possess specific in-depth knowledge of different security methods, technologies and tools. However, for these important security professionals it is far from being an absolute requirement.

We could not resist the temptation to cite quite a lengthy excerpt from Clausewitz's *On War,* discussing the qualities a top military commander should wield:

The Commander of an army neither requires to be a learned explorer of history nor a publicist, but he must be well versed in the higher affairs of State; he must know and be able to judge correctly of traditional tendencies, interests at stake, the immediate questions at issue, and the characters of leading persons; he need not be a close observer of men, a sharp dissector of human character, but he must know the character, the feelings, the habits, the peculiar faults and inclinations of those whom he is to command. He need not understand anything about the make of a carriage, or the harness of a Battery horse, but he must know how to calculate exactly the march of a column, under different circumstances, according to the time it requires. These are things the knowledge of which cannot be forced out by an apparatus of scientific formula and machinery: they are only to be gained by the exercise of an accurate judgement in the observation of things and of men, aided by a special talent for the apprehension of both.

This, in our humble opinion, is a very precise description which is easily transferable into the language of modern technology. The CISOs should be able to identify five AES (Advanced Encryption Standard) selection finalist ciphers, but do not need to know how many rounds of iteration or S-boxes these ciphers have. They should know the difference between WPA (Wireless Protected Access) versions one and two, and the distinctions between their SOHO and Enterprise implementations. However, detailed knowledge of the RADIUS (Remote Authentication Dial In User Service) protocol used by WPA Enterprise is not needed. They should understand the principles behind buffer overflow, SQL injection, cross-site scripting and other common software-centric attack means. Nevertheless, a CISO does not have to read, write, patch or even execute code. Speaking of the 'management part' of the aforesaid *On War* excerpt, you only need to replace the 'State' with 'company' or 'organisation' to apply its intended meaning to our situation. The parts dealing with the human issues can be safely left intact.

The real role of the CISO is the one of a bridge or, to be more technically meticulous, a router that supports multiple communication protocols. The CISO 'routes' between those who operate on a large scale and know what to protect in general terms (the top management) and those who function within their limited scopes and know the details of *where* and *how* to safeguard it in practice. The CISOs must be able to capture the senior management's directions and intent, and translate them into a clear and precise language of security policies, standards and guidelines. Then they have to work on implementing, enforcing, maintaining and improving these policies and their operational applications, with more junior security specialists, as well as professionals from other departments. These departments include, but are not limited to, human resources, IT, risk management, legal and compliance. Figure 3 shows the classical top-down flow of information security guidance and intent in a large entity, the CISO being its 'core router'.

Figure 3: The personalised top-down flow

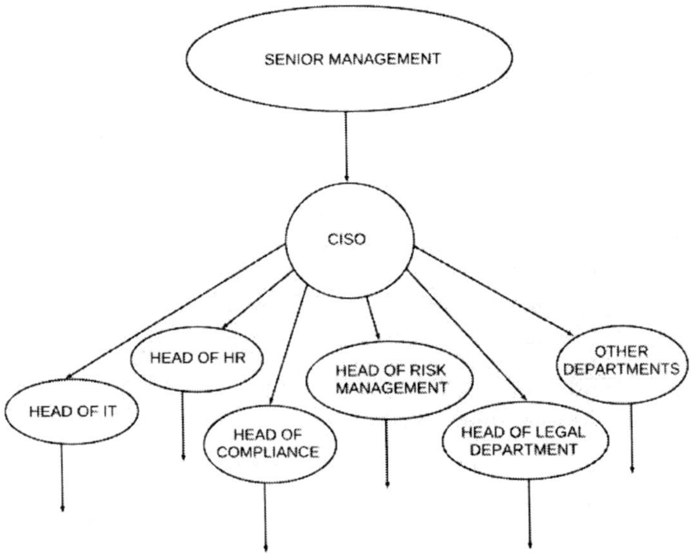

To summarise, the role and expected skill set of the CISO must be clearly understood by information security auditors of all specialisations and backgrounds. This is absolutely crucial for the assessment and their follow-up reactions success, since the auditors will closely work with the auditee CISO from the very beginning to the very end, and probably afterwards.

As for the company directors and other top managers, they should have some understanding of general information security principles and issues. For example, as primary data owners they should be well-familiar with how the company information is classified to assign and alter appropriate classification levels themselves, or authorise others to do so. Overall, this is similar to what Clausewitz has said about the Cabinet members of a state: '*a certain knowledge of the nature of war is essential to the management of political commerce*'.

By the way, did it cross your mind that since 'any action is reciprocal and triggers reaction', the scheme in Figure 3 is fundamentally flawed?

When things go bottom-up

'The occurrences of war will not unfold like clockwork. We cannot hope to impose precise, positive control over events. The best we can hope for is to impose a general framework of order on the disorder, to influence the general flow of action rather than to try to control each event. If we are to win, we must be able to operate in a disorderly environment.'

MCDP 1 *Warfighting*

Information security management, unfortunately, tends to lean to one of two extremes. One is to be too lax. Another is to be too severe. 'Taking information security seriously' is usually associated with the latter. The stricter, the better. If you ask many security specialists what is most vital in their field, you will no doubt receive plentiful answers like 'control', 'discipline', 'enforcing the policies' and 'that the rules are followed'. Some may recall the infamous 'deny all' principle. However, building and maintaining a viable ISMS is not configuring a firewall.

Surely, unrestricted top-down flow of control is highly important. As Sun Tzu pointed out, '*maintain discipline and adapt to the enemy in order to determine the outcome of the war*'. The aforementioned 'flow of control' and following the established rules, maintains discipline. But what about adapting to the enemy?

In his *Patterns of Conflict* Col. John Boyd has stated: '*Napoleon, Clausewitz, and Jomini viewed the conduct of war and related operations in essentially one direction – from the top down – emphasising adaptability at the top and regularity at the bottom*'. This is the essence of the 'top-down' principle. The 'top' adopts, writes and edits policies and standards. The 'bottom' must follow them with the utmost precision. If this is how you think the effective ISMS should work, than you are in the same company as 'Napoleon, Clausewitz and Jomini (a famous 19th Century French strategist)'. But don't be so proud. Recall that we have previously compared active adversaries to guerrillas or insurgents. Marching in perfectly organised columns against mobile guerrilla groups is utterly useless. They will dissipate and wait for an appropriate moment to strike. The moment will come. This effective approach decimated Napoleon's armies in Spain, Russia and Austria. He did not know how to address the problem and compared guerrilla warfare the Grande Armée faced, to an ulcer.

This, and not the lack of specific technical skills, is the reason why malicious hackers and cybercriminals often mock security systems and infrastructures they face, as well as professionals who oversee them. Attackers view these systems as bulky, inflexible and slow-reacting, with the costs of safeguards not justifying their practical worth. The only real danger modern day guerrillas face when encountered by a Napoleonic era column charging towards them, is to die from laughter. Yet this is, metaphorically speaking, what numerous information security specialists and whole organisations are currently doing. This is how it looks like from the outside attacker's perspective. When discussing absolute Command and Control (many CISOs sacred dream!), Col. John Boyd has astutely pointed out that the traditional 'C&C (Command and Control) *represents a top-down mentality applied in a rigid or mechanical way that ignores as well as stifles the implicit nature of human beings to deal with uncertainty, change, and stress*'.

These factors of 'uncertainty, change and stress' bring to attention the issue of friction. As we have previously discussed, friction is something we should strive to diminish. Figure 4 demonstrates that it could be completely the opposite if one adopts the 'control freak' or, to put it more politely, the 'rigid C&C' paradigm.

Figure 4: Friction and excessive control

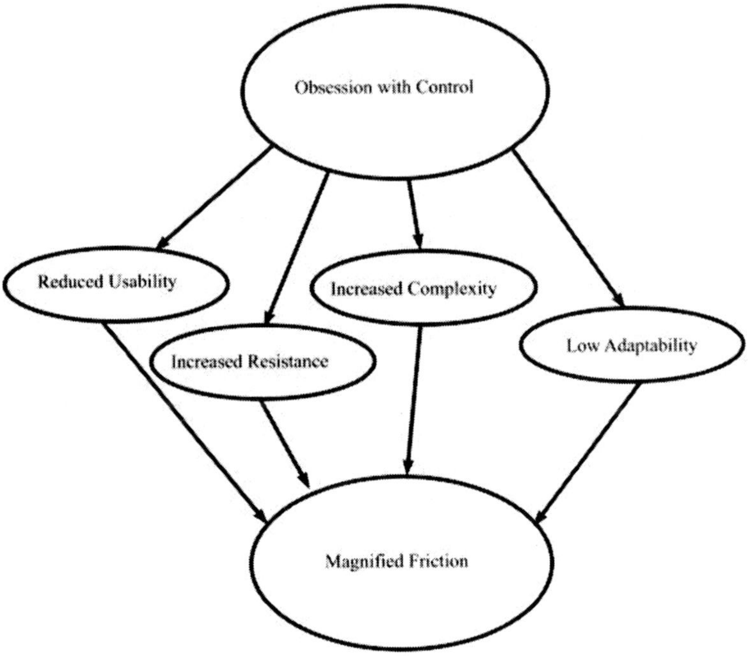

The most commonly addressed technological manifestation of this issue is 'security versus usability'. Recall the 'difficult password problem'. The majority of security professionals will suggest using two-factor authentication to resolve it. This suggestion is generally correct. However, we have seen people literally wearing necklaces of authentication tokens like stereotypical tribal chefs wear shark teeth. The accursed complexity has returned, alas on a different level.

Then an advice to employ a two-factor authentication scheme that uses mobile phones may follow. This technology allows you to receive authentication PINs via SMS. Thus, all PINs will be received by a single device. However, everything comes with a trade-off. To simplify matters, phone-based two factor authentication systems allow the reuse of a PIN. That is, the same PIN number can be utilised several times, or multiple times for a pre-defined duration. No doubt, many companies and organisations will opt for this. However, such an implementation is less secure than the more traditional authentication tokens. Besides, a mobile phone is not a little specialised dongle. Mobile phones are lucrative targets for thieves. They can also be hacked into via Bluetooth (and many smartphones – via WiFi) or infected by malware. If the PIN is reusable and did not expire, an adversary who has got (or has got into) the phone can abuse it. Thus, a very thorough analysis of benefits and risks must be performed prior to deciding which authentication system is optimal for every specific case.

This was a purely technical example. At times, technology can resolve such issues by applying unorthodox (at their introduction age) means. Before the event of asymmetric encryption, a common way to protect the shared keys was by using a KEK (Key Encryption Key). But then, logically, the problem of enciphering the KEK with some KEKEK would arise, and then the KEKEKEK and so forth towards the infinity. The introduction of Diffie-Hellman and similar secure mutual authentication algorithms has successfully solved this issue. However, there is no magical silver bullet for eliminating its human counterparts.

When employees are exposed to harsh and obstructive regulations and controls, the following can, and will happen:

- They would passively resist (ignore) the controls.
- They would actively resist (circumvent) the controls.
- They would obey them to the letter, which usually comes down to endless execution of mindless drills.

At the end of the day, they will completely lose any initiative and become dissatisfied, if not disgruntled.

Contemplating flexible command and control

The MCDP 1 *Warfighting* asserts that '*we must not try to maintain excessive control over subordinates since this will necessarily slow our tempo and inhibit initiative*'. It also reinforces this thought with the following statement: '*The senior intervenes in a subordinate's execution only by exception. It is this freedom for initiative that permits the high tempo of operations that we desire. Uninhibited by excessive restrictions from above, subordinates can adapt their actions to the changing situation*'. Surely, what is acceptable and recommended for the Marines should satisfy even the most authoritarian CISO in the world!

Figure 5 shows the 'boydian' reciprocal approach to information security management as we see it.

Figure 5: Bidirectional flow in a nutshell

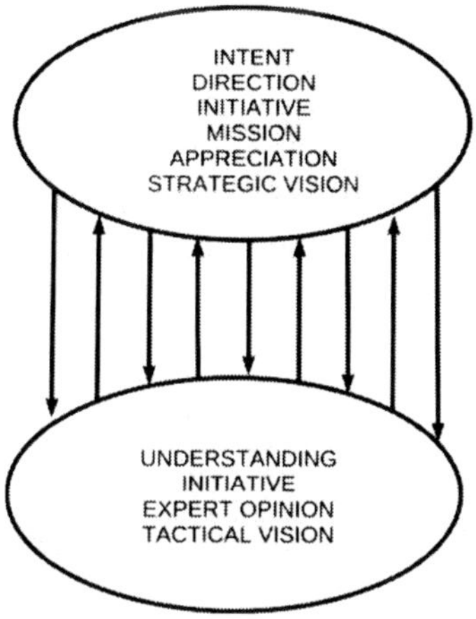

The 'top' should generate intent, provide direction and formulate missions to accomplish. It must see information security of the entity as a whole, and from the business perspective. The 'bottom' should clearly understand these intent, direction and mission assignments flowing from the top, but it should not be silent. It has the expertise that the 'top' lacks. Thus, it should provide an upward flow of such expertise, and the management should actively appreciate and encourage it. Technical, human resources and other specialists know the details the management is naturally unable to see. And, as the folk wisdom goes, the devil is in the details. The 'bottom' is obliged to listen by the rules the 'top' sets. The sensible 'top' is obliged to listen by reason and circumstances. *Lack of effective communication in any direction is a serious security gap*. Finally, but most importantly, both the 'bottom' and the 'top' must exhibit appropriate initiative.

When outlining a possible solution for the 'top-down-top' question, Col. John Boyd has proposed that the inflexible top-down command and control should be substituted with a swiftly adaptable 'leadership-monitoring-appreciation-error correction' flow. This is a highly sensible approach, which is fully applicable to modern information security management. As the MCDP 1 *Warfighting* precisely formulates, '*we seek unity not principally through imposed control, but through harmonious initiative and lateral coordination within the context provided by guidance from above*'.

To conclude, what is casually viewed as the most stringent and hard-boiled 'thou shalt not' structure of enforcement and control should be, to the contrary, one of the most flexible corporate or organisational management systems. In its rapid adaptability to changing environments it can, perhaps, be compared to stock market trading. Thus, the auditors must verify that the ISMS and the way it is run maintains the necessary degree of initiative, flexibility, fluidity, adaptability, harmony and pace to be truly proficient. This could easily be the main strategic goal of any ISMS assessment. Meanwhile, '*the autocratic control and drill-machine approach*' has just joined the club of glaring strategic faults to look for during information security audits.

On analysing ISMS strategies and flows

'It may sound strange, but for all who know war in this respect it is a fact beyond doubt, that much more strength of will is required to make an important decision in strategy than in tactics.'

Carl von Clausewitz

If we know what to assess and how it should function to be effective, the audit is not a difficult task. Assuming that the auditors are familiar with how a robust ISMS is constructed and should operate, the major obstacle to auditing information security strategies is the situational orientation. All security programmes and strategies of a company or organisation should be in perfect resonance with its business model, modes of operation and aims. Prior to performing the assessment, the auditors should learn as much as possible about these decisive factors. They should get a good grasp of corporate politics and study the 'terrain', as *the first step of any ISMS audit shall always be analysing and verifying the aforesaid resonance*. If information security strategies and programmes do not correspond to the business model and planned developments of a company, they are non-viable and there is no point in studying them any further. The same applies to their accord with operational models and strategic aims of any non-commercial organisations, from charities to government agencies.

What about real-life examples of such situations? We can recall a corporation that built its ISMS and security infrastructure in accordance with the textbook rules. It did not take into account the fact that about 70% of its staff were temporary contractors who, on average, didn't stay employed for more than a year. This was completely overlooked on all levels, from security policies to access lists, authentication methods, personnel monitoring and physical controls. As a result, they had at least a few cases of major confidential data leaks, as well as rampaging plain old theft of IT equipment, stationery and other goods. Another instance that can be rather illustrative, is a company that was undergoing a major merger which was not sufficiently addressed in its information security programmes and plans until it actually happened. The management of the new entity had to restructure the ISMS reactively and in haste. Expectedly, this created multiple security shortcomings, a few of which still remained unresolved a year after the merger took place.

To outline *the next strategy assessment step*, we will return to the previous section's discussion topic, namely to the 'leadership-monitoring-appreciation-error correction' flow. The first question is whether it exists at all. If it appears so, check its functionality and sufficiency, starting from the leadership part.

There are plentiful modern definitions and theories of leadership which are useful to know, but are clearly outside this work's scope. One such definition, coming from Warren Bennis' and Dan Goldsmith's *Learning to Lead* is '*a good manager does things right. A leader does the right things*'. It underlines initiative and active decision making, instead of following the prescribed word. Sun Tzu provided probably the most ancient definition of 'leadership': '*The Way means inducing the people to have the same aim as the leaders*'. His follower, Cao Cao, later commented: '*This means guiding them by instruction and direction*'. All this requires having a strategic goal or goals which can serve as rallying point(s) of effective strategic information security programmes. As John Boyd pointed out, '*for success over the long haul and under the most difficult conditions, one needs some unifying vision that can be used to attract the uncommitted as well as pump-up friendly resolve and drive and drain-away or subvert adversary resolve and drive*'.

Such rallying points must be clearly defined, explained and communicated. Compliance can help, especially if it is strongly ISMS-related. Becoming ISO27001 compliant within a year is a perfect rally point. Making all employees security aware and able to spot and duly report all suspicious activities is a good rally point. Recalling the aforementioned negative example, in case of a merger or acquisition, creating an effective ISMS for the newborn corporate entity by absorbing the best from the amalgamating companies, is an excellent rally point. Reducing the number of information security incidents below a certain level can be a good rally point, if one is able to define this level with clarity and solid reason. Our division of security incidents into passive and active may help. The management could first address the reduction and mitigation of the former, and then deal with the latter. The following excerpt from the MCDP 1 *Warfighting* provides a good summary for this discourse:

- *Top-down flow of intent provides consistency and continuity to our actions and establishes the context that is essential for the proper bottom-up exercise of initiative. A subordinate should be ever conscious of a senior's intent so that it guides every decision. An intent that is involved or complicated will fail to accomplish this purpose.*

Providing that such a flow of direction and intent exists, the strategic goals and plans are reasonable, clearly defined, and are thoroughly synchronised with their governing 'political' counterparts; what remains to be *assessed is whether it all actually works as intended.* This relates to the 'monitoring-appreciation-error correction' part of our flexible security management chain. Its analysis amounts to reviewing information security processes and their end results. In this chapter we shall concentrate on the former, leaving the latter for more technical discussions to follow.

High level dissection of security processes

The peculiarities of separate specific processes, for example the processes of secure software development or change control, belong to the realm of tactics. This section is dedicated to the strategic dimension, which covers the ISMS as a whole. ISO/IEC27001 explicitly incorporates that ISMS processes must follow the classical Deming, or PDCA (Plan-Do-Check-Act) cycle. COBIT promotes its adapted variety. To refresh your memory, the cycle is shown in Figure 6.

Figure 6: The all-familiar PDCA

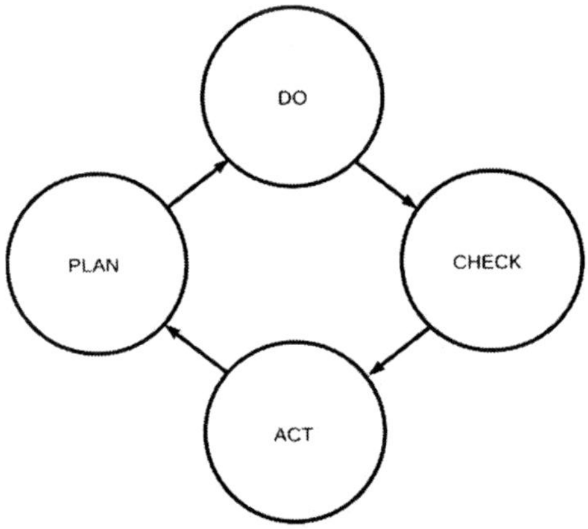

In practical terms, a typical Deming cycle of the ISMS process is characterised by a combination of relatively large amplitude and slow pace. In particular, thorough planning and in-depth checking must absorb and analyse a large number of variables, which inevitably consumes plenty of time. An information security audit can fit the Deming cycle well, when looked at from the auditee perspective. Which is, as we have noted in the beginning of Chapter 1, *more strategic in nature*. The assessment is first planned, then executed, then its outcome is studied, and finally appropriate follow-up actions are performed. However, from the auditor's viewpoint, the OODA loop is far more suitable to describe and structure the process of assessment. Also, take note that typically attackers 'operate in OODA loops' rather than follow 'the Deming'. OODA loops can be slow and fast, covering vast or narrow ranges; they can be tactical or strategic. So, how do OODA loops and the Deming cycle mix together on a grand scale of things? Figure 7 depicts our vision of this dynamic union.

Figure 7: Unfolding of a complete strategic process

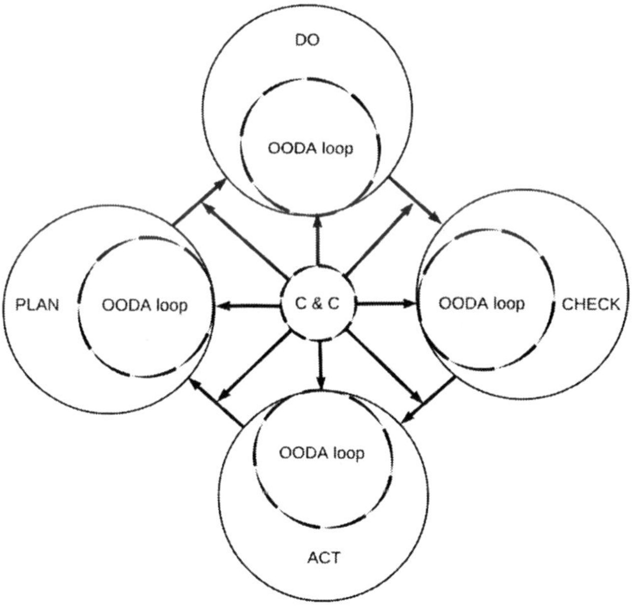

The flexible 'command and control' in the centre of the scheme, spins its own OODA loops. There are OODA loops within every single stage of the Deming cycle. There could be as many of them as necessary, both in the 'C&C centre' and within the separate cycle phases. They can be embedded one within the other like Russian dolls. A very important part of the scheme is that the central 'flexible C&C loops' influence every Deming cycle stage and its inner OODAs. Even more, they also influence the transition between the phases, which is represented on the scheme by the diagonal arrows. By 'influence' we imply a whole plethora of possible effects: trigger, direct, control, monitor, correct, appreciate, accelerate, delay, etc. This is how, in highly simplified terms, such a process would work in the ideal world:

1 The central C&C OODA loop revolves. Its Action becomes the Deming PLAN stage.
2 The PLAN OODA loop now spins. The end results of its Action (plans) are fed back to the C&C.
3 The C&C OODA loop revolves. If the plans are disapproved, we return to two. If the plans are deemed satisfactory, its Action becomes the Deming DO stage and triggers the inner DO OODA loop.
4 Repeat this block for the whole Deming cycle until its successful completion.

But in the ideal world we won't need any information security assessments whatsoever.

In reality, the auditors must check where and how our security process goes wrong and suggest a suitable remedy. In severe cases the whole stages of the Deming cycle, not to mention separate OODA loops, can simply go amiss. But the issues you will most commonly encounter are the problems of synchronisation. Note, that the scheme shown in Figure 7 looks like a combination of clocks that converge into a single all-permeating pattern. If some of these clocks become desynchronised, the whole process may fall apart, or its efficacy can be dramatically reduced. In the words of Col. John Boyd, that have actually inspired this scheme, '*faster tempo, or rhythm, at lower levels should work within the slower rhythm but larger pattern at higher levels so that the overall system does not lose its cohesion or coherency*'.

Thus, look for what is missing and what is desynchronised. Check where the C&C OODA loop didn't spin to initiate a Deming phase or supervise the transition between them (*laissez-faire*!). Verify that nothing has stuck 'at the stuttering sound of 'OO-OO-OO' as described by Dr. Ullman in his CrossTalk Journal article (available at *www.stsc.hill.af.mil/CrossTalk/2007/04/0704Ullman.html*). Examine that one loop didn't start to spin before its logical predecessor has completed its revolution (a typical case of de-synchronisation). And so forth.

Nevertheless, always keep in mind that we are not dealing with some infallible rigid clockwork mechanism of medieval deists or theatrical military parades. Re-read the epigraph to 'When things go bottom-up' section of this chapter one more time. Contemplate it. Synchronisation, for instance, does not mean that all our 'clocks' are ticking with exactly the same speed. Or that this tempo would *always* be slow at higher levels and rapid at their lower reflections and counterparts. Our synchronisation is a matter of functionality, operability and efficacy. It is not striving for some *über*-Platonic perfection that would inevitably destroy all initiative. Some deviations could, or even should, be acceptable. The auditors should always keep it in mind. After all, '*information security assessment always operates with probabilities*' and is a way of analysing and prioritising risks. Low risk issues can be tolerated and retained, as eliminating them might introduce more problems than such issues present.

When gauging the balance of factors, such as those discussed above, experienced security auditors firmly enter the realm of art.

On security assessments and security policies

'War is an instrument of policy; it must necessarily bear its character, it must measure with its scale: the conduct of war, in its great features, is therefore ***policy itself, which takes up the sword in place of the pen, but does not on that account cease to think according to its own laws****.'*

Carl von Clausewitz

One of the most straightforward elements of assessing the ISMS and information security strategies in general, is auditing security policies of a company or organisation. Security policies are rightfully viewed as a centre and a cornerstone of any ISMS, outlining and connecting into a whole a variety of its elements. This can be compared with the role national policies have in the conduct of a state:

- '*War is to be regarded as an organic whole, from which the single branches are not to be separated, in which therefore every individual activity flows into the whole, and also has its origin in the idea of this whole, then it becomes certain and palpable to us that the superior stand-point for the conduct of the war, from which its leading lines must proceed, can be no other than that of policy*' (Clausewitz).

If you substitute 'war' with 'information security' in this excerpt, it would outline our situation very well. Being the founding father and a vigorous proponent of the political concept of warfare, Carl von Clausewitz contemplated a lot on the role of (state) policies in 'taking up the sword in place of the pen'. That is, moving from the guidance of the policies to resolute action. Many of his conclusions deserve honourable place in information security management textbooks. Therefore, we have decided to dedicate some of this section's space to a brief 'Clausewitz substitution exercise'. Consider the following statements:

- *If war belongs to policy, it will naturally take its character from thence. If policy is grand and powerful, so will also be the war, and this may be carried to the point at which war attains to its absolute form.*

If the security policies are 'grand and powerful', so will be the ISMS and the entity's information security state, which can even come close to an 'absolute form'. By an 'absolute form of war', Clausewitz implied a total mobilisation of all citizens and resources of the state, towards a unified military goal. In our case, participation of every employee in information security programmes and enabling reasonable safeguards for all systems, networks, physical premises and sensitive documentation, would suffice.

- *Only through this kind of view, war recovers unity; only by it can we see all wars as things of one kind; and it is only through it that the judgement can obtain the true and perfect basis and point of view from which great plans may be traced out and determined upon. It is true the political element does not sink deep into the details of war, vedettes (listening-posts) are not planted, patrols do not make their rounds from political considerations, but small as is its influence in this respect, it is great in the formation of a plan for a whole war, or a campaign, and often even for a battle.*

Only through the policy-centric approach, information security of an entity becomes complete and plans for effective security programmes can be laid. It also enables us to see various human, technical and operational actions and countermeasures as 'things of one kind', guided by the same direction, intent, philosophy and logic. While it is true that information security policies 'do not sink deep into the details' of personnel vetting or database input validation controls, organisation and planning of all these measures and even the separate acts, are governed by the policies.

- *If, therefore, in drawing up a plan of a war it is not allowable to have a two-fold or three-fold point of view, from which things may be looked at, now with the eye of a soldier, then with that of an administrator, and then again with that of a politician, etc., then the next question is, whether policy is necessarily paramount, and everything else subordinate to it.*

Security policies cannot have 'a two-fold or three-fold point of view', looking at the issues they address with the eye of an IT specialist, then with that of a human resources manager, and then again with that of a CEO. They must effectively translate information security intent, direction and initiative of the entity's top management into a clearly expressed written form.

General security policy shortcomings

Having said all of the above, we have encountered numerous sufficiently large companies that don't have any information security policies whatsoever. We have seen even more businesses that have security policies to observe formalities ('the compliance demands it!') or for the sake of appearance ('look, we care about security, we have a beautifully bound 400-page policies tome!'). The policies exist but are completely ignored. They are not read, updated, followed and, of course, not reviewed and reassessed. Many security specialists, in particular on the technical side, view the policies as a 'mere formality', 'annoying bureaucracy' and even simply as a 'waste of time'. If the situation is similar to the ones we have just outlined, these opinions of policies are entirely correct. One of the key aims of information security assessments must be to ensure that such a state of affairs is avoided or abolished.

We will review more specific details regarding hands-on security policies auditing in the upcoming chapter of this book. This chapter is dedicated to security governance, thus the strategic side. When performing a general assessment, the first thing the auditors should look for is whether the security policies are generated via some clueless automated tool, or by taking a publicly available template or someone else's policy and using the 'find and replace' function of a text editor. If you have looked at such tools and written numerous security policies consulting various templates yourself, this should not be difficult. It should not be harder than spotting plagiarism in a student's works is to an experienced lecturer.

A hallmark of a mindless template or other's policies adaptation is the presence of elements that are completely irrelevant for the company or organisation. This signifies the cardinal sin of the ISMS (if actually existent!) being out of touch with the business model, modes of operation and aims of a company. The irrelevant elements can vary. It could be assigning responsibilities to positions, or even whole departments and teams not available within the company. It might be covering areas of business operations that are completely absent. To remind, ISO/IEC27001 suggest the following general 15-part set of security policies aligned with this standard:

- Chapter 1. Information security organisation
- Chapter 2. Classifying information and data
- Chapter 3. Controlling access to information and systems
- Chapter 4. Processing information and documents
- Chapter 5. Purchasing and maintaining commercial software
- Chapter 6. Securing hardware, peripherals and other equipment
- Chapter 7. Combating cybercrime
- Chapter 8. Controlling e-commerce information security
- Chapter 9. Developing and maintaining in-house software
- Chapter 10. Dealing with premises-related considerations
- Chapter 11. Addressing personnel issues related to security
- Chapter 12. Delivering training and staff awareness
- Chapter 13. Complying with legal and policy requirements
- Chapter 14. Detecting and responding to information security incidents
- Chapter 15. Planning for business continuity.

In the past, we audited a company that had security policies dedicated to in-house software development (Chapter 9 of the above), and another that possessed a fully-blown e-commerce (Chapter 8) policy set. However, the first company did not develop *or plan to develop* any software in the foreseeable future. The second did not perform *or plan to perform* any e-commerce activities. Above, we have marked the planning intent in italics because sometimes things are done in advance in scalability's sake. These were clearly not such cases. If the standard recommends so, it does not mean that you have to do it, even if only to become compliant. Practical demands should be addressed first, and if a severe security incident takes place, being compliant can actually make things worse from a legal viewpoint.

After the auditors have finished searching for unnecessary *and obsolete* elements within the policies, they should start looking for gaps. The most obvious gap is when a whole chapter or subject section is missing. The proposed ISO27001 list of policy chapters provides a good reference point, but is by no means complete. For example, if a company heavily relies on telecommuters or staff on business trips, a separate telecommuter security policy set or, more generally, a remote employee security policy set should be developed. If the company strongly depends on wireless networks in its everyday business operations, a sound wireless security policy should be created. Both remote employee and wireless security policies have sufficient scope to become separate policy chapters. Such chapters are not listed in the 15-part set. Nevertheless, in the situations we have outlined, not having them would constitute serious gaps.

The next overall security policy review stage will need to weight the chapters against each other. You may find out that while all relevant topics are covered, this coverage is highly uneven. Such irregularity often discloses the policy author's main background which can be management, technical, human resources, or even legal. By analysing which policy chapters are well-cultivated and to the point, and which are frankly poor, this background is easy to deduce. When contemplating on Clausewitz's wisdom earlier in this section, we have explicitly stated that 'security policies cannot have a two-fold or three-fold point of view'. Being the top management's written expression of information security direction and intent, they cannot afford to have one of the lower level specialist's views as prevalent. Thus, irregular coverage of various information security topics is also a serious strategic gap, second only to not covering some of the areas at all. If this unevenness is very high, it is a clear indication that the 'Maginot Line mentality' is present. Too much effort is dedicated to a specific scope of activity and field of knowledge, at the expense of its equally important counterparts.

When checking the policies, pay due attention to their general style and depth. Clarity is easy to verify. For instance, '*computer and network appliance premises must be safeguarded against unlawful and unauthorised physical intrusion. All visitors to these premises must be physically supervised*' is a very clear premises security policy statement. The evaluation of depth, however, is somewhat of a delicate issue that requires experience and expertise to reach the needed balance.

It is common knowledge that information security policy statements must be general, if not generic. The 'technicalities' should be left for the corresponding guidelines, standards, manuals, etc. It is very easy to slip from the 'strategic' level of the policies to the 'tactical' level of such specialist documentation. This is a typical error of security professionals who get carried away by their special background-related knowledge when composing the policy statements. However, it is not a particularly dreadful error. It only means that as the implementation inevitably changes, the correlating policy will have to be reviewed, rewritten and re-approved.

Statements that are too general present a much larger problem. They are also a good indication that some standard policy template was used without giving much thought to its relevance for the business. '*All sensitive data must be encrypted*' is not a security policy statement, but simply an expression of common sense. '*All back-ups of highly confidential data must be protected with strong cryptography*' is a good policy statement. It shows precisely which defined data classification category ('highly confidential') is covered, and where ('all back-ups') it must be protected. The word 'strong' also makes a huge difference, providing that a downstream standard or guideline defines what is acceptable as 'strong cryptography' in the company, and what isn't. For example, it might say that when it comes to symmetric block ciphers, only AES with a minimal 128-bit key size can be used. This discussion has inevitably brought us to the subject of verifying whether every security policy is properly supported with necessary downstream documentation, as well as corresponding processes and countermeasures. It will be reviewed in the less 'strategic' chapters of this book.

Addressing security audits in policy statements

To accomplish the discourse on general assessments of information security policies, we still need to address the coverage of security assessments in the policies. Chapter 13, Complying with Legal and Policy Requirements,

Complying with Security Policies subsection appears to be the most appropriate part of ISO/IEC27001 streamlined information security policy to cover the subject of security audits. Just as an example, its corresponding statements might look like:

- *The <responsible senior manager, CISO, Chief Compliance Officer> shall initiate periodic information security assessments and employ trusted third party auditors to evaluate the degree of compliance with the current Information Security Policy.*
- *These information security assessments can be external, internal or otherwise specialised as determined and approved by <company name> senior management.*
- *All files and documents related to the Information Security Policy compliance and audits are considered to be 'highly confidential' and must be appropriately safeguarded. A register of their location and ownership is to be created, maintained and safeguarded as 'highly confidential' data.*
- *A re-assessment of the threats and risks involved relating to <company name> business activities must take place periodically to ensure that the company is adequately insured at all times.*
- *Managers and system owners must ensure compliance with information security policies and standards through regular platform security reviews, penetration tests and other relevant activities undertaken by competent testers.*
- *Information security audits should be carefully planned to minimise disruption to operational processes and systems.*

Periodic or triggered assessments of security policies must be covered in the Chapter 1, Information Security

Organisation, Information Security Policy review subsection. Its statements might be similar to:

- *<company name> Information Security Policy shall undergo an annual review.*
- *The management shall form an ad-hoc review committee to create, update, or review policies when significant changes are necessary prior to the regular (annual) review.*
- *The Information Security Policy review procedure shall be endorsed and supported by <company name> senior management, and signed-off by the <responsible senior manager position> prior to initiation.*
- *Trusted and competent third party consultants can be employed to assist with the Information Security Policy review if deemed necessary by <company name> senior management.*

Additional policy entries might cover who is responsible for supervising information security audits, depending on their scope and specific nature. More often than not this is a direct responsibility of the company's CISO.

On security assessments and compliance

'Regulation-SOX, HIPAA, GLB, the credit-card industry's PCI, the various disclosure laws, the European Data Protection Act, whatever – has been the best stick the industry has found to beat companies over the head with. And it works. Regulation forces companies to take security more seriously, and sells more products and services.'

Bruce Schneier

Regulations and standards are the top-down approach taken to the absolute. The top (from which the regulations and standards are hammered down) is literally removed from the company or organisation to the realm of a higher authority. This is somewhat similar to the role of the United Nations in the world's political affairs. But at least in the UN the representatives of different nations can vote. In contrast, any down-top flow in information security regulations and standards is extremely limited. There is usually little you can do to alter them, unless you are a part of the regulatory body yourself. However, sometimes it is possible to contribute at least to the relevant guidelines. For example, if you have sufficient experience in ISMS assessments, you can provide input to ISO/IEC27007, Guidelines for ISMS Auditing (currently a draft), and its complementary ISO/IEC27008, Guidance for Auditors on ISMS Controls (also still a draft).

Compliance to industry standards and legal regulations is, overall, a good thing. As Bruce Schneier pointed out, it forces companies and organisations to do something about information security or face various penalties. It aspires to provide a defined security baseline for the whole variety of business operations. It sells products, but beware of the 'shiny box with flashing lights' mindset. Being compliant while some of your rivals aren't can provide a significant competitive advantage. Sometimes, it can open the whole market. For the auditors, compliance demands are beneficial, not only because they provide their bread and butter by forcing companies to subscribe for security assessments. Technically speaking, at least some standards and regulations provide highly useful reference points for assessing processes and controls while streamlining them across entire industries. Or so the theory goes.

In practice, the UN analogy seems to be a reasonable one. Sometimes the intervention of the UN stops wars and mitigates disasters. Sometimes it completely fails to do so. The predecessor of the UN was completely toothless to prevent the Second World War. There are many companies and organisations which are fully compliant to various standards from ISO/IEC27001:2005 to PCI DSS, and yet had severe security breaches that made large media waves. The UK FSA Detailed IT Controls Form (Annex 1) has dozens of pages dedicated to information security requirements, including independent penetration testing. Nonetheless, we have encountered plenty of companies that were fully FSA-compliant but didn't even have a security policy. Needless to say, the actual 'hands-on' controls were also close to abysmal. In fact, we have never seen any detailed statistics comparing both the number and impact of security incidents between companies compliant and non-compliant to a selected industry standard. Doing such statistical research would be a difficult task. Its results could be easily biased.

The erroneous path to compliance

In some situations, regulations and standards can become a part of a problem rather than its intended solution. Just like information security in general, they are frequently treated as necessary (enforced) evil that must be shaken off with minimal resources and time expenditure. This leads to a very formal and superficial approach. The auditees build 'Potemkin villages' or, to say more precisely, 'Potemkin fortresses', for compliance auditors to see. Unfortunately, the latter are often perfunctory themselves. They go through a prefabricated checklist of 'how-it-should-be's', apply it to the presented 'Potemkin fortress', and churn out another 'everything is OK, you are compliant' report. The behaviour of such auditees is very similar to that of the crammer students who mechanically memorise answers to the expected exam questions instead of properly studying and comprehending the examined subject. When encountering real-life issues pertinent to this subject, such graduates are commonly lost.

When the auditees are, at least, honest to themselves and understand that their 'Potemkin fortresses' do not provide any *actual* protection, the aforementioned issue is half the trouble. The real calamity unfolds when the auditees start believing their own smoke-and-mirrors. Then the false sense of security slips in. It is your mortal foe. The military parallel is thinking that a certain section of the front line is reasonably defended while it lays bare in front of the opponent. Never underestimate the adversaries: they will find such gaps and ruthlessly exploit them. And if we look at passive security incidents only, the thread will break where it is the weakest. When applied to information security auditing, the 'something is better than nothing' principle is blatantly wrong. It is wrong because it is incomplete. The complete version should be '*something is better than nothing only if it does not encourage a false sense of security in any shape and form*'. Thus, even if the auditee did a very good job at satisfying all compliance demands, and the auditors truly excelled at verifying every single inch of it, do not sit back and cheer. Being fully compliant to any existing information security standard should never instil a scruple of a false sense of security. It is only a step on a long way to becoming adequately secure, even if making this step requires tremendous efforts from the company management and its subordinates. However, these pains are largely justified.

Keeping in mind the problems we have just discussed, perhaps there is a need to single out the 'narrow compliance-centric approach' as one of the strategic flaws to look for during ISMS assessments. Sometimes, when a company does not have a CISO or equivalent, its information security management is handled by the compliance officer. In other cases, the compliance issues are so hard-pressing that all resources are re-oriented to resolve them. In these situations the general security orientation may suffer from severe confusion. However harsh and unsettling the compliance auditors might be, they are not the enemy. The main aim of any information security act and safeguard is to protect data and systems – not to get certified. Information security standards and regulations also serve the same goal: they are not a noumenalist thing-in-itself. Armies exist to fight battles rather than successfully pass inspections of the general staff. Apart from possible disorientation, the 'narrow compliance-centric approach' can also promote what we have earlier called a 'drill-machine mentality'. This is not surprising, considering that the down-top flow is restricted and the primary source of initiative lies outside the entity, being a regulatory body or a standard committee. To avoid such shortfalls, the following suggestions could be helpful:

- *The senior management of the company or organisation must intercept the compliance initiative and become its main source.*
- *There must be a clear understanding that while the compliance demands shape security programmes and*

systems, their 'command and control' are still internal and must serve the specific aims of the business first.

- *An attitude of getting the most and the best out of any security compliance audits and their follow-up reactions,* ***in terms of actual/practical information security*** *should be developed.*

In our earlier metaphor of world politics, the UN undoubtedly shapes the political landscape, but does not violate sovereignty of its member states (with a few possible force majeure exceptions). The states, on the other hand, are trying to get maximal benefits for themselves out of different UN initiatives.

Getting down to earth

The paradox of information security-related standards and regulations is that while being stringent and rigorous in essence and on paper, they can be very lax when it comes to practical implementations and their assessments. The main reason for this looseness is that they are too general and do not go deep under the bonnet from many security specialists' perspective. On the other hand, some of the regulations address only the limited areas of information security, and don't even do it directly.

One should always keep in mind, that at the end of the day regulations like the Sarbanes-Oxley Act, Basel II Accord and GLBA are financial by their very nature. For them, information security is auxiliary. It should be reviewed, but is not likely to be the decisive factor in getting compliant. It is one thing of many. Sarbanes-Oxley 404 assessment approach is a very good illustration of this statement. These regulation's demands do not explicitly enforce many specific, highly important types of hands-on information security audits, like penetration tests or social engineering checks. In our experience, sometimes auditors that verify compliance to such regulations pick on these matters, but more often they do not. In a similar manner, FSA auditors in the UK often ignore the presence or absence of specific security assessment services. Quite recently, auditors from one of the 'Big Four' ran FSA compliance-triggered security assessments of a company we have been supplying with internal and external penetration tests for years. They were totally unaware of these tests and didn't even ask the auditee for the most recent test report. If they did, it would have saved them plenty of time. Besides, they could have synchronised with us in verifying whether various security issues we have previously discovered, are fixed prior to the next planned penetration test. The auditee company could have gained additional benefits from such collaboration.

Now let us turn to information security-specific standards, namely ISO/IEC27001 and PCI DSS. ISO/IEC27001, as one would expect, is fully ISMS-centred. There is no point in reiterating the whole ISO27001 certification process in this brief section. Just like the standard itself, its descriptions are widely available in the public domain. For example, a clear scheme of the certification process can be found at *www.27000.org/ismsprocess.htm*. In regard to building and assessing information security management architecture of an entity, ISO27001 does a pretty good job. What is important to understand, though, is that the ISMS is only a part of the overall information security of a company. It is a crucial backbone, core, organising, structuring part, but not the entire thing. While this could sound highly obvious, at least some security professionals with mainly managerial backgrounds, tend to neglect this basic truth. Returning to our warfare analogy, ISMS can be compared to the C&C chain, and security policies to military regulations, codes of discipline and field manuals. History knows many great armies that possessed the most perfect chain of command, organisation, orderliness, the books, etc. and were completely defeated.

ISO27001 compliance audits traditionally concentrate on policies, other security documentation, ISMS processes and controls. Assessing the actual implementations of the above is not their strongest trait. Neither should it be. Security policies, standards and guidelines have to prescribe more specific implementation-targeting audit types. Reviews of these important documents must verify that they are prescribed correctly. Such specialised security assessments, like penetration testing and social engineering checks mentioned above, must complement the verification of ISMS. In fact, they are a down-top (implementation – process – policy) hands-on way of this verification. Only when the harmony between both top-down and down-top approaches is achieved, will the 'security audit architecture' attain its '*absolute form*'.

PCI DSS, however, is expected to get under the bonnet with a greasy toolkit. It explicitly prescribes specific technical security controls, safeguards and their regular audits. This is what PCI DSS states regarding the latter in accordance with the defined merchant tiers:

- *Level 1 – Any merchant processing more than six million transactions per year, merchants identified by any card association as Level 1 or merchants that have suffered a hack or an attack that resulted in an account data compromise. Level 1 Merchants validate by undergoing an Annual On-Site Security Audit by a Qualified Security*

Assessor and carry out a Quarterly Network Scan utilising an Approved Scanning Vendor.

- *Level 2 – Any merchant processing one million to six million transactions per year.*
- *Level 3 – Any merchant processing between 20,000 and one million transactions per year. Merchants with Levels 2 and 3 validate PCI Compliance by completing an Annual PCI Self-Assessment Questionnaire and carry out a Quarterly Network Scan utilising an Approved Scanning Vendor.*
- *Level 4 – Up to 20,000 transactions per year. Level 4 merchants validate PCI Compliance by completing an Annual PCI Self-Assessment Questionnaire and carry out a Quarterly Network Scan utilising an Approved Scanning Vendor.*

Sounds good, especially considering the fact that those who suffered from a severe active security incident are automatically assigned to Level 1.

To refresh your memories, Table 1 presents 12 requirements for PCI DSS compliance, organised into six logically related groups called 'control objectives.' These are also PCI DSS audit targets.

Table 1: PCI DSS requirements

Control objectives	Control objectives
Build and maintain a secure network	1: Install and maintain a firewall configuration to protect cardholder data.
	2: Do not use vendor-supplied defaults for system passwords and other security parameters.
Protect cardholder data	3: Protect stored cardholder data
	4: Encrypt transmission of cardholder data across open, public networks.
Maintain a vulnerability management programme	5: Use and regularly update anti-virus software or programmes.
	6: Develop and maintain secure systems and applications.
Implement strong access control measures	7: Restrict access to cardholder data by business need-to-know.
	8: Assign a unique ID to each person with computer access.
	9: Restrict physical access to cardholder data.
Regularly monitor and test networks	10: Track and monitor all access to network resources and cardholder data.

	11: Regularly test security systems and processes.
Maintain an information security policy	12: Maintain a policy that addresses information security for employees and contractors.

There are also six milestones for prioritising PCI DSS compliance efforts, which are shown in Table 2.

Table 2: PCI DSS prioritised approach

Milestone	PCI DSS compliance goal
1	Remove sensitive authentication data and limit data retention.
2	Protect the perimeter, internal, and wireless networks.
3	Secure payment card applications.
4	Monitor and control access to your systems.
5	Protect stored cardholder data.
6	Finalise remaining compliance efforts, and ensure all controls are in place.

In relation to Requirement 11 (Regularly test security systems and processes), the prioritised approach sets forth the following prerequisites:

11.1 Test for the presence of wireless access points by using a wireless analyser at least quarterly or deploying a wireless IDS/IPS to identify all wireless devices in use.

11.2 Run internal and external network vulnerability scans at least quarterly and after any significant change in the network (such as new system component installations, changes in network topology, firewall rule modifications, product upgrades).

11.3 Perform external and internal penetration testing at least once a year and after any significant infrastructure or application upgrade or modification (such as an operating system upgrade, a sub-network added to the environment, or a Web server added to the environment). These penetration tests must include the following:

11.3.1 Network-layer penetration tests.

11.3.2 Application-layer penetration tests.

11.4 Use intrusion detection systems, and/or intrusion prevention systems, to monitor all traffic in the cardholder data environment and alert personnel to suspected compromises. Keep all intrusion detection and prevention engines up to date.

11.5 Deploy file integrity monitoring software to alert personnel to unauthorised modification of critical system files, configuration files or content files; and configure the software to perform critical file comparisons at least weekly.

We should note that PCI DSS Requirement 12 is not only about creating and maintaining appropriate information security policies. It also covers other elements of the ISMS, even though in this aspect it is not as complete as ISO/IEC27001 and its corresponding ISO/IEC27002 guidelines. Besides, at least some parts of PCI DSS Requirements, such as Requirements 9 and 12, address issues of social engineering attacks.

Is PCI DSS perfect? Nothing is. One can still be technically meticulous and note a few problems lurking within the standard. For instance, Requirement 4 Section 4.1.1 tells that:

- *For new wireless implementations, it is prohibited to implement WEP after 31 March 2009.*
- *For current wireless implementations, it is prohibited to use WEP after 30 June 2010.*

The vulnerabilities of WEP have been known for nearly a decade. More than a year before 31 March 2009 we could easily break WEP in about three minutes when performing wireless security audits. However, this is not the leitmotif of this governance and strategy-dedicated chapter. Technical discrepancies happen. Using WEP even in June 2010 is not the end of the world, providing that strong higher layer countermeasures (hint: IPSec) are concurrently applied. The matters which are more relevant for the current discussion are:

- *PCI DSS standard has a limited scope. Only the companies and organisations that accept payment cards, store or transmit card or transaction data, are covered.*

Producing a PCI DSS-like compulsory standard that would affect all industries that hold sensitive data (for example, personal data), would be a tremendous step forward in upholding a high level of information security and combating cybercrime. Even better, such a standard could combine the strong sides of both ISO/IEC27001 and PCI DSS.

- *This limited scope is transferred downwards within a single company or organisation. Only the systems, premises and communication channels that belong to the 'cardholder data environment' (CDE) need to be compliant.*

This opens up a potential gap for lateral attacks and may lead to the development of 'Maginot Line mentality' within the affected entities. We will heavily review the subject of 'outflanking' attacks in Chapter 5 of this book. By the way, note how the 'grand politics' (the business goals and reasons behind PCI DSS) influence the 'battlefield technicalities' (which parts of the IT infrastructure of a separate company are protected in accordance with PCI DSS demands, and which are not).

- *At the very least, PCI DSS network scans and their reporting formats, still need optimisation and streamlining.*

This statement comes from pure experience. We have seen many scans and reports from PCI DSS Approved Scanning Vendors (ASVs). There are, of course, PCI Security Standards Council requirements for the ASVs. The ASVs have to be re-approved annually. But the real quality of these scans and their reporting is not the same. Some ASVs seem to perform well within the limited scope of quarterly security scanning. Others use freeware public domain vulnerability scanners that are known to miss the whole classes of security flaws and produce numerous false positive results. Some scanning reports are sufficiently detailed. Other may simply say 'these hosts are secure' and supplement it with fragments of a common scanning tool output without even bothering to edit them. Remember, that in information security auditing '*something is better than nothing only if it does not encourage a false sense of security in any shape and form*'. Can you sense the ghastly spectre of the false sense of security creeping in?

CHAPTER 3: SECURITY ASSESSMENTS CLASSIFICATION

'If tactical facts in one case are entirely different from those in another, then the strategic must be so also, if they are to continue consistent and reasonable.'

Carl von Clausewitz

In theory, everything must be thoroughly assessed and verified to eliminate all kinds of security vulnerabilities and gaps. In the real world, however, there are limitations imposed by both budget and time. Because of these restrictions, the most critical areas must be identified to be audited first. Or, unfortunately, to be the only areas where information security state is going to be assessed for the foreseeable future. Making a correct, well-informed decision concerning the needed information security audits scope, priorities, spectrum and characteristics can be an intricate task. We shall thoroughly address it in the next chapter of this book. To be well-prepared for it, though, the auditees need to familiarise themselves with the assessments à la carte. The menu is quite extensive, and on numerous occasions the differences between the starter and the dessert are blurred and vague.

There is no universal panacea against information security incidents, whether passive or active. Thus, in the words of Col. John Boyd, '*it is advantageous to possess a variety of responses that can be applied rapidly to gain sustenance, avoid danger, and diminish adversary's capacity for independent action*'. The available variety of information security assessments can be broken up into separate categories in accordance with their targets, aims, methodologies and depth. If judged by applying these multiple parameters, a specific security audit can belong to several categories at once. When selecting the most appropriate information security assessment type, it is advantageous to move from the more general categories towards their specialised analogues. Accordingly, we shall review the global classifications first.

On broad categories of security audits

'Strategy may follow a great diversity of objects, for everything which appears an advantage may be the object of a combat.'

Carl von Clausewitz

The systematics discussed in this section are sufficiently common to apply to nearly all types of information security assessments. Previously, we have already divided the assessment activities into passive and active on the basis of their approach to tackling security issues. To rehearse:

- *A passive information security assessment is based upon verification against prefabricated checklists.*
- *An active information security assessment is based upon vigorously searching for vulnerabilities and gaps, employing all relevant knowledge, experience, creativity and insight.*

Another approach-based division is characterising security audits as *intrusive or non-intrusive*. Intrusive assessments can, but not necessarily will, heavily interfere with the audited systems or processes. As such, it is generally not recommended to perform intrusive audits against live production systems or important business processes and operations. Nevertheless, since non-intrusive tests usually lack the depth of their counterparts, and testing or pilot set-ups are not always available or feasible, the above advice is frequently ignored. When the estimated impact of a threat is incomparably higher than any disruption an intrusive audit that counters this threat can bring, such passing-by is entirely justified. In any case, intrusive assessments should be more carefully planned, monitored and supervised. Commonly, but not always, by their nature the intrusive audits are active, and non-intrusive are passive. Interviewing employees, checking physical security of premises, vigorous social engineering and penetration tests are typical examples of intrusive assessment activities. Reviewing security documentation, access lists, audit trails and configuration files are usually not intrusive.

Based on the auditors and their targets location, all information security assessments can be divided into *internal and external*. This should not be confused with the assessments being performed by in-house or third party consultants. There is nothing unusual about external assessments run by an in-house team using rented premises and remotely hosted systems. External assessments are often active and emulate exterior attackers trying to breach perimeter defences and penetrate into the *information security zone* of the auditee anywhere it extends. As such, they are penetration testing and social engineering-centred. Regular network vulnerability scans like those required to be PCI DSS compliant and provided by the ASVs are another common example of external security audits.

Internal assessments can come in all shapes and forms, targeting policy, operational, human and technical security issues. They are usually done on-site, but this is not obvious. The auditors can review some of the assessed data in their office, if the contract and NDA conditions permit it. It is also possible to install a separate testing system or software kit on the internal auditee network and use it to run a variety of technical checks initiated and controlled remotely over a well-protected VPN link. However, we strongly discourage taking any sensitive data, including personal employee, configuration and password files, off the auditee premises. It doesn't matter how strong the auditor's defences and controls can be, all actions that could create additional security incident opportunities must be avoided. *The information security zone* should be kept as shrunk as possible. At the end of the day, who audits the auditors? Besides, being on-site ensures robust communication between all parties involved, which is crucial in any information security audit's success.

Black, grey and white box tests

According to the initial level of the auditor's access, information security assessments are divided into *black box, grey box and white box* varieties. This classification is traditionally applied to purely technical activities from which it has originated. Nevertheless, we feel it can assume a wider scope and should be viewed as general. To define:

- *Black box assessments refer to situations where the auditors have no access rights at all and possess very limited information about the audit targets.*
- *When performing grey box assessments, the auditors start with having some form of limited, unprivileged access.*
- *White box assessments signify that full access to all analysed data, networks and systems is granted throughout the whole audit.*

To a certain extent, this classification can be applied to non-technical activities. For example, social engineering checks can be black or grey box. If the list of preferred targets is supplied and some physical access to the auditee premises is granted, a social engineering check no longer belongs to the black box category. In theory, ISMS reviews should always fall under the white box category. However, in practice many of them are more close to the shades of grey. This happens because more often than not, for a variety of reasons, the auditors are not provided with complete and unrestricted access to all relevant processes and documentation.

To summarise, black box tests are directed at assessing risks presented by typical external opponents with no insider knowledge. A great deal of vulnerability scanning, penetration testing and social engineering audit services belong to this category. The reconnaissance phase plays the pivotal role in any black box activities: to find gaps in the *information security zone* one has to know its boundaries and terrain very well.

Grey box tests evaluate risks stemming from adversaries who are legitimately allowed at least some access rights and admittance to internal information. Such opponents can be rogue employees, as well as customers, guests, external consultants and partner companies' staff. Or, as a matter of fact, *anyone who successfully hijacks their access, whether technically, socially or physically*. When contemplating on the 'insider threat', it is of utmost importance to remember that *any external attacker who managed to get a foothold within becomes a part of this threat*. Thus, *grey box tests are invaluable in assessing defence, in-depth countermeasures and safeguards beyond the protected perimeter*. All testing activities that involve *privilege escalation* are, by definition, grey box.

Finally, white box assessments aim at achieving the highest efficacy of discovering security flaws in a given period of time. The auditors do not have to spend any time on reconnaissance and can get straight to the unabridged matter. Thus, *white box checks present a superb form of quality control, but are usually poor as a form of practical risk assessment*. The white box approach is somewhat of a 'testing lab exercise' that lacks situational realism. Even the internal attackers that hold highly advantageous positions do not have full access to anything they desire. Neither do they use the majority of hands-on methodologies that typical white box assessments employ. Reviewing security policies and other relevant documentation, or scrutinising the source code of applications and configuration files of systems, are classical examples of white box tests.

Assessments specialisations and actual scopes

The most obvious general classification of information security assessments is splitting them into 'technical', 'human resources', 'operational' and 'management'. This division takes into account the audit targets, methods and required professional expertise. At the same time, when discussing the fundamentals we have explicitly specified that any security assessment inevitably addresses all major information security areas simultaneously. The difference seems to be through which specific realm and its applicable methodologies it is *primarily* done in practical terms. The 'chain diagrams' in Figures 8, 9 and 10 illustrate this point of view using typical examples of what is considered to be purely 'technical', 'human' or 'security management' auditing tasks.

Figure 8: The 'technical' chain example

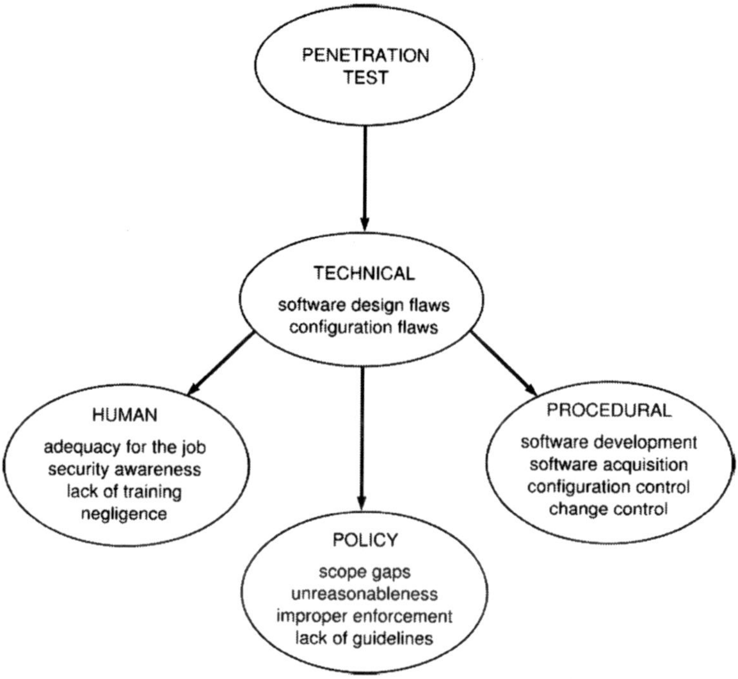

Through purely technical gaps our penetration test evaluates other information security realms. The sources of software design or configuration flaws commonly originate from problems in these non-technical areas. For example, before the patch is released by a vulnerable software vendor, the problem is largely technical. As soon as the fix becomes widely available, the issue turns operational, as in 'not following efficient patch, or vulnerability management procedures'.

Figure 9: The 'human' chain example

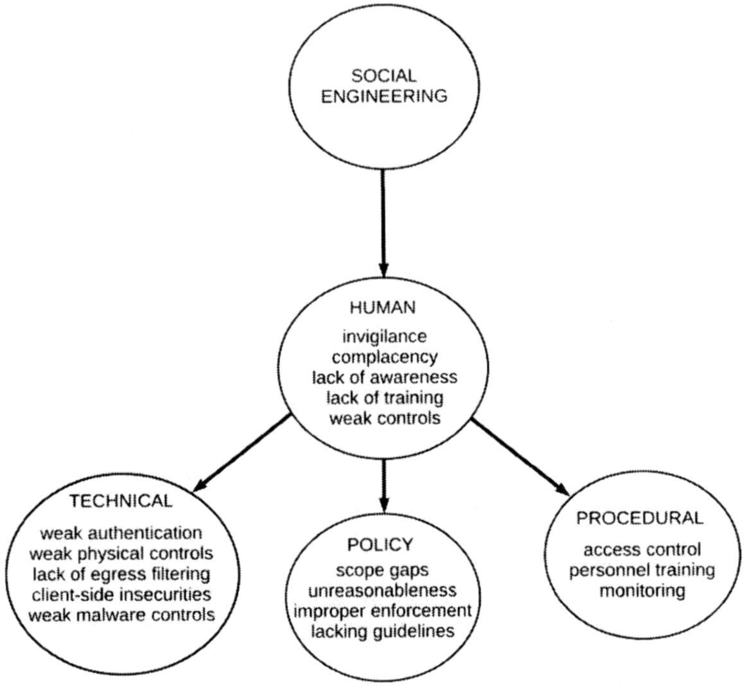

Some people are naturally complacent and naive, but more often than not, vulnerability to social engineering is a result of improper security awareness and related training. Also note that a variety of technical countermeasures and security procedures can be used to mitigate social engineering risks. For example, a combination of strong physical controls with strict identity verification procedures, is efficient in thwarting physical intrusion attempts. Proper two, or even three ('what you have, what you know, and what you are') factor authentication can also prevent many social engineering attacks.

Figure 10: The 'management' chain example

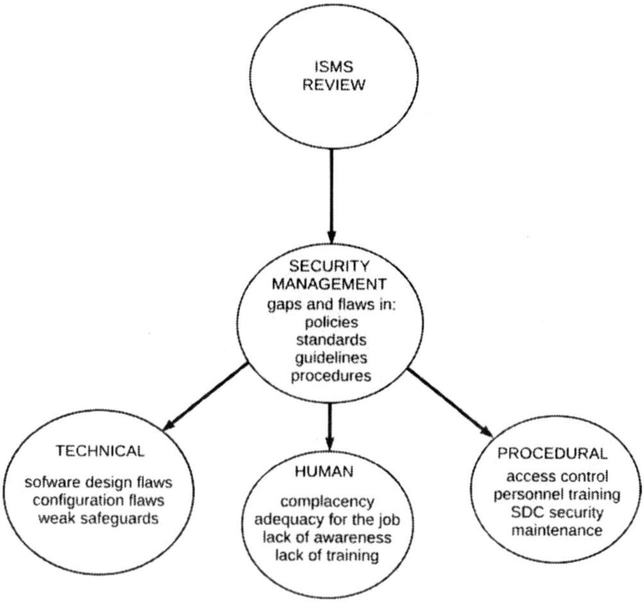

The SDC on the diagram refers to the 'Software Development Cycle', while 'maintenance' applies to maintaining software, systems and networks. Practically any security flaw can be (and often is) the end result of information security management gaps.

These schemes are by no means complete. You can add as many factors as you see fit to them. For example, far more procedures or processes can be listed in Figure 10. Nevertheless, the diagrams clearly demonstrate that the actual separation of information security assessments into technical, human, procedural, policy, etc. is, indeed, vague. Besides, many real-world security assessments can be described as semi-technical, semi-human, or semi-security management, or use a combination of these general areas approaches and methodologies. It will become more apparent in the remaining sections of this chapter.

On technical information security assessments

Different types of technical security audits are casually defined by what is assessed in the first place. The 'what' determines the 'how'. A notable exception is the division between vulnerability scanning and penetration testing, which is based upon the level of depth. This separation, and the definitions of vulnerability scanning and penetration testing services in general, has created plenty of confusion even amongst the auditors who perform such tasks. In his popular *Schneier on Security* book, Bruce Schneier pointed out that '*Penetration testing is a broad term. It might mean breaking into a network to demonstrate you can. It might mean trying to break into the network to document vulnerabilities. It might involve a remote attack, physical penetration of a data centre, or social engineering attacks. It might use commercial or proprietary vulnerability scanning tools, or rely on skilled white-hat hackers. It might just evaluate software version numbers and patch levels, and make inferences about vulnerabilities*'.

We believe that by introducing the overall division of information security assessments into 'passive' and 'active', we have successfully resolved this issue. *Vulnerability scanning is passive. Penetration testing is active*. The rest is technical details. Thus, to '*just evaluate software version numbers and patch levels, and make inferences about vulnerabilities*' is to perform a typical vulnerability scan. The rest of the activities listed by the security guru are different forms of penetration testing. For the sake of clarity, we discuss social engineering and technical penetration testing as separate types of information security assessments. Thus, the latter in this book refers to the technical activities only.

Server, client and network-centric tests

By their general targets and corresponding methodologies, technical security tests can be separated into three large groups:

- Server-side tests
- Client-side tests
- Network-centric tests.

Server-side tests are the most traditional form of penetration testing and vulnerability scanning. Centralised services provided by corporate or organisational servers always presented the most lucrative trophy for any attacker. At the same time, breach of their confidentiality, integrity and availability usually has the highest negative impact for owners of these systems. Server-side attacks (and their emulation by the auditors) traditionally involve feeding maliciously modified 'client-side' input to the targeted services. It is easier to launch typical server-side attacks since they do not require installation and configuration of any services on the assailant's systems. Such attacks are highly mature and well-researched. The countermeasures against them are also numerous and widely implemented. Due to the latter fact, in recent years the trend began to shift towards client-side (in)security.

Client-side attacks (and their emulation by the auditors) are centred on installation of rogue services that feed maliciously modified 'server-side' input to the targeted end-user applications. Web browsers are the most frequently targeted user applications of today. To execute client-side attacks with success, the assailants need to lure users of a vulnerable application to connect to their rogue servers. This is usually done via the following avenues:

1 Phishing.
2 Social engineering utilising e-mails, instant messengers, social networks, message boards, etc.
3 Intercepting and redirecting network traffic so that the users end up visiting the rogue service.

The latter approach requires network traffic access, thus being applicable only when the connections are insecure (shared cable and wireless) or for internally positioned attackers. Alternatively, the assailants can try to poison DNS caches to alter the records, so that the users of vulnerable DNS servers can be redirected to a malicious service. At the moment, client-side attacks that involve aforesaid approaches 1 and 2 are heavily employed by cybercriminals worldwide.

The network-centric tests can be subdivided into two categories: testing network appliances and checking security of communication protocols. As servers became harder to crack, the attention was diverted not only to their clients, but also to various network appliances deployed nearby. Security of network appliances is still frequently overlooked. Many system administrators treat them in accordance with the infamous 'if it works do not break it' principle. As a result, there are many routers, switches and more specialised appliances that run obsolete systems with known security issues. We have heavily elaborated on this problem in our earlier *Hacking Exposed Cisco Networks* book, where we also blatantly stated that 'who controls the router, controls the network'. This was written five years ago, but the problem still remains at large.

As for the security of network protocols, it has entered the spotlight due to two major factors:

- Comprehending and popularising the 'insider threat'.
- The spread of wireless networks.

While network appliances security can be accessed from anywhere, providing the connectivity exists, to check for network protocols vulnerabilities the auditors must be directly plugged into the auditee network. There are a few notable exceptions to this statement, but we won't go into the technical details here. As a general rule, network protocols assessments belong to the realm of internal and wireless security audits.

IT security testing levels and target areas

There are three general levels to which a variety of IT security checks can be applied. These levels are shown in Figure 11.

Figure 11: Three planes of technical security assessments

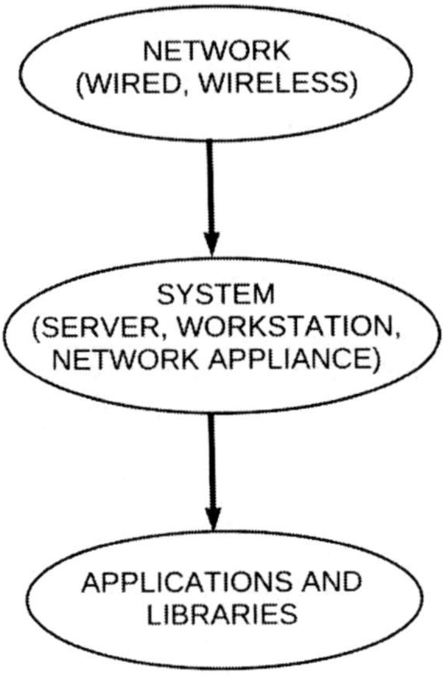

The highest level is the network. All access to corporate or organisational networks can be in-band or out-of-band. In-band connections are links to the Internet and other networks casually used in the everyday business practice. Out-of-band connections are auxiliary links used for specific purposes, such as troubleshooting in cases of major in-band lines failure. External wireless connectivity can be viewed as out-of-band, unless we are talking about connections to last mile wireless providers. The most traditional out-of-band form of connectivity is dial-in via POTS (Plain Old Telephone Service). Nowadays, old slow dial-in lines for connecting remote users or, for example, payment systems, are dying out, being superseded by VPNs. Nevertheless, reserve dial-in lines are still used for network appliances maintenance. Thus, one of the most ancient attack types, the wardialing, should not be discarded as a source of potential risks. Where applicable, wardialing tests should be performed.

The middle level is various networked systems. This means absolutely any network-connected device, not just servers, workstations, routers and switches! To keep a wide perspective of things, these include:

- Mobile hosts such as PDAs and smartphones.
- Networked printers and scanners.
- Networked cameras, including CCTV.
- VOIP phones and other tele- and videoconferencing equipment.
- Networked data storage and back-up devices.
- Networked environment control sensors.
- Wireless access points and bridges.
- Load balancing and Quality of Service (QoS) appliances.
- Specialised security appliances, including, but not limited to, firewalls, VPN concentrators, Intrusion Prevention Systems (IPS) and their sensors.

Security gaps can lurk anywhere. If 'it' is connected, or could be connected to any network, its security state must be verified.

Unless we look for purely configuration-centric gaps, like enabling insecure network protocols or weak authentication means, security testing of systems always ends up in searching for gaps in various software they run. This is the lowest and the most detailed level of the three. The applications tested can be of a system, service or end-user types. Security of the environment in which the tested application runs must always be taken into consideration. A serious flaw in a common library used by multiple applications is major trouble brewing.

In application security testing, the differences between black and white box approaches are probably the most pronounced. Thorough black box application security testing has to involve different fuzzing and reverse engineering methodologies. We will elaborate more on fuzzing, its types and scope, in Chapter 5 of this book. White box application testing refers to its manual and automated source code reviews. Grey box application testing can apply to situations when some of its modules are open source, and some are proprietary and can't be disclosed to third parties. If the application is not open source and the auditee is not its vendor, than all application testing is legally restricted to observing how it behaves in different environments and under various types of input. Asking the auditors to perform even the most minimalistic reverse engineering of proprietary software is pushing them to break the law. This can be reported. On the other hand, if the auditors themselves offer to reverse engineer a close source application, the situation is fishy and you should stay away from it as far as you can.

A casual overall technical information security assessment evaluates all three levels, progressing in a top-down direction from scanning the network to verifying separate systems, their configuration settings and applications they run. This provides a good slice across the general technical information security state of a company or organisation, and is instrumental in realistic assessment of related risks.

However, in the majority of situations you cannot have both the all-encompassing scope and breathtaking assessment depth. Not with the imposed limitations of budget and time, anyway. Typically, external and internal tests are treated as completely separate categories, and rightly so. Black, grey and white box audits are also performed separately, or in stages proceeding from black to white. For instance, after security scans of the internal network infrastructure (black or grey box testing), a thorough review of hand-picked appliances configuration files can be performed (white box). Nevertheless, these general classification-based split-ups can be insufficient. So, highly specific technical security audits are sometimes called for, to address what is perceived as the area of highest concern. Most commonly encountered types of such specialised assessment services are selected application security testing and wireless network audits.

Above, we have already reviewed application security testing in brief. When a specific application is crucial for business operations and carries significant risks if compromised, its detailed security assessments are routinely ordered. Such audits must be performed at the pre-production stage against pilot installations of the tested application. They should be repeated as a part of the change control process when significant alterations to the application's architecture and functionality are introduced. Casually, these audits are supplemented with penetration tests of the infrastructure that supports the application in the production environment. There is no point in having strong security of the application itself, if the server it is hosted on or a back-end database it communicates with, can be successfully breached. More often than not, the applications which are explicitly assessed are online shopping cards and other software used to perform financial transactions or collect customer data over public untrusted networks. Though, in practice it can take all kinds. For instance, we have performed an in-depth evaluation of a novel wireless authentication software aimed at bringing the benefits of WPA Enterprise security for SOHO users.

Talking about wireless security assessments, they do imply using highly specific methodologies that strongly differ from their wired counterparts. It is even difficult to say whether wireless assessments are external or internal. The auditors must be present within the coverage zone of the analysed network, which typically spreads across and beyond the auditee premises. Physical location is important. Wireless network defences can be analysed in a more comfortable manner while staying in the auditee offices. However, we recommend running off-premises tests using specialised equipment, such as antennas and amplifiers. This allows one to discover where the fuzzy borders of the network or wireless signals from standalone client devices spread. It means knowing where the attackers can position themselves. Are such locations, such as the company's car park, within the security guard's reach or is there outdoors CCTV coverage?

At least some wireless security issues are physical, as in 'radiophysics', and require a degree of knowledge in this subject. The encryption protocols employed by WPA to protect wireless networks differ from their wired siblings. Most importantly, wireless security testing is typically fully black box, with the auditors not having any initial connectivity to the assessed network at all. Note, that while the majority of today's wireless tests are WiFi-centric, the issues of wireless security are not limited to WiFi. For example, Bluetooth and WiMax also present their share of potential security risks. Below we will also mention security problems of commonly used wireless keyboards.

'Idiosyncratic' technical security tests

There are whole ranges of technical information security assessments that have little or no relation to any networks and networking hosts. These assessments can include:

- Technical evaluation of physical premises controls.
- Verifying security of RFIDs.
- TSCM (Technical Surveillance Counter-Measures) or, to put it simply, bug and frequency sweeping.

A lot of corporate physical entry controls are still based on RFIDs, and only some are biometric. RFIDs, obviously, have plenty of other uses, from asset tracking to mobile and transportation payments. They also have their growing share of insecurities, mainly directed towards cloning the actual RFID tag or reproducing its signal. Then, in our example, successful unauthorised entry becomes possible. Fully blown RFID exploits are reported, and the talk of RFID viruses and worms is in the air. Thus, if a company or organisation depends on the heavy use of RFIDs, and any disruption or compromise of this use may present high impact risks, auditing security of the deployed RFID solution becomes a priority. In general, RFID security is an increasingly popular and actively developing field. Pay attention to what it brings, especially if you are a professional technical security auditor or manage the auditor team. It could be that you will have to expand your arsenal of everyday tools and techniques soon.

TSCM, though, is an entirely different ball game. Electronic surveillance is usually of a great concern when industrial espionage from powerful competitors or even foreign governments, is high on the list of risks. In such cases the premises must be built with blocking all compromising radio, optical and acoustic emanations in mind. All unauthorised electronic devices such as personal mobile phones or pagers must be banned. Power and phone lines must have appropriate filters and/or white noise generators applied and so on, until it becomes a fully-blown TEMPEST bunker. TCSM sweeps must be performed by highly professional teams that possess very costly equipment. When we checked a few years ago, the NSA stated that a qualified TSCM team must spend at least 250,000 US$ on necessary hardware. Since then this sum has probably gone up by quite a margin. Operating this hardware requires skills that need formal training and years of experience to hone. Do not be deluded by someone who will offer you a spy shop tools-based sweep. It might only discover bugs you can buy in a local Maplin store.

We are not TSCM experts and do not perform professional bug sweeps. However, there are two relevant issues we would like to address. The first one is you might, after all, encounter the use of low grade, spy shop bugs within your corporation. It would be 'personal'. Driven by internal skirmishes and squabbles, employees can use them to snoop on their colleagues. Most likely you don't even need a proper TSCM sweep to discover these feeble devices. Your technical specialists would be able to do so with some exciting bed-time reading and an inexpensive wideband radio frequency scanner. Or, most likely, they would be discovered physically after the unusual leaks of information become apparent. Casually, their discovery results from purely human failures of the corporate James Bond wannabes.

The second issue is far more interesting and challenging. More than five years ago we used to amuse guests by playing music with a PC monitor and a free software tool that controls it. The signal could be picked up in a neighbouring room with a wideband scanner at about 10 MHz frequency. Wrapping the screen in tin foil did not help. Years passed since. The trend of 'traditional TSCM' steadily merging with 'conventional IT security' becomes progressively evident. For example, keystrokes can be relatively easily captured and decoded by:

- Intercepting the signals sent by wireless keyboards.
- Directing a laser beam at the back of a laptop.
- Monitoring the minute voltage changes of a power line to which a computer is plugged.

All of this can be done using cheap DIY hardware and public domain open source software tools to go with it. We have also seen a proof-of-concept software backdoor that could transmit data from the system on which it is installed at 10-12 MHz, using a serial port jack as an antenna. Thus, methods and approaches that firmly belonged to the realm of government agents or professional corporate spies in earlier times, are becoming fully accessible to 'Joe the hacker'. It should not be ignored. When internal and physical premises security audits are performed, the auditors should look out for all unusual activities and contraptions they might encounter. The latter are easy to discover, for now.

On non-technical information security audits

Just like their more 'geeky' siblings, all non-technical information security assessments are subdivided in accordance with their primary targets. These targets inevitably determine the methodologies utilised. A non-technical security audit can concentrate on:

- Premises

- People
- Documentation
- Operations and procedures.

With the previous section finishing on auditing wireless security, some aspects of physical access control and TSCM, it makes perfect sense to proceed with the premises reviews first.

Premises and physical security checks

Assessing the security of premises can be a stand-alone task. But most of all, it is an important element of more general internal information security audits. As such, it supplements their technical, human, policy and operational components, and is reciprocally reinforced by them. Figure 12 depicts the main areas addressed by security assessments of corporate or organisational premises.

Figure 12: Five domains of premises security checks

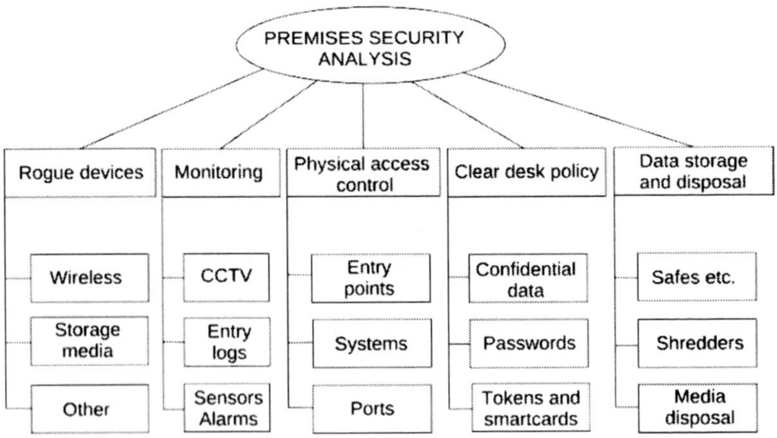

Physical access control means having control over all forms of physical admittance to premises, systems and networks. It does not limit itself to doors, receptions, keys and swipe cards. Of course, all traditional physical entry points must have sufficient authentication and supervision means. The strictest controls must be applied to:

- All outside entries.
- All entries to server rooms.
- All entries to other premises where confidential data and critical systems are stored.

Such entry points must be constantly monitored. The doors should withstand all unlawful entry attempts that do not involve a serious welding job or dynamite. If an entry code is used, it must be difficult to guess. Check how often this code is changed, who is allowed to know it and why. These 'who' and 'why' also apply to all other physical authentication means, including ID and swipe cards, RFID tokens and biometrics. How are they issued and withdrawn if an employee leaves? What are the procedures for cancelling and replacing stolen or lost tokens and cards? How is third party and guest access granted and supervised? As you can see, we have already crossed the border into the realm of physical access control policies, guidelines and operations.

Controlling physical access to systems most commonly means that:

- Mobile computers cannot be stolen.
- Unsupervised systems are protected with a screen lock.
- Bootloader and BIOS passwords are applied.

Using biometric (fingerprint-based) and two factor authentication for physical computer access is gaining popularity and will hopefully join the above list soon. When verifying security of physical system access, always check that:

- The screensaver would lock the screen in 10 minutes or so.
- Screen lock, BIOS or bootloader passwords are strong.
- Computers are configured to boot from the hard drive first.
- When dealing with multi-boot computers, boot time protection is equivalent for all operating systems installed.

Besides, if countermeasures against connecting USB and other devices are implemented, their efficacy should be verified.

Controlling physical access to ports means that unauthorised devices cannot be plugged into the network. As a general rule, all physical ports which are not in use must be turned off on the corresponding switches. All physical ports used to manage network appliances or for monitoring purposes (e.g. Cisco SPAN) must be adequately protected. At least, strong passwords must be applied. When analysing physical access to systems and network ports, we inevitably plunge into the realm of technical internal audits. And of course, all these vital countermeasures against physical intrusion must be reflected in the relevant security policies and guidelines.

Monitoring goes hand in hand with physical access control. Traditionally, physical monitoring refers to CCTV coverage of physical points of entry and all areas where confidential data and critical systems are present. When reviewing CCTV security it is important to check:

- Which areas are properly covered.
- Whether movement sensing and night vision functionalities are implemented.
- How secure the communications between CCTV cameras and monitoring stations are.
- Who is reviewing CCTV records and how often it is done.
- Who has access to the *records and systems that store them.*
- Whether the records are properly time stamped.
- How the records are kept and backed up.

In a nutshell, CCTV records should be treated in a similar manner as systems logs. However, unlike logs, video clips take up a lot of space. We have seen many companies where the server storing the records ran out of space. As a result, older records were simply lost, being overwritten by more recent ones. A correct implementation of the system must include secure regular back-ups of the older records, as well as *redundant servers,* in case a crash happens. Another problem we have regularly encountered is access to record-storing systems being granted to anyone in the IT support team. This is not a good security practice. The records should be treated as confidential data with need-to-know, role-based access to it.

In a very similar way, all logs from physical entry control systems must be maintained, protected and preserved. Since these logs are not video or audio data, encrypting them would not present any technical inconvenience and is highly recommended. From our practice, we can recall a forensic investigation in which the entry logs were decisive in determining and later prosecuting a malicious insider. He had actually managed to delete the logs, but in the process of investigation they were successfully restored.

A few words should be said about verifying environment monitoring and controls. While this may not sound like a relevant security subject, don't be so sure. First of all, availability is still a part of the CIA triad. If environment support systems fail, a major collapse of servers and appliances is likely to occur, resulting in severe disruption of availability, or even loss of valuable data. After all, CISSP textbooks always include a section on fire, flood and other disaster and elements-related issues. Do you actually have a fire extinguisher not further than 30 yards away from the server room?

What makes this topic a much hotter one, is that nowadays many environment monitoring and control systems operate via IP networks. As such, they present a very interesting (and often insufficiently defended) target for hacking. Evaluating this issue properly belongs to the area of internal penetration testing. When performing a physical premises audit, do not limit the checks to verifying that the environmental and building control systems are operating as expected. Verify whether they are managed over a wired or wireless IP network. If such is the case, enquire how the management access to such systems is protected and who is authorised to access them.

Another important domain of physical information security audits is to assess that the clear desk policies are followed. Unattended confidential data should not tumble about in any shape or form, on paper or in electronic format. This applies not only to the employees' desks, but also to networked printers or scanners, where such documents are sometimes forgotten or lie for a long time before being picked up. It helps to have a separate 'confidential' printer or scanner, which is physically supervised.

Passwords are, of course, confidential data. Since the problem of them being written down is so excruciatingly common, in Figure 12 we have placed passwords into a separate box. Below, authentication tokens, smart cards and, potentially, other physical authentication gimmicks are noted. Whether used for the premises entry or system and network access, they must be kept in a secure place where they cannot be stolen or lost.

Two remaining domains of physical information security checks are in a way related to clear desk policies. If confidential data is not lying around, then where is it stored? Is it properly locked? Is the location supervised? Who can access it? Are there back-up copies? How are these copies secured? After checking for these basic facts, verify if such data is disposed of in a secure manner. Technical destruction of sensitive data in electronic format can be logical or physical. Here we are interested in the latter. In a nutshell, it comes down to mechanical grinding of data carriers, like hard drives or CDs. We can recall an instance of a company that had a room literally filled to the ceiling with old hard drives awaiting physical destruction to be done by a third party. In the meantime, the room was not properly secured and any employee could pick up a hard drive or two.

Both paper documents and CDs are destroyed by shredding. It is good practice to have separate 'confidential' shredders and bins. Office shredders are not considered to be a party icebreaker topic. However, it is useful to know that different types of shredders exist, and there are currently six security levels of their classification in accordance with the DIN32757-1 standard:

- Level 1 = 12mm paper strips
- Level 2 = 6mm strips
- Level 3 = 2mm strips (Confidential)
- Level 4 = 2 x 15mm paper particles (Commercially Sensitive)
- Level 5 = 0.8 x 12mm particles (Top Secret or Classified)
- Level 6 = 0.8 x 4mm particles (Top Secret or Classified).

So, a shredder for confidential documents should at least satisfy level 3 requirements. It must not be one of the cheap strip-cut devices which slice pages into narrow strips as long as the original sheet of paper. It should, of course, support the shredding of CDs.

Finally, the premises must be thoroughly checked for rogue devices. In general, the term 'rogue device' can apply to any unauthorised equipment that presents security risks. In the past, the accent was on rogue modems that could fall prey to wardialing. In this day and age this term became nearly synonymous with 'wireless rogue device'. By providing unaccounted out-of-band connectivity, *both rogue wireless access points and unauthorised client devices* do constitute a grave threat. The best way to discover and pinpoint them is, of course, through wireless security scans or intrusion detection systems. However, to some extent, physical security checks can also counter this nuisance.

One of the most blatant issues to check for when performing a physical premises audit is the presence and use of various removable storage media. Nowadays, it ranges from the ordinary USB memory sticks and external hard drives, to media players, mobile phones and digital cameras. These humble 'rogue devices' present one of the most formidable security threats of today. Via them, confidential data trickles out, bypassing any egress filtering, and malware crawls in, outflanking gateway anti-virus controls. Prior to performing a physical assessment, the auditors should consult existing security policies to find out the auditee position on using removable storage media on their premises. If the policies are lax, they should at least enquire whether there are any specific systems to which connecting removable media is highly undesirable. If the policies explicitly forbid the use of removable media, then any suspicious device must be scrutinised. It does not matter if a discovered USB stick, external hard drive or *any other removable storage media* merely lies on a desk, not being plugged into a nearby computer. In Anton Chekhov's words, '*one must not put a loaded rifle on the stage if no one is thinking of firing it*'. In a similar manner, do the acceptable use policies allow employees to burn CDs (which are also a common source of sensitive information leaks)? If not, check for any computers that have CD burners. *Physical security assessments are immensely policy-driven.*

What are the other types of rogue devices one should look for? When discussing TSCM, we have stated that the auditors should always expect the unexpected. However, physical keystroke loggers are a danger you should always expect and check for. Usually, these minute nasty devices come in four possible varieties:

- USB-to-USB
- PS/2-to-PS/2

- USB-to-PS/2
- PS/2-to-USB.

However, it is possible to buy a whole keyboard with an in-built keystroke logger. If all keyboards in a large office are of the same make and type, but a single one sticks out like a sore thumb, we, as auditors, would start asking questions. Similarly, if there are three laptops on the system administrator's desk it looks perfectly normal. At the same time, if three laptops lie on a desk of an accountant or sales manager, there is a good probability that at least one of the three is personal. Are employees allowed to bring in and connect their own computers? Again, enquiries will follow and the policies will be consulted.

Two factors seem to be of the utmost importance when security assessments of premises are performed. The first is verifying if all necessary controls are in place and humming. The other is being able to spot things that somehow break the general pattern and are out of place. The former requires very thorough checklists, as premises assessments are usually passive. Hopefully, the information discussed in this section can help you to create or improve these lists. The latter challenges this view, as the sense it requires grows with experience and is on the verge of art.

Social engineering tests

Information security assessments that centre exclusively on the human factor, involve different forms of social engineering. Additionally, ISMS assessments commonly have a strong human component dictated by relevant policies, standards and guidelines. Recall the ISO/IEC27001-aligned policy set. Chapters 11 and 12 are fully directed at the personnel issues, while the rest inevitably address them to a larger or smaller extent. Likewise, assessing actual information security operations and procedures is impossible without auditing the performance of all employees involved in their execution, either by observing or by interviewing them.

A considerable volume of information security publications are dedicated to discussing social engineering and emphasising that 'humans are the weakest link'. We wholeheartedly agree with this statement – for as long as it out-steps any specific boundaries and applies to the overall human folly and its role in allowing security incidents to occur. As far as social engineering is concerned, it is simply the oldest and most tested and tried method of breaching confidentiality, integrity and, at times, availability of any imaginable target. Or, to simplify and resonate with the introductory discourse, of bending and overcoming the opponents will by deceit. Practically any social engineering attack can be described with a simple scheme shown in Figure 13.

Figure 13: A general outline of social engineering attacks

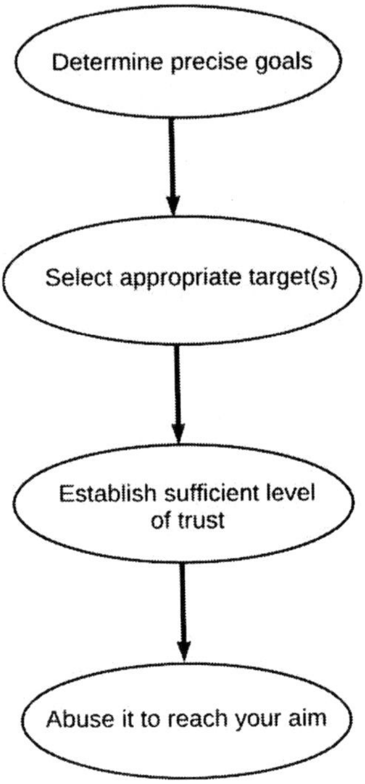

That is, you decide what you want, select the most appropriate person that can lead you to it, establish the necessary level of trust, and then abuse this trust when the time is due. Unlike legitimate security assessments, real-life social engineering attacks have an additional stage – getting away with what you've got. This can be more difficult if compared to purely technical security breaches. Social engineering casually involves a much higher degree of human contact and interaction, which often leaves a pronounced give-away trace. In contrast, remote attackers that rely on technical means only, are faceless until caught.

Practical social engineering methodologies are very strongly affected by its defined aims. Compare the following tasks a security test can be expected to complete:

1 Getting into the company premises.
2 Getting into the server rooms.
3 Getting into the server room and retrieving a configuration file (or any other data).

The first is easy to accomplish, providing that sufficient public information about the auditee employees, suppliers, customers, etc. is available. The second significantly raises the bar. People are not expected to hang around server rooms without a valid reason. As we have already reviewed, such premises must be protected with strong physical authentication means and stay constantly monitored. The third option inevitably brings in the element of technology. Our social engineer will have to be able to bypass physical authentication of a system and copy the file. This may require some specific technical skills and an appropriate console cable in your pocket. It also takes time. 'Hey, you, what are you doing there?!' The more specific is the aim faced by a social engineer, the harder it is to accomplish. This is precisely the opposite in many other areas of information security testing.

The major goals of social engineering tests are summarised in Figure 14.

Figure 14: Social engineering aims

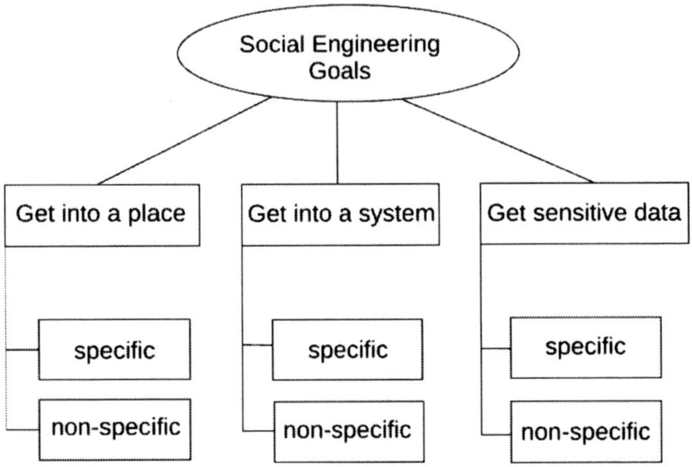

An attack may reach them directly, or via a chain of intermediate targets. Through the social engineer's sights all people can be subdivided into two large categories:

1 Those which possess desirable data or access rights.
2 Those which are highly susceptible to social engineering tricks.

When a single person belongs to both groups at the same time, it is called luck, or, a negligence of those who trusted valuable data or systems to such employees and did not provide necessary security awareness training. As one cannot base effective attack strategies and tactics upon the assumption of favourable fortune or complacent opposition, a correct approach of getting to 1) via 2) must be found and successfully exploited. This might require a hefty dose of elaborate planning and research.

In establishing the necessary contact with the targeted employees, all types of communication channels can be used. The more of these channels that are open, the better for the attacker. This allows sufficient manoeuvre space while increasing the area of possible influence. Quite often, the behaviour and perception of people strongly differs between personal, telephone and online intercourse. In the process of developing rapport and gaining trust, all three ways can be tried to select the most optimal one. Common sense dictates that the online – phone – personal contact sequence should be followed where possible. The earlier in this chain the breakthrough occurs, the more insecure our targets are. However, in practice, such succession may not be the best, or might not work at all. Technology also imposes its mighty amendments. Nowadays, the quality of streaming video-conferencing can be so high, that it comes close to a personal contact.

Just like with the 'conventional' IT security and electronic surveillance, we are observing active interpenetration between social engineering and technical attack means. In some areas this transfusion is practically complete. Above, an example where some technical skills are needed to bypass system authentication after physical access has been gained, was noted. Now we would like you to consider the following looming factors:

- RFID hacking can be employed to assist in physical premises penetration.
- Rogue wireless devices of all kinds can be plugged in by physical intruders to provide out-of-band connectivity.
- Client-side attacks often rely on social engineering means. The opposite is also true.

Currently, the latter case seems to be of particular relevance. Old good social engineering tricks using e-mails claiming to be the IT department representative asking to change passwords or click on the attached 'update' file, may still work. Some people just never learn. Nevertheless, an explosion in client-side attack methods and techniques allows far more efficient ways of exploitation. A link to a phishing or browser exploits-hosting site can be carefully hidden in a long URL of a well-composed 'click-this-and-receive-a-candy' e-mail. It can be posted to social networks or sent through instant messengers. Flaws like cross-site scripting (XSS) allow the stealing of authentication cookies to your corporate or third party sites as soon as such a potentially interesting link is clicked. And do not forget that nowadays trojans can be concealed in practically any file format. Would you resist if an MP3 of a yet unreleased hit of your most favourite band, is sent to you by this exceptionally friendly young lady you enjoyed chatting with on Skype so much? A pity her microphone is broken. She absolutely adores the same band and this is why, obviously, you have met online. Don't you have the band listed in your profile? Would you not listen to that MP3 'she' has just sent? It is only a double-click away.

We shall return to the subject of social engineering in Chapter 5 of this book, where some applicable terminology, strategies and tactics will be introduced first.

Security documentation reviews

The final class of non-technical information security assessments that needs to be reviewed in brief is auditing ISMS of a company or organisation. It was already covered in the previous chapter on the strategic scale. Verifying the 'tactical ISMS level' means checking that all agreed strategies are effectively implemented in everyday practice. After all, '*the art of war in its highest point of view is policy, but, no doubt, a policy which fights battles, instead of writing notes*' (Clausewitz).

In terms of assessing security documentation it all comes down to verifying whether the policies are supplemented with all necessary downstream documents and these documents are feasible and correct. Figure 15 outlines the 'classical' security documentation chain.

Figure 15: Three planes of security documentation

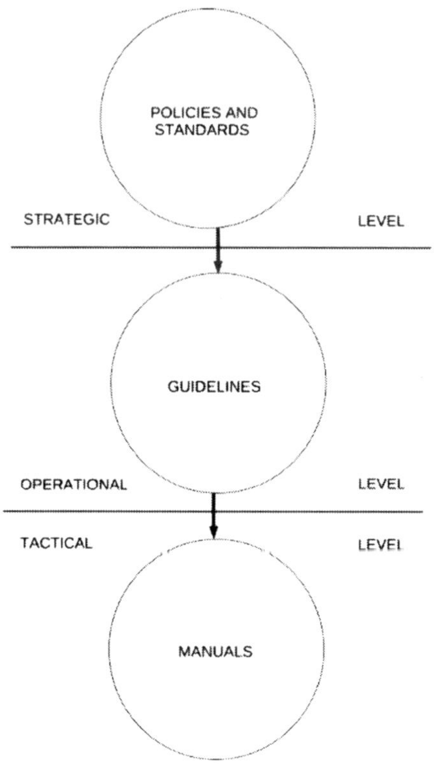

Take notice that the standards are placed at the strategic level, together with security policies. While being subordinate to and driven by the policies, information security standards are casually company or organisation-wide and must affect all relevant areas of practice. For example, data classification standards apply to all data within an entity. Cryptography standards apply to all use of any ciphers for any purpose. Weak or lacking standards are just as disastrous as poor security policies can be.

Analysing the standards requires specialised expertise. When checking the cryptography standards mentioned above, the auditors must know which encryption algorithms *and their applicable modes of operation* are considered to be strong and weak in today's industry and government sectors. Even more, it is highly advantageous to be able to forecast which ciphers are unlikely to be broken in the near future. Such ciphers are expected to have a *high security margin*, implement *whitening* and *avalanche effects*, allow for *large key sizes* and have tested and tried structural elements. In the meantime, we are already talking the language of applied cryptography.

Figure 15 positions guidelines at the intermediate *operational* plane. In military terms, the operational level lies between strategy and tactics and deals with campaigns, rather than the whole conflict or its separate battles. Guidelines apply to specific information security areas e.g. an employee vetting guideline, a secure password guideline, or an incident response guideline. They define and shape separate processes and operations that can consist of multiple individual elements. Thus, the guidelines are clearly not strategic in nature. But neither are they tactical – the manuals are.

For instance, a firewall configuration guideline should state which particular networks, systems and services are allowed to be accessed, and from where such access is permitted. It can go into great technical detail outlining which types of network traffic are considered to be malicious and must be blocked under any circumstances. It ought to cover how access to the firewall itself must be protected and how it should handle various event logs. However, such guidelines must be applicable to all major firewall types of any make, whether Cisco ASA, CheckPoint, Microsoft ISA, Juniper, Linux Netfilter or anything else. So, it should not contain commands, screenshots or chunks of configuration files. This would turn it into a manual.

- *The auditors should always point out if a guideline is too generic, like a policy, or, in contrast, is too manual-like. In other words, it should not slip up or down, into the strategic or tactical planes.*

In the first case it will completely fail to fulfil its purpose. In the second case it can become obsolete and incorrect if the specific means it addresses change. Just like the policies, you don't want to rewrite security guidelines with every upgrade. And, just like the policies, sufficient attention should be paid to their clarity. When looking through the guidelines, always think whether a newcomer employee with a relevant background will understand them, without additional instructions and explanations.

Auditing security guidelines is 'semi-technical', in a sense of demanding necessary specialist knowledge in the applicable area. It is not necessarily passive. Having detailed checklists may not cover all aspects of a proper guideline assessment. When analysing security guidelines, sometimes you have to think out of the box. Consider the following typical password guideline excerpt:

- The password must not be in any dictionary.
- The password must be at least eight characters in length.
- The password must contain both lower case and capital letters.
- The password must contain numbers.
- It must strongly differ from the previous password.

Is it reasonably complete? Is it secure? If you think so, have a look at these ways of generating passwords:

- CompanyName01(2,3,4,5 ...).

Providing that the name of the company is dissimilar to a previous password, is not in a dictionary, contains at least eight characters and is written using caps, this password fully satisfies the above criteria.

- SystemDomainName01(2,3,4,5 ...).

This would also fulfil them.

- DeviceVendor01(2,3,4,5 ...).

Is the vendor name not in the dictionaries? Is it longer than eight characters and has caps? Fine.

We can also recall many passwords that contain, for example, the fragments of employee's names or system's IP addresses. All of them are unsafe. Current password list generating tools are very powerful, and can easily make extensive dictionary files filled with such passwords in minutes. When performing various internal and external security audits, we have successfully cracked thousands of such passwords without spending much effort. What is the actual source of this security issue? Incomplete, poor password guidelines. In your spare time, think what these guidelines must contain to avoid these and similar problems. How should it be worded? How else seemingly complex, yet profoundly insecure passwords, could come into existence?

Manuals usually come from vendors and are straightforward. Unless there are clear indications that a source of insecurity can be a manual error, they are rarely checked. The real tactical level verification of ISMS and its documentation cascade is assessing all nuts-and-bolts implementations and processes. 'By ye fruits shall you know them.' In practice, it comes down to security scanning, penetration testing, social engineering, physical security checks and other hands-on activities we have already discussed. However, separate audits of information security processes can also be performed. In a nutshell, they aim at detailed verification of how the unfolding of a strategic process (*see Figure 7*) is reflected on all interrelated planes.

Assessing security processes

Unlike security documentation, we cannot divide security processes into strategic, operational or tactical. Rather, a separate process would permeate all three levels having strategic, operational and tactical parts (Figure 16).

Figure 16: A typical process flow

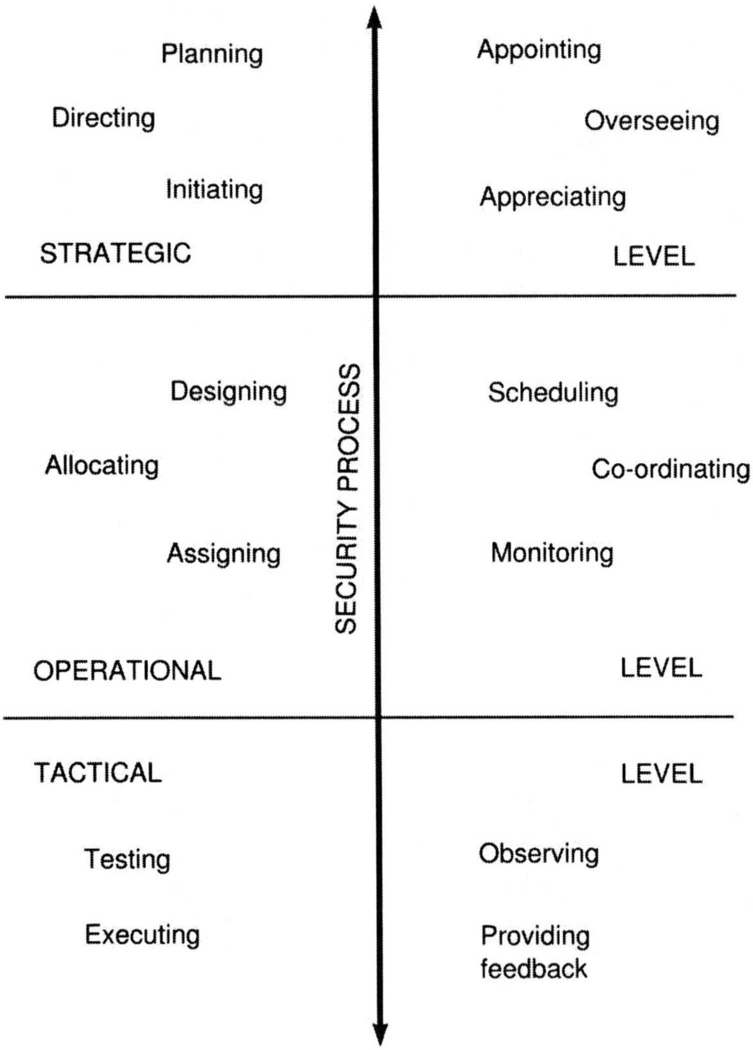

Note, that the flow on the scheme is bidirectional. This reflects the previous chapter's discussion of the top-bottom relationships and resonates with Figure 5. It would have been tempting to speculate that specific positions of responsibility can correspond to our process levels. It is even more enticing to superimpose it onto the Figure 7 scheme and state that the central 'C&C' OODA loop is 'strategic', the Deming cycle is more 'operational', and its separate stages loops are 'tactical'. However, that would be an oversimplification, and a fatal one indeed. There are information security processes of different scale, involvement, depth and scope. Applied information security itself is a process. Information security auditing is its sub-process. There are a great deal of specific processes that must be assessed security-wise, such as access control and identity management, change control, configuration and patch management, software development and acquisition, incident response, security awareness and training, personnel screening and vetting, etc. An individual approach to every process is required.

Overall, a process assessment is threefold, as Figure 17 shows.

Figure 17: Three components of a process assessment

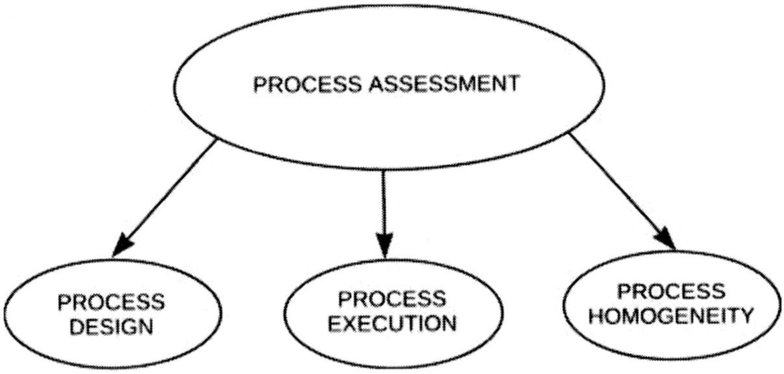

Auditing the process design concentrates on verifying its completeness, correctness and feasibility. Does it have all the components needed to be workable and effective? Are these elements efficiently interlinked? Do they correspond well to the environment in which the process operates? Are the responsibilities for executing different stages of the process correctly assigned? Is it all properly documented? The full Figure 7 strategic cycle is most evident, manifested and should be verified, when you analyse the process design from the very conception to the minuscule technicalities and latest improvements. Designing a fully fledged process inevitably requires going through the Deming cycle, exactly as ISO/IEC27001 prescribes. In contrast, when auditing processes execution and processes homogeneity, you are more likely to encounter a collection of OODA loops.

Process execution review aims at checking whether different stages of a selected process are performed in practice without unacceptable shortfalls. In a more active form it also means verifying if these stages can be successfully circumvented or abused by attackers of all kind. We will use the access management process as an example.

The ITILv3 'Service Operation' paragraph 4.5.1 states that '*Access Management provides the right for users to be able to use a service or group of services. It is therefore the execution of policies and actions defined in Security and Availability Management*'. Further it continues that '*Access Management does not decide who has access to which IT services. Rather, Access Management executes the policies and regulations defined during Service Strategy and Service Design. Access Management enforces decisions to restrict or provide access, rather than making the decision*' (paragraph 4.5.5.3). Thus, when elaborating on Access Management, ITIL deals only with the *operational* and *tactical* stages of a much larger *information security process* of Access Control. If we were to review the process design, we would have to assess the whole Access Control without such limitations, review the relevant policies and regulations, analyse decision making, and walk through all the Deming stages. However, assessing the access management process execution can be limited to the ITIL-defined scope. It includes the following parts:

1 Requesting access.

Verify how request generation mechanisms work. Take into account not only the requests to obtain access, but also requests to restrict it, or to change (especially elevate) access privileges. Can anyone fake access requests? How?

2 Request verification.

How does it work? Can it be tricked and deceived by any technical or non-technical means?

3 Providing rights.

How does it operate? Which roles and groups exist? Can extra rights be easily granted to someone by mistake? Can conscious attempts to get extra rights succeed?

4 Monitoring identity status.

How is it performed? Can any changes of status be missed? Can employees do something to conceal such changes, especially if they are related to demotion, disciplinary action and dismissal?

5 Logging and tracking access.

How does it work? Can these activities and mechanisms be circumvented? How are the exceptions handled?

6 Removing or restricting rights.

How is it done? Is it easy to remove or not to remove someone's rights by error? Are the restrictions as tight as they should be? Is it possible to avoid or reverse removal or restriction of rights?

A *passive* approach to auditing such a process would be to go through a specific and extensive list of 'must dos' and 'must nots'. An *active* approach is separating OODA loops for each process part (if you look at these stages carefully, you would clearly see these loops) and analysing them, applying a variety of 'what ifs'. Is observation done properly? Is orientation complete? Is the decision right? Was the action seamlessly performed? What if we submit a fake request? What if we alter a legitimate request to get into a user group we are not authorised to be in? What if we try to copy another user's data without authorisation? Would this attempt trigger an alarm? What if ...?

If a process appears to work fine, it does not mean it will do so the next time, or with someone else, or anywhere else. Verifying such things is what we refer to as assessing process homogeneity. A process must be reproducible. It must work in a virtually identical way when applied to different departments, company branches, other employee roles and teams. As pointed out by Chinese strategist Du Mu, '*when it comes to establishing rules and regulations, everyone, high and low, should be treated alike*'. The same applies to processes that put these rules and regulations to practice. Exceptions do happen, but must apply to equally exceptional circumstances, being strongly justified and endorsed at the very top.

Assessing and judging process homogeneity can be tricky. Heraclitus observed that we can never step into the same river twice. Neither would it be the same up- or downstream. Demanding that a process must be reproduced every time and in every department, in exactly the same manner, down to every microscopic detail, is unrealistic. Even more, it would be promoting that very 'autocratic control and drill-machine approach' that we actively criticised in Chapter 2. Friction exists. *Processes should operate effectively and smoothly while being affected by friction.* In fact, they should have a needed degree of friction resilience and redundancy built-in. The auditors must sound the alarm only when the homogeneity deviations threaten to impede the process, or clearly increase the risk of a security incident.

We must note that concentration on, and understanding of the processes involved, gives additional impetus and direction to other information security assessment types. When you audit any security elements, you always assess a part of some staged process, and usually more than a single process at once. You also assess the interaction between different processes and all friction born from it. This would be taken into account when we discuss the nature of different vulnerabilities and evaluating risks they present.

The final ISMS-related subject that needs be addressed here is the matter of secrecy. No aspects of your ISMS, including security policies, standards, guidelines, procedures, descriptions of processes and so on, must be disclosed to any outsiders, or unauthorised persons, unless required by law. Sometimes, security policies are disclosed to partners or customers, the disclosure being subject to a specific contract condition. In such case the receiving party is authorised, and an appropriate NDA must be signed prior to granting the authorisation. All of this is, generally, common sense known from the ancient times:

- *Matters are dealt with strictly at headquarters (Sun Tzu).*
- *Strictness at headquarters in the planning stage refers to secrecy (Mei Yaochen).*

Nevertheless, we often find various security documentation of companies and organisations being published online. Some of these policies, guidelines, schemes, etc. contain definite security gaps. We can see these gaps. So can the potential attackers. Besides, you have spent effort, time and money developing these documents, as well as the ideas, plans and processes they describe. Now your competitors, who probably operate in a similar manner, can copy and adopt them for free. When any ISMS assessment is performed, the auditors must verify that such information is not unnecessarily exposed.

CHAPTER 4: ADVANCED PRE-ASSESSMENT PLANNING

'It is best to thwart people by intelligent planning.'

Wang Xi

Planning is vital. Planning is vision, direction and structure incarnate. However, in the rapidly changing sphere of information security, it has to be done with utmost care. Plans must always make allowance for the turn of the tide and our inevitable companion 'friction'. If they fail so, plans will become rigid. From a strategic advantage they will turn into an obstacle of equally grand proportions. There are situations in which having inadequate plans is worse than having no plans at all. At least, in the latter case there are still some possibilities of swift adaptation. Enforcement of stagnant plans will kill any useful initiative on the spot.

Different versions of the '*no plan survives contact with the enemy*' statement are ascribed to a disciple of von Clausewitz, Prussian Generalfeldmarschall Helmuth von Moltke the Elder. This is what this renowned strategist actually wrote on the subject:

- *No plan of operations extends with certainty beyond the first encounter with the enemy's main strength. Only the layman sees in the course of a campaign a consistent execution of a preconceived and highly detailed original concept pursued consistently to the end. Certainly the commander in chief will keep his great objective continuously in mind, undisturbed by the vicissitudes of events. But the path on which he hopes to reach it can never be firmly established in advance. Throughout the campaign he must make a series of decisions on the basis of situations that cannot be foreseen. The successive acts of war are thus not premeditated designs, but on the contrary are spontaneous acts guided by military measures. Everything depends on penetrating the uncertainty of veiled situations to evaluate the facts, to clarify the unknown, to make decisions rapidly, and then to carry them out with strength and constancy.*

Helmuth von Moltke was obviously inspired by the following thoughts of his fellow countryman and strategy guru:

- *War is the province of chance. In no sphere of human activity is such a margin to be left for this intruder, because none is so much in constant contact with him on all sides. He increases the uncertainty of every circumstance, and deranges the course of events. From this uncertainty of all intelligence and suppositions, this continual interposition of chance, the actor in war constantly finds things different to his expectations; and this cannot fail to have an influence on his plans, or at least on the presumptions connected with these plans.*
- *... in the course of action circumstances press for immediate decision, and allow no time to look about for fresh data, often not enough for mature consideration. But it much more often happens that the correction of one premise, and the knowledge of chance events which have arisen, are not quite sufficient to overthrow our plans completely, but only suffice to produce hesitation.*

The modern take on this formidable issue is perfectly summarised in the MCDP 1 *Warfighting*:

- *Because we can never eliminate uncertainty, we must learn to fight effectively despite it. We can do this by developing simple, flexible plans; planning for likely contingencies; developing standing operating procedures; and fostering initiative among subordinates.*

Perform the 'substitution exercise' against the aforesaid reasonings. Its results shall be the philosophic backbone of our discussion of information security assessments planning and preparations in this chapter.

On pre-audit gap analysis

'Every war should be viewed above all things according to the probability of its character, and its leading features as they are to be deduced from the political forces and proportions.'

Carl von Clausewitz

The first thing to do prior to any information security assessment is to determine its scope, objectives and targets. The scope is characterised by both width and depth of the audit. The objectives could range from meeting specific compliance demands, to assessing risks presented by deploying a novel process or technology. The targets can be anything that presents information security risks, from systems to people, and organisation of processes. As heavily emphasised in the previous chapters, with a proper auditing approach more targets than defined by a narrow initial scope, would be verified and, ultimately, different aspects of the ISMS will be assessed.

The scope of an audit is heavily shaped by its budget, time frame and objectives. If the objectives are to generate an overall security baseline of systems and networks, a sweeping vulnerability scan will suffice. In the same manner, a mass-mailing social engineering test can be applied to all employees to see how many of them would open an attachment or click on a supplied 'malicious' link. The results of such a test can then be used to verify the efficiency of the existing security awareness programme, and pinpoint staff in need of additional awareness training. On the other hand, if the objective is to test a crucial system, application or process, the assessment must concentrate on this element going into maximum depth and possibly, including white box testing.

The four stage framework

Ideally, you would want to go as wide and as deep as you can. In practice, some form of a gap analysis is required to define the assessment priorities, and thus – its type, scope and targets. The audit itself is, of course, the pinnacle of analysing information security gaps. However, prior to its solicitation the auditee team has to do some important homework. This is similar to a common academic opinion that a good student comes to a lecture or seminar already knowing at least some of its material and with a few topical questions prepared. A proposed pre-audit gap analysis four stage general framework is shown in Figure 18.

Figure 18: The basic anatomy of a pre-assessment gap analysis

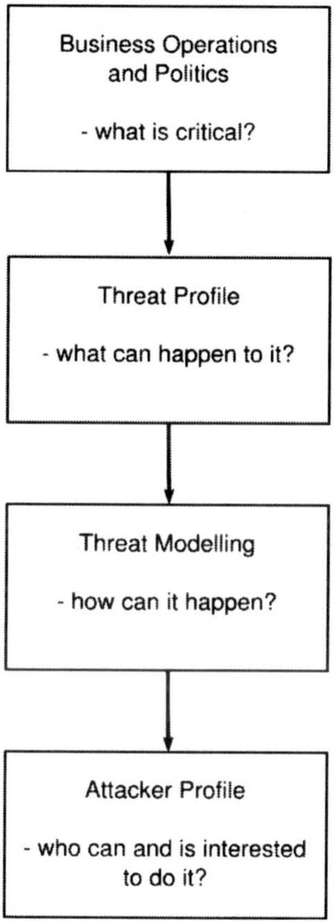

The first step is to find out what is most vital for the company or organisation. Is it a certain trade secret? Is it the customer database? Could it be the public image? Or, perhaps, being compliant with specific standards and regulations? What about records covered by the Data Protection Act in the UK or its equivalents abroad? Such critical elements can be both tangible and intangible. They may, or may not, be related to any estimated monetary values. The key is the seriousness of damage that can be done if they are affected by a security incident of any kind, whether passive or active. Try to compile a priority list, going from the most to the least critical factors and components.

The next step is to estimate and prioritise the threats. A threat is an action that leads to a security incident. You should not confuse threats with their sources (attackers, accidents), which is a common error, or permitting factors (vulnerabilities and gaps). A threat in information security terms is similar to 'infection' in medicine, which is neither the germ nor the lack of immunity, but 'the growth of a parasitic organism within the body' (*Webster's Medical Dictionary* definition). In relation to active security incidents, a threat is what the assailants want. This could be 'selling confidential data to competitors', 'a fraudulent transaction', 'ruining the company image', 'blocking access to online resources', etc. Reviewing the information security history of the entity is a good starting point in estimating threats. Which incidents happened in the past? What was affected? Are such issues still challenging? Assign the appropriate threats to the priority list of critical factors compiled during the previous step. It is also advisable to prioritise the threats assigned to every single critical factor on the list.

Once you have reviewed and prioritised a variety of threats, think of how your information security nightmares can become reality. We are not talking about any actual vulnerabilities and the ways to abuse them. Finding and assessing them is the auditor's task. When discussing social engineering in the previous chapter, we noted that often to get what the social engineers want, they have to exploit a chain of opportunities, moving from who is vulnerable to who has the desired trophy. If you substitute 'who' by 'what', this approach is fully applicable to any technically-centred attacks. Thus, review (and if you don't have them – create and review) data flow, process, network and other applicable diagrams and schemes. You can construct a personnel communication diagram to understand how confidential data flows between people and how the employees are interconnected in overall terms. This can be called a human data flow scheme. Think what is exposed, where it is exposed, how and to whom. Relate it to the critical elements and threats evaluated during the two previous gap analysis steps. Then attempt to build the attack trees. Think through which specific points and in which particular sequence, either external or internal adversaries can get what they want. Draw these points and connect them. Remember, that both the points and links in between can be technical, operational, human, or combined.

Finally, it is time to make some educated guesses about the nature of conceivable adversaries. The following main characteristics must be taken into account:

- *The starting position.*

Are the most likely attackers external, internal, or both? How much can they know about their presumable targets? What level of access do they have? Can they open guest or customer accounts? Are outsiders casually permitted to enter your company or organisation's premises?

- *The motivation.*

Remember, it's all about the clash of wills. If the motivation is low, a general technical or social engineering sweep and its follow-up actions should be sufficient to prevent most attacks from such people or malware they use. If the motivation is high, only active in-depth security testing will suffice. Motivation, based on personal or political hatred directed against the company, organisation, or its selected employees, is usually strong. If you are a lucrative target or a chief competitor, greed can also be the source of a powerful motivation. Impersonal motivation, like trying to steal what is easy to get one's hands on, is weak.

- *The inclinations.*

Are the presumable assailants technically inclined? Or are they more likely to exploit the human factor? What about physical premises intrusion? Can they combine these approaches? While this may be hard to forecast for the external adversaries, as the fog of war is dense out there, this is not so with various types of internal malcontents.

- *The means.*

Try to guess what the likely opponents may have at their disposal. Are they resourceful? Are they technically savvy? Are they experienced? Can they work as a team? Can they have or gain internal allies within your company or organisation? Would they be willing and able to pay highly skilled professionals in either networks, systems and applications hacking, electronic surveillance or social engineering to do the job?

Different types of adversaries can be distinguished by a combination of these important characteristics. However, their conjunction is situational, even within a separate attacker group and may always change. For example, typical cybercriminals are usually external, technically inclined and sufficiently technically savvy, but have weak motivation, hunting for a low hanging fruit. Although, some could specialise in social engineering instead of the technical attack methodologies. However, should any of them realise that your company is a very fruitful, profitable target, their motivation can sky-rocket. The felons will try everything to become intrinsic, which may even include attempts to get employed to gain internal access. Besides, if the motivation is high, but the actual skills are insufficient, the opponents will thrive to learn. So, do not let estimated low skills of the potential attackers put you off guard.

Selecting the targets of assessment

If you have vigorously followed these four steps of the pre-assessment gap analysis, you should have at least approximate answers to the four main questions they pose. Then you can draw the plans outlining what should be audited, how (in general terms) it should be audited, and in what depth. When it comes to the actual selection of specific security assessment targets, the following approaches are casually applied:

1 Audit what is valuable.
2 Test what is perceived as potentially vulnerable.
3 Check what is exposed.
4 Assess what is unknown.

The first approach is most commonly recommended in all relevant information security publications. It is highly sensible, being directly related to step one of the pre-assessment gap analysis. Alas, it is not infallible. The issue, which has already received extensive coverage elsewhere, is estimating the value of data or systems that hold it.

Sometimes, it is easy to do (e.g. trade secrets, or downtime of the e-commerce server of an online shop). However, there are multiple cases of intangibles which are hard to measure in monetary terms, e.g. those related to company image or customer's trust. There are also situations in which the data classification policies and standards are either incomplete or not properly enforced. This leads to confidential data not being labelled as such, which means it will be treated with laxity.

Using the example of a trade secret, there can be bits and pieces of information which do not constitute it directly, but can provide competitors with a hint to what the secret could be. Are they labelled as highly confidential or, at least, confidential data? Are systems that store them and channels that transmit them, sufficiently secure? Are people who know them reliable and security aware? And how do you value such fragments of data monetarily? They may supply outsiders with important clues that will allow them to reconstruct your most guarded treasure. Then again, they may not.

This brings the discussion to the matter of friction and its close associate, the fog of war. Are you sure that the systems which store valuable data are the only systems to hold it? Are you completely confident that it was not disseminated to any other systems? How about paper documents, removable media and people? Data tends to spread across the *information security zone*. It shrinks and expands with it. It propagates along the interlinked chains of computer and human hosts. It's fuzzy. It's chaotic. Confidential data, unfortunately, is not exempt from this observation. At times, it can be found in places you would never expect it to be. This must be taken into account when you zero in on the security assessment targets on the basis of their value and criticality.

Also, what about neighbouring systems or people? All right, they may not hold highly sensitive data, for now. But can it leak to them? Besides, they make perfect proxies for attacks against their secret-holding counterparts, bringing the assailants much closer to their aim and dramatically increasing their chances of success. Check your attack trees. How spacious should the *secure buffer* around the most critical points be? Does it have to cover only the most valuable and crucial elements? Do you really need to expand it further? How far? Can you afford such an expansion and thus, the corresponding scope of any security assessment-to-be? Figure 19 provides some food for thought, with a few of the possible secure buffer borders drawn in dashes and labelled with question marks.

Figure 19: Where does your secure buffer spread?

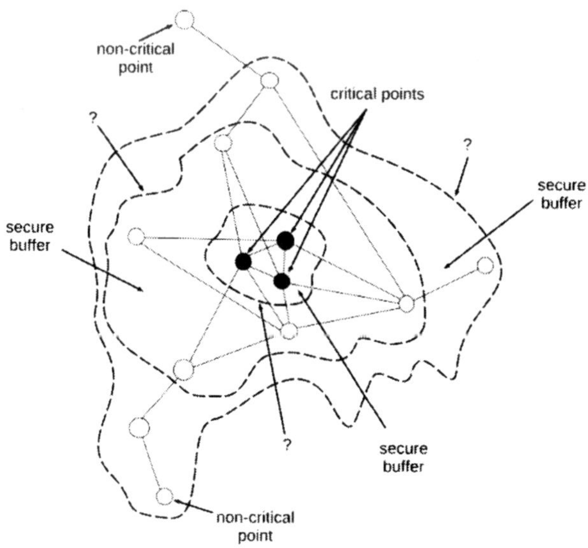

The second approach is based upon either the expert advice of internal specialists, the history of security incidents, or both. It does not appear as sensible as its predecessor on the target selection list. However, it may well be justified. If the problem was not completely resolved, it is likely to repeat again. Besides, technical, human resources, or other professionals of the auditee, can be completely right. But since they don't view themselves as security experts, they would like to see an independent verification of their worries. Perhaps as a manager *you should listen and appreciate such top-bottom initiative*. In addition, there are information security zone elements which are commonly and rightfully perceived as potentially unsafe. On the human level this applies to contractors and temporary workers. On the technical level – to complex Web applications, wireless networks and various forms of telecommuter and other remote employee access. It makes perfect sense to include such shaky borders of the information security zone within the scope of a security audit.

The third approach is highly common and is one of the major justifications for subscribing to external security audits of all kinds. Testing the defences that the attackers will encounter first is perfectly reasonable, providing that the opponents are outside. Check the security of all entry points, be that physical doors, employee vetting, remote connections, or open ports, but do not fall for the 'Maginot Line mentality'. Always keep the defence-in-depth doctrine in perspective. What if the pre-assessment gap analysis indicates that an internal incident is more imminent and certain? What if the externally exposed systems are not highly valuable and critical, and do not communicate with any important networks and hosts? This scenario is perfectly possible if a company website is very simple and hosted by a third party. At the same time, there are no public services open on the internal company network. What about the ever-present fog of war? Are you sure that you are fully aware of all externally accessible services and points of entry? Should you impose any scope limitations on external security scans? Or, in contrast, give the auditors complete freedom of trying to get in anywhere by any possible means? These issues must be seriously weighted prior to making your final decision on the assessment scope and type.

Finally, you can opt to target what is the least certain and understood. This usually means the areas and segments where the internal expertise and corresponding controls are lacking. As compared to the three previous target selection points, this one might appear to be rather strange. Yet, when we recall our military strategy implications, it is perfectly logical. If security assessments reduce friction, and this is what we want, targeting the spots where the friction is at a maximum and fog of war is immense, is wise. Recall our example of the IT security director who ordered a wide scope internal security assessment to get a good grasp of what was going on the network from an independent source. This was a good decision that helped him with resolving multiple issues, some of which were not directly related to security. Reconnaissance is a vital part of any information security audit. It must be put to effective use anywhere the intelligence data is lacking and unexpected can lurk.

The four target selection approaches we have listed work in perfect concert. They can be employed to create a simple point-based system. Make a list of potential security audit targets. Place the criticality/value, perceived vulnerability, exposure and uncertainty against them as table rows. Give one to each of the criteria if you think the target is critical, potentially vulnerable, exposed to attacks, and you are not really sure about security risks it may present. This basic exercise is represented in Table 3.

Table 3: A possible way of selecting feasible audit targets

Criteria	Target 1	Target 2	Target 3	Target 4
Criticality or value	0	1	0	0
Perceived vulnerability	1	0	0	1
Exposure	1	0	1	0
Uncertainty	1	1	0	0
Total	3	2	1	1

The more points a potential target scores, the higher its assessment priority should be. In the illustration of Table 3, Targets 1 and 2 should be security verified. Targets 3 and 4 can probably wait. You can always devise a more complex target selection grading that will use, for example, marks from one to 10, if you see it as more fitting.

On auditing the auditors

'– Maestro, what is more essential in art: 'how?' or 'what'?

'– The most essential is 'who'.'

Pierre-Auguste Renoir to one of his disciples

Once you have decided on the scope, objectives, targets and other desired characteristics of a security assessment, it is time to pick the most appropriate auditors. This task can be far more complex than you might think. It is critical not only for the planned assessment and its follow up, but for the future information security projects and plans of the entire company or organisation. Thus, it must not be taken lightly.

If the audit team is internal, then all you must do is to assign its members to the tasks, in accordance with their specialisations and abilities. A most suitable selection of the team personnel should have been done beforehand. Nevertheless, if the scope and character of the planned assessment is dramatically different from what the internal team usually does, hiring new professionals or, at least, providing additional training, must be considered. This is not so with the more common third party security audits. You cannot rely on advertisements that companies proudly parade. Naturally, everyone would claim they are the best. Of course, sales people do not lie, they just exaggerate a bit. And often, they don't have exact technical or operational understanding of the specialised services they advertise. How can we approach this problem?

First of all, having a long-term overall information security programme that covers the assessments as its important part is the key to many gates. Today, you may need one type of an audit. Tomorrow, it could be completely different. Unless absolutely necessary, or you can afford the luxury of one auditor company verifying the results of another, you would want to work with a security company that can provide for all your assessment needs. Having multiple suppliers for different assessment types increases costs and bureaucracy, while diminishing the possibility to standardise the audit results. In one word, it's an overhead. Unless you need top-notch specialists for a highly peculiar task, it is best to avoid it.

Evaluating what is on offer

In the previous chapter we have thoroughly discussed various security assessment classes and types. In fact, information security assessments are like ... pizza. In a good pizzeria you would be offered a set menu of options, as well as the wide selection of separate pizza toppings to make your own for a fastidious taste. Of course, you also need a delicious crunchy pizza base for all of these. The fundamentals we discussed in Chapter 1 form this base. They must go with any choice you make. The classes and types outlined in Chapter 2 allow an educated selection of the 'toppings'. However, we did not discuss the 'set menu'. Here are the standard audit types you can find in information security companies' adverts:

- ISMS audits
  - Documentation reviews
  - Process reviews
  - Overall security management reviews

- Human-related audits
  - Social engineering
- Premises and physical checks
  - Overall premises security audit
  - Physical systems security audit
  - Social engineering
- Technical security audits
  - External penetration testing
  - External vulnerability scanning
  - Internal penetration testing
  - Internal vulnerability scanning
  - Application security testing
  - Source code review
  - Wireless security testing.

These are the most common pre-set combinations of our 'toppings'. If you are not a security auditor, do practise going through this list, analysing which typical assessment types can be black, grey or white box. Guess which are likely to be passive or active, intrusive or non-intrusive. But the specific point to make here is: *the selection offered by a security company you consider must contain all audit types that are, or can be demanded by, your long-term information security programme*. The more extensive is the spectrum of specific audits offered by a company, the better. Things change, and you cannot be sure what exactly you would need in a longer run. Alas, we do acknowledge that even a specialised security company cannot cover everything and may itself resort to outsourcing. And, in some cases, narrow scope, highly specific, sole security assessment services offered, can bring great advantage. For example, there are security companies that are based around a team of highly skilled programmers which specialise in source code reviews for software vendors.

The second point is: *a security company must offer both the 'set' and the 'custom' menus*. If all they have available is the set, than it is a good indication that all testing is done in a mechanical way. In other words, it can only be passive. This is not a good sign. Because we operate in a fluid, rapidly changing, highly variable environment, security testing procedures often need to be modified in accordance with the auditee peculiarities and unfolding circumstances. Sometimes, they may need to be adjusted 'on the fly'. A rigid selection of predefined services will not meet such a purpose. There must be a possibility of mix-and-match, of a transition in the flow. A typical technical example of such a situation would be if potentially insecure wireless connectivity is detected during an internal penetration test. Then the test will have to involve at least a partial wireless security assessment and a brief security policy review. Finally, if the testing has specific implications for compliance, they must be addressed. For instance, PCI DSS security scanning must be done by the ASVs, and it is only among them that you can make your choice. This concludes the part of the discussion dedicated to the offered security assessments scopes and types.

Judging the assessor's suitability

The next issue is rather tricky. Somehow, you need to estimate the potential security auditor's skills. Note, that this is pertinent for both the auditee and the auditor (when hiring the personnel). We will briefly review it as such. But before delving into the skill sets of people and teams, remember to do at least some background checks to avoid unpleasant surprises. Background checks can vary from contracting to specialised companies like Kroll and PeopleCheck, to Googling and using more attuned online people and companies search sites. At the very least, sweep for common public knowledge regarding companies and people whom you are reviewing as potential security auditors. The auditors will inevitably access and handle sensitive data. The assessment report itself is highly confidential. You can't risk it. So, check if the companies you are reviewing were involved in any scandals, machinations, major security incidents, etc. Are there any publicised customer complaints? If you know the names of the auditor candidates, check their reputation does not include any malicious hacking, cybercrime or other fraudulent activities. You might be astonished. We knew and reported entire companies operated by scammers that looked legitimate at first sight. Alas, they weren't information security specialists.

Probably the most reliable way of determining the auditor's knowledge and skills is to have appropriate and trusted professionals from your company or organisation to check them. This means bypassing the auditor marketing team and arranging a direct meeting between the specialists from both parties. Typically, it should not present a problem. If it does then, perhaps, the auditor company is doubtful about their expert's proficiency, and has instructed the sales reps to hold the ground, which is also not a good sign. Note, that apart from fitting the profile of the audit (e.g. network engineers, if it is network security-centred), the internal professionals selected to communicate with the potential auditors must be trusted. In the context of this discussion it refers to their genuine interest in getting the best assessment results. A situation in which the company specialists may try to favour weak auditors out of fear that the assessment can uncover their faults, is entirely possible. It must be taken into an account when you pick personnel for this specific task and debrief them afterwards.

Professional certifications and education

Next you need to look at different credentials and other achievements the auditor's possess. These may include:

- Certifications
- Education
- Publications
- Tools and exploits.

The relevant certifications provided by the industry standard bodies, etc. can be divided into four major categories:

1 General information security certifications
2 Specific information security certifications
3 Specific security-centred technical certifications
4 Other professional certifications.

Currently, there are far too many applicable certifications to be reviewed in this book. We suggest studying the appropriate certification authority sources to gain necessary knowledge about each particular instance. However, some pertinent common examples need to be addressed.

CISSP and its concentrations are a good example of category one. The concentrations make it more area-directed, but only in rather general terms. SANS GIAC is closer to category two, with its separate specialisations in security administration, security management, software security and security auditing, with further subdivisions within these spheres of knowledge. Another example of a certification par excellence directed at security auditing is Certified Ethical Hacker (CEH) from the EC-Council. ISECOM (Institute for Security and Open Methodologies), most known for providing and maintaining OSSTMM (Open Source Security Testing Methodology Manual), also certifies security assessors in accordance with the OSSTMM practices. The cert is OPST (OSSTMM Professional Security Tester); other ISECOM certifications are Security Analyst, Security Expert and Wireless Security Expert.

Security+ is an example of an entry level certification covering various technical aspects of information security. More specific security-centred technical certifications can concentrate on separate technology or vendors. CWSP (Certified Wireless Security Professional) is an instance of the former, CCIE (Cisco Certified Internetwork Expert) Security – of the latter. Nowadays, practically all major security equipment and software manufacturers offer certifications pertaining to their blockbuster products. Also, vendor certifications not centred on information security, still include significant parts on it that pertain to the specific technologies and products the cert addresses. There are security sections within MCSE, CCNP, RHCE (Red Hat Certified Engineer), etc. Such certs form the fourth category listed above.

Apart from a huge variety of professional certifications, there is higher education in information security or relevant specific areas, ranging from human resources management to software engineering. MSc programmes in information security have become increasingly popular, with more and more universities around the world following the trend. The ‘academic’ areas in which these programmes are typically strong are information security organisation, management and principles, relevant theories, and cryptography, in both theory and practice. Sometimes, university programmes concentrate on specific technologies subject to lecturers' expertise, available sponsorships and grants. But in general, we tend to view current information security MSc degrees as 'CISSP on steroids'.

When assessing security auditor's credentials, like certifications and degrees, whether for signing a service (the auditee) or an employment (the auditor) contract, one has to take into account a variety of factors. Some of these factors, more pertinent to the auditor party, will be reviewed in more detail in the last chapter of this book. For the purpose of the current chapter, the following matters are essential.

- *It is better to have certifications and degrees than not. At least, they provide reasonable proof that a certain proficiency baseline exists. In this case, something is clearly better than nothing.*
- *More often than not, certifications and degrees relate to knowledge, rather than skills.*

Very specific accreditations that require passing practical, hands-on exam tests are the possible exceptions.

- *Despite what many technical specialists think about their usefulness, having general information security certifications and degrees is advantageous for the auditors.*

Finding vulnerabilities is one thing, establishing their true sources and evaluating risks is another. The former firmly belongs to the realm of tactics, the latter crosses into the strategic domain. Both must be present, operating in concert. Nevertheless:

- *For executing specific audit types highly pertinent qualifications and respective accreditations are vital, even if they are not security-centred.*

For a source code security review a good degree in software engineering is likely to be far more important than any information security-centred education or cert.

- *Having too many certifications and (more rarely) degrees is suspicious, especially if the declared work experience period is rather limited.*

Is this person really walking the talk? Is it not the case of cramming-for-the-exam we have used as an allegory when discussing compliance issues in Chapter 2? How much is too many? We have seen people boasting to have more than a dozen certs in totally unrelated areas. On the other hand, if a professional is known to have worked with a specific vendor solution for a decade and has plentiful certifications from this vendor, it makes perfect sense. Study it because you like it and need it in everyday work, not for the fancy letters on a business card.

- *Some of the best hackers known, or unknown to the world, have no relevant certifications and degrees. The same can apply to prominent security researchers and developers.*
- *Finally, there is no cert in social engineering.*

Publications and tools

Apart from certifications and university diplomas, the auditors can also demonstrate a variety of publications, software or hardware tools, and exploit code. In our opinion, these are highly important since they clearly point at ongoing hands-on work. Publications are casually divided into:

- Journal articles and books
- Security advisories
- Posts on professional forums and groups.

Articles demonstrate knowledge (or, at times, lack of thereof) in a specific area they cover. If they are written in a HOWTO style being essentially printed manuals, they indicate practical skills as well. Alternatively, a security team can release a specific tool and supplement it with detailed manuals. Check what the tool does. Think whether it, or any similar applications, can be used to assess your systems and networks, addressing the likely problems they might face.

Of course, *the ultimate publication you should ask for is a sample of the relevant assessment report*. A security company must be able to provide it ASAP and for every specific audit type they advertise. It should not be obsolete, reflecting methods and vulnerabilities of a lustre past. It must not contain any sensitive *or potentially sensitive* data related to current or previous customers. Such information can often include network addresses and diagrams, or employee's positions. If it contains theirs, than where is the guarantee that some day it would not embody yours? Analyse the assessment report together with the respective specialists. Is it what you expect to receive from the planned audit? Does it correspond well to the descriptions and requirements we outline in Chapter 7, dedicated to reporting the outcome of security assessments?

Books are similar to articles, but have a much wider scope and often go into more depth. They casually hint at long-standing experience or original research, since respected publishers would not accept a proposition from anyone. Quite often, practical books are supplemented with a few tools, or whole toolkits. Talking of which, you may encounter an information security company centred around producing and maintaining a powerful and complex tool. Again, verify what such tool does and which specific or unique abilities that you need, it offers. Authoring a mighty security tool clearly shows profound knowledge and skill in the area to which these abilities pertain. On the other hand, it may also turn the company into, essentially, the tool vendor. This will undoubtedly limit its assessment scope, strongly relating it to the tool capabilities.

Security advisories indicate active hands-on investigations and are, in this sense, similar to the exploit code. In fact, they are regularly supplemented with the exploit code. Check which specific issues are reported in the advisories and are targeted by the exploits. Is it somehow relevant to your networks, systems and critical applications? Also, check the element of ethics. A standard procedure is to report a new vulnerability to the affected software vendor, wait until the patch or fixed version is released, and only then publicly disclose the information, not to mention the exploit code. Disclosing vulnerability information before the fix is out in sake of personal fame indicates serious ego problems. Stay away from such people, since they can put your systems at risk by making their flaws public before they are eliminated. To do this, they don't have to publish a full advisory to open disclosure mail lists. Bragging to friends about 'how masterly did we get in' is more than enough. However, there are exceptions to everything. If the vendor did not release the fix in a year or so's time, deciding to publish information about the flaw is entirely justified. Vendors should be reprimanded for their negligence. If it was a serious bug of utility or function, the customers would have already switched to a different supplier or even sued. Why should security, an essential part of warranty according to the ITIL, be any different?

In the recent past we would have said: if the auditor company has continuously published new security advisories, exploit code, and tools, go for it if technical assessments is all you need. Nowadays, things are not so simple. First of all, numerous companies and organisations that buy exploit code and information about novel vulnerabilities have come to life. Once it is bought, it becomes a property of such a company and will remain confidential for a long time, perhaps, forever. So, many security researchers of today quietly sell their 'sploits and vulns', instead of publishing them to public disclosure lists like Open Disclosure and Bugtraq, or at their company's sites. Then, more and more client companies enforce very strict NDAs that prohibit such publications. For instance, we cannot disclose a few critical holes in a certain network appliance because of such an NDA, even though the appliance retired about three years ago and is no longer maintained. Also, do not be astonished by the amount of security advisories published by some researchers and teams. Have your specialists examine them. Currently, many security holes in Web applications can be discovered by powerful scanning tools, without much effort on the auditor's side. These flaws are underlined by common algorithms and are sufficiently basic to be uncovered by automated scans. Publishing them en masse demonstrates that the auditing team has a decent Web application scanner, but does not necessarily indicate a high level of proficiency and skill. So, *it is always a good sign if a security company publishes some security advisories, tools and exploits. However, it does not have to spit out tonnes of them all the time.*

The bottom line of this discussion is: *if a company has released security advisories, exploits and tools, it means that its team is capable of performing meaningful and efficient* ***active*** *technical security assessments*. Which is something you probably need now or in the not-so-distant future. On the other hand, it does not say a lot about its capabilities in non-technical security auditing. You should also question whether they are proficient in analysing risks and establishing the actual sources of the uncovered flaws. As we have stated above, discovering the vulnerabilities is surely crucial, but at the end of the day, it is only a half of the whole job. If the matters are not put into the strategic perspective, important factors can go amiss. You can get trapped in the endless scan-report-patch-scan-report-patch-scan- ... loop while it is entirely possible to break this nagging pattern by finding and eliminating the problem's true root cause.

The auditor company history and size

What about the security firm itself, not just its auditing team expertise? The first thing you should look at after verifying the company's and its specialist's reputation, is for how long the company has been operational. Common sense tells us: the longer, the better. If it has not gone out of business, than its services are either unique and have captured their niche, or are of a high quality, or both. There are exemptions that thrive entirely on highly aggressive marketing or strong personal connections of their directors, but these are few in number. If a company has operated for a long time, it must have developed an internal 'school of thought and skill', as well as an extensive knowledge base. This ensures that the newcomers to such a company are properly trained by joining the continuity. In spite of the rapidly evolving nature of the information security science and art, having strong 'internal tradition' is worthwhile. If possible, find out about the rotation of personnel in the reviewed security company. Public searches for current and former employees are the easiest way of doing it. A high level of retention of experienced professionals within the company indicates that such tradition is present and very well alive.

Over the time of its operation, the company should have amassed various references and accumulated a sizeable client base. Always ask for the references and review the client base profile. Many companies and organisations are unwilling to provide their name for privacy reasons and supply written reference letters. Information security is a sensitive area. Nevertheless, some customers may well do, or even advertise it on their websites. You have probably seen many of these stating 'this site was security checked by <Company Name>'. Besides, references do not have to be formal. What amounts to a reliable reference can be passed by word of mouth in a private conversation or via e-mail. Apart from proving (or disproving) the quality of the performed work, the rumour mill can also provide invaluable information regarding the ethical aspects. We live in a small world. The professional information security world is even more like a village. If someone has being involved in dubious activities, like leaking confidential data or charging for non-existing services, it will be known and spread from lip to lip. The more contacts you have with the scrutinised security company acquaintances, the better. Especially if they were (or are) its customers. As for the advertised base of the existing and former clients, it should at least state to which industry or government sectors they belong. Is there a certain pattern of preference? How does your company or organisation fit into this pattern?

The final question to be addressed is how large the auditor team is. The judgement by size is not straightforward. A lot depends on what kind of security assessments you really need and what their perceived and planned scope is. The reality is that the number of highly skilled auditors in any company or organisation is going to be limited. Admittedly, there are not a lot of them on the whole and they are thinly spread around the world. Their services are usually expensive. Besides, such professionals are typically driven by passion and would thrive to do what interests them the most. Thus, if some security company claims to have dozens of top-end security specialists in a team, we would naturally have strong doubts. They aren't the NSA, after all.

Most likely, there is a small dedicated yolk surrounded by a mass of the less knowledgeable and skilled colleagues, who in the best case can be the disciples of the core 'maestros'. No one has ever mastered to assemble an entire army of 'ninjas'. Neither is it likely to happen in the foreseeable future. So, providing that the presence of necessary expertise is evident, the actual choice is between the 'naked' core and the core enveloped by numerous acolytes. If you opt for the latter, you will have more people to do a massive scope job. If you choose the former, you can be more confident that you are getting the service from the wizards and not the apprentices. It is reasonable to assume that active testing is going to (and should) be performed by the first, and passive – by the second. So, if you need wide-ranging passive checks, especially if they demand physical presence of the auditors at your premises, a large team is a definite advantage. However, if limited scale but great depth active testing is required, a small highly professional team could be a better option. Remember, that many wide scope technical or semi-technical passive tests can be successfully performed by a smaller team employing effective automation (scripting). Nevertheless, as classic Chinese strategist Wu Qi pointed out millenniums ago, '*when employing a few, concentrate upon narrows*'.

On arranging the audit process

'First establish your plans, then prepare your equipment.'

Li Quan

Once the assessment characteristics are decided upon and the appropriate auditors are selected, it is time to pull up the sleeves to plan and arrange the assessment process. On the auditor side it is straightforward:

1 Review the customer requirements and all information (schedules, deadlines, target lists, etc.) provided.
2 Make sure everything is understood, agreed and no arrangements are unrealistic.
3 Select specialists and assign their roles in the upcoming assessment.
4 Select who is going to communicate with the auditee during the whole process.
5 Select appropriate methodologies and techniques.
6 Now select the tools, if the assessment is technical.
7 Make sure that all chosen tools are fully operational, stable and are upgraded to the latest versions. You don't

want to tweak, update and reinstall during the tests. Time is precious.

8 Wait for the green light.

Verify that you clearly comprehend all the objectives and aims of the audit. Check that the timetable for it is reasonable and won't force you to rush with either the assessment itself or with producing the audit report. Ensure that all necessary instruments are humming smoothly. Finally, check several times when exactly you can kick off. We have seen far too much confusion when the audit began earlier than the auditee personnel were prepared for. Of course, by preparedness we do not mean any frantic attempts to 'clean up' and conceal possible issues just before the testing starts. Such behaviour must be strongly discouraged, not at least because it is actually more likely to introduce more errors than existed before. What we imply is simply being ready to react to the assessment process and its immediate discoveries. The key words are 'effective communication'.

Final auditee preparations and planning

The auditee arrangements and planning tasks carry a higher responsibility and involve greater decision-making. First of all, is the assessment done against a live or testing environment? This applies to technical audits only. If the assessment targets the testing environment, its milieu must be created beforehand, allowing sufficient time for the construction and review. Then it must be thoroughly verified to emulate the real thing to the maximum possible extent. If the assessment targets the live environment, always prepare for the unexpected. What if the tested systems collapse? What if a social engineer is caught red-handed and reported to the police? What if the internal audit turns out to be too disruptive? What if key participants of the audit fail to turn up on both sides? What if the assessment uncovers illicit behaviour or an outright criminal offence? The friction is higher at the auditee side. Always prepare for a sudden change of plans. Have spare plans. Plan for contingency.

The next thing is to decide who will communicate with the auditors and how it should be done. Common sense tells that it should be the CISO or equivalent. However, it also suggests that relevant technical or non-technical specialists must be involved. Thus, define who will be in touch with the auditors. It could be more than one person, but you should avoid large communication teams susceptible to miscommunication and confusion. Three is a sensible number that ensures that someone will always stay in touch. For example, the involved trinity can be the CISO, head of the department which is affected the most (e.g. IT, human resources, compliance/risk), and a selected relevant specialist, or the departmental administrator/secretary. In any case they must be able to respond quickly to any auditor's requests or status updates. Keep more than one channel of communication constantly open – phone, e-mail, instant messengers, if necessary – personal contact. Verify its efficiency. Send the auditors a few mails, or give a few phone calls asking for news and updates. See how quickly they would respond. Immediate response is highly desirable. If it lags for more than a day, it is a bad sign. Log a complaint.

Talk to the auditors and agree on the assessment phases, schedules, timetables, deadlines, debriefs and emergency breakpoint events. A security audit can consist of a few phases. The separation into such stages can be done in accordance to numerous criteria and will be addressed in more detail in the next chapter. A recent audit we have performed for one of our clients was split into the following steps:

- Assess a critical application.
- Debrief, wait for the follow-up reaction.
- Assess the systems that host the application.
- Debrief, wait for the follow-up reaction.
- Assess the network on which these systems are deployed.
- Debrief, wait for the follow-up reaction.
- Arrange the next round of testing.

It is important to define the stages in a logical sequence and provide sufficient and meaningful intervals between them. When planning the audit schedules, think at which points the status updates are necessary. For example, update after the reconnaissance is done, then after the vulnerability scanning is done, then after the risk analysis is performed, and finally when the report is submitted. With every status update received, ask the auditors about the estimated time of the next assessment stage. Are they ahead or behind the schedule? This brings us to the topic of security assessment timetables and deadlines.

You might have a variety of urgent pressures. For instance, a compliance check can be looming. Besides, time is invaluable anyway, and the quicker a security problem is discovered and dealt with, the lower are the associated risks. At the end of the day, it is up to the auditee to decide on both the time-frame and the deadline of the assessment process. Nonetheless, don't be mean and demand the impossible. Keep your required deadlines in sight, but also negotiate with the auditors. Find out how much time they *think* they need to do a proper job. Consult your professionals and relevant third party sources regarding it. There are plenty of useful publications that describe similar testing and its peculiarities. Form your own opinion. You do not want to be overcharged or have a delayed assessment report. On the other hand, haste can be detrimental to the audit quality. *Bargain for time as you would for cash.* Decide on the absolute deadline when everything must be accomplished in full. Then consider a *realistic slack*. Shift the deadline back and present it to the auditors. Listen to their reasonings. Adjust the slack, trying to keep it sufficient. Then, as suggested above, keep your finger on the pulse checking the assessment progress with every single status update. If you see that the *very final and absolute deadline* is unlikely to be met for *objective reasons*, reconsider your plans. Perhaps, some things are not that critical and can be assessed the next time. Possibly, it is you that have overestimated the audit scope. However, if there are no apparent reasons for the severe delay, consider using a different audit supplier next time.

Dealing with common assessment emergencies

The last topic that needs to be discussed is what we call the emergency breakpoints. *An emergency breakpoint event is the event that leads to the halt of the audit process and a sudden change of plans.* Review the following possibilities, some of which we have already noted in this section:

- A severe, high risk vulnerability has been discovered
- A critical live system has crashed
- A clear-cut security incident is detected.

All three issues provide strong reasons for stopping the assessment and redirecting attention and resources to their immediate resolution. They must be promptly reported by either party that discovers the problem (usually the auditors). In such a case, waiting until the planned audit process is over and the full report is submitted can do more harm than good. It risks becoming a textbook example of damage done by following rigid, inflexible plans. After the issue is successfully solved, a continuation of the audit can be arranged.

The simplest case is a critical system crash. Usually, the tests performed against such systems are non-intrusive. Nevertheless, there is always a chance of such an unfortunate event taking place. If strong redundancy and fault tolerance is built in (as it should be), and the fall-back system is not subject to similar tests, the assessment can continue. It will have to, of course, concentrate on establishing the cause of the crash and evaluate whether only availability is affected by this security problem. In other words, the auditors will have to investigate what caused an effective Denial of Service (DoS) attack and whether the issue is exploitable any further. In our practice, there were occasions on which important systems collapsed during the security assessment. However, the real causes of the crashes turned out to be completely unrelated to the tests. Always keep this possibility in mind: coincidence does not always mean a definite link and can be a mere manifestation of friction.

If, however, the availability is severely disrupted, the assessment will have to stop. The operation of the affected system will have to be restored ASAP. The next steps should include:

- Trying to establish what caused the crash in the first place, using all information at hand.
- Writing a report based on the incomplete assessment results and outlining in detail what has happened.
- Arranging a continuation of the checks against a stand-alone testing system that will completely mirror the affected one.

All of this must be done as quickly as you can. Meanwhile, the assessment report might have to point out the lack of proper redundancy and failover as a serious security gap, putting data and services availability in jeopardy.

The next common type of an emergency breakpoint event is discovering a highly critical, exploitable vulnerability. Prior to the audit start, a preliminary arrangement covering this important issue should be reached. The typical action plan dealing with it is:

1 The auditors must immediately report such vulnerability to the auditee contact.
2 They must clearly outline its severity, associated impact and estimated risks.
3 The assessment must be stopped.
4 The vulnerability must be fixed.
5 The assessment can now continue, starting from verification that the breakpoint cause vulnerability is now fully eliminated.
6 Rapid status update must inform the auditee contact that the issue is now resolved.
7 The assessment report must still outline this vulnerability and address the actions performed to remove it.

Back in our university times, one of the author's friends installed a new Solaris system on a network-connected server. He left it at the default configuration and went for coffee, planning to configure the box properly right after that. When he returned, the system had port 666 open and a root shell bound to it. It took the time of drinking a single coffee mug to get hacked. If such a possibility is very likely, do not wait for the rest of the tests to complete. Inform and correct. Remember the OODA loop and getting ahead of the adversaries. If you don't, there is a fair chance that the audit will have to be followed by an entirely different service of a forensic investigation.

This is what actually happens in the third aforementioned emergency breakpoint case. Alas, the assessment is not followed by the forensic service. Rather, it flows straight into it. Imagine, that the auditors find out that one of the systems checked is already hacked and backdoored. Or highly confidential documents have disappeared without a trace. Or the auditee employees are doing something in a clear violation of the acceptable use policy. For example, they can abuse network resources to run their own unrelated business, or store child pornography, or else. The assessment will have to be stopped. The uncovered security incident must be discussed with the highest auditee contact, usually the CISO, *in strict confidence*. All evidence of the incident found by the auditors must be documented and provided to this contact in full. The rest would depend on the incident response and investigation policies and procedures of the auditee. If the auditors possess appropriate qualifications and the auditee deems it necessary, they can be employed as third party consultants to assist with forensics.

These are probably the most common examples of the security assessment emergency breakpoints we can recall. No doubt, other disruptive possibilities that can reshuffle even the most delicate arrangements and plans, do exist.

Nevertheless, it is entirely possible to anticipate and adapt to the inevitable interference of friction. In the words of Carl von Clausewitz, *if we go further in the demands which war makes on its votaries, then we find the powers of the understanding predominating. War is the province of uncertainty: three-fourths of those things upon which action in war must be calculated, are hidden more or less in the clouds of great uncertainty.* ***Here, then, above all a fine and penetrating mind is called for, to grope out the truth by the tact of its judgement.***

CHAPTER 5: SECURITY AUDIT STRATEGIES AND TACTICS

'In military operations, what is valued is foiling the opponent's strategy, not pitched battle.'

Wang Xi.

The previous chapters put heavy emphasis on governance, management and policy issues in relation to assessing information security. They are also heavily centred on the issues of strategic significance. It is time to pull up the sleeves and dive into the realm of tactics. Inevitably, this means that the upcoming discourse will have to be more technically inclined. However, as stated in this book's preface, providing detailed checklists or hands-on testing manuals is not the intended goal. We are not competing with, for example, OSSTMM (Open Source Security Testing Methodology Manual), not to mention more specific in-depth guides like OWASP (The Open Web Application Security Project). Rather, we create a layer of applicable logic above and through such guides, by explaining how the fundamentals and strategies previously discussed can be implemented in practice.

When discussing the differences between a strategic and tactical approach, Carl von Clausewitz wrote the following:

- *Combat consists of a greater or lesser number of individual acts, each complete in itself, which we call engagements, which constitute new things. This gives rise to an entirely different activity, namely, individually planning and conducting these engagements and joining*

> *them together to achieve the objective of the war. The first is called tactics, the second, strategy.*

This provides a defined separation line between 'strategic' and 'tactical' when applied to information security assessments. A separate test, or a testing phase, amounts to an engagement in the above quote. Every engagement is an entity '*complete in itself*', meaning it has its own OODA loop. This loop should revolve seamlessly to ensure the engagement's efficacy. '*Joining them together to achieve the objective*' of the assessment is the audit's strategy. A large part of it amounts to pulling all assessment findings together and performing an all-encompassing synthetic risk analysis, which is the subject of the next chapter.

Another take on what is strategic is presented in the MCDP 1 *Warfighting*, which states that '*strategy involves establishing goals, assigning forces, providing assets, and imposing conditions on the use of force in theatres of war*'. This relates to defining the objectives and planning we have already addressed in detail. Note, that from the auditee viewpoint, hopefully based upon running large-scale long-term information security programmes, a stand-alone audit appears to be a tactical assignment. Nevertheless, security assessments have their own, if somewhat restricted, language and logic of strategy. Aforementioned audit planning and synthesis of its approaches, methods and results to generate the whole picture are its vital parts. The same applies to all general methodologies and frameworks that can be applicable to security assessments of a different nature. For instance, the basic audit sequence outlined in the very beginning of Chapter 1 is suitable for technical, process and social engineering tests. It is clearly strategic, just as all the fundamental principles discussed in that chapter are. Keep them in mind when planning and performing any information security audits, and you will find them all-permeating. No matter what you do, if you are doing it right '*strategy can therefore never take its hand from the work for a moment*' (Clausewitz).

On critical points

'There's only one principle of war and that's this. Hit the other fellow, as quick as you can, and as hard as you can, where it hurts him most, when he ain't lookin'!'

Sir William Slim

The immediate practical aim of any information security audit is to discover as many vulnerabilities, weaknesses and gaps as possible, within the defined assessment limits. In the cases of active assessment approach, simple discovery of flaws is usually insufficient. The vulnerabilities must be exploited. To do so in an effective way, it is important to pinpoint the weakest links in a chain and direct maximum effort at breaching them with further expansion of success. Since the hoar of innumerable ages, '*there is no more imperative and simpler law for strategy than to keep the forces concentrated*' (Clausewitz) against the opponent's critical points. But how do we define them? Is it something (or someone), which is the most vulnerable? Or, perhaps, the most valuable? Or, has a specific position in a general scheme of things? Could it possess a peculiar combination of these and, perhaps, some other important characteristics?

Centres of gravity and their types

In the previous chapter we elaborated on a possible way of allocating priority targets for an upcoming security assessment. The problem is: the perspective of the auditors on both criticality and prioritisation of specific items can be significantly different from that of the auditee. This is expected – the mindset and vision of both sides are typically highly dissimilar. Thus, there is a need to discuss the subject of critical points in more detail, this time primarily from the auditor's side. To do it in a logical and organised way without slipping into technical specificity, we shall borrow a few more important terms from military science. These terms are '*centre of gravity*', '*Schwerpunkt*', '*Nebenpunkt*' and '*Systempunkt*'. Just as '*friction*' and '*fog of war*' are highly applicative for describing the effects of uncertainty, the unknown, chaos and chance, these terms are honed to perfection to address vital, deciding points *from the attacker perspective*.

The modern definition of the *centre of gravity* is provided in the MCDP 1 *Warfighting* (just replace 'the enemy' with 'the auditee', 'eliminated' with 'breached', and 'our will' with 'attackers will'):

- *We ask ourselves: Which factors are critical to the enemy? Which can the enemy not do without? Which, if eliminated, will bend him most quickly to our will? These are centres of gravity.*

Thoroughly review all the information the auditee contacts have supplied. Then perform the reconnaissance testing phase, and answer these questions for yourself on the basis of its results. When doing so, dissociate yourself from the initial information provided by the auditee. You may already find that some of your answers do not match the auditee opinions. Continue with the vulnerability discovery and exploitation. During the risk analysis stage that follows, perform another round of 'centre of gravity questions'. Do their final answers correspond to the auditee estimations? What about your own post-reconnaissance assertions? How many centres of gravity were confirmed or determined by the tests? Can you prioritise them?

Centre of gravity is a 200-year old concept introduced by Carl von Clausewitz. He acknowledged that there could be more than a single centre and recommended to direct maximum effort at what seemed to be the most vital one:

- *Therefore, the first consideration in drafting a plan of war is to recognise the centres of gravity of the enemy power, and to reduce them to one, if possible.*

Nevertheless, the grand strategist did realise that sometimes concentrating all effort to what is perceived as the main centre of gravity, is not practically feasible:

- *There is only one exception to the principle of directing all one's forces against the centre of gravity of the enemy force, and that is if secondary operations promise extraordinary benefits.*

The idea of prioritising centres of gravity to determine those likely to *cause a total collapse of the opponent's defences* was further developed by blitzkrieg strategists. Blitz, as we know from history, is a highly effective offensive approach, recapitulated in the famous '*Nicht kleckern, klotzen!*' (Don't fiddle, smash!) of Heinz Guderian. Blitzkrieg generals used the germane terms of *Schwerpunkt* and *Nebenpunkt* to harmonise their operations.

- *Schwerpunkt is the centre of gravity towards which the main effort of the attack is focused so that the desirable objectives are met.*
- *Nebenpunkt is the centre of gravity towards which secondary activities supporting the primary effort are*

> *directed. These activities often involve distracting the opponents or 'softening' their defences.*

In a penetration or social engineering test, *a Schwerpunkt is the primary point that allows effective breach of data and systems confidentiality, integrity and/or availability.* It could be a system, application, network protocol, authentication mechanism or even someone's personal trait. The key is: *it must be more mission critical and sufficiently exploitable as compared to other identified centres of gravity*. Only that warrants the time, attention and measure of concentration it demands. Thus, like in a real war, establishing a security assessment's Schwerpunkt requires decent reconnaissance and good judgement. Note, that since the concept of Schwerpunkt provides a crystallisation point for mission, direction and intent, it can be highly applicable for organising any information security programmes, not just running the audits. Also note the dependence of selecting the Schwerpunkt on the objectives, which can differ.

In a sophisticated hacking attack, the assailants can flood intrusion detection and monitoring systems with junk traffic or fake attack signatures to render them useless. They can even try to exploit and subvert them. At the same time, the true targets of the attack are clearly not the IDS/IPS sensors or syslog servers. This constitutes a technical instance of the *Nebenpunkt*. Emulating such subterfuge as a part of a penetration test can be highly effective in assessing the deployed safeguards. In Chapter 1 we noted an example of a wireless penetration test in which the IPS was tricked to attack legitimate hosts, effectively becoming a problem itself. In a real hacking attack that could have forced network administrators to turn off the 'misbehaving' IPS, thus softening the defences.

Social engineering can supply us with plentiful illustrations of using the Nebenpunkt to alleviate tension, distract attention and reduce suspicion. If an astute social engineer expects that the very contact with the 'Schwerpunkt person' will raise some eyebrows, she can simultaneously connect with a bunch of other people. No matter if they are totally unrelated to the engagement's aims or the person our social engineer is after. In fact, it could only create advantage by diverting attention and presenting the contact as natural and unsuspicious. All communication with the 'mission-critical person(s)' will inevitably involve lavish Nebenpunkt. Further still, it might consist of 'pure Nebenpunkt' without any specific attempts to get to the point, until the needed sensitive data is 'incidentally' revealed. Sometimes, the absence of any direct head-on approach to the target is the best approach of all.

The latter case is Guderian reversed: '*Fiddle until it smashes*'. One of the Nebenpunkt suddenly becomes the Schwerpunkt, which falls prey to an attack: bingo! It also bears associations with the fuzzing method discussed later in this chapter when addressing application vulnerability discovery. But above all, it brings into the spotlight the most modern of all the discussed terms – the Systempunkt. It is derived from the combination of German 'Schwerpunkt' and English 'system' (in general and not the IT-specific sense). A characteristic Systempunkt exhibits the following traits:

- *It is critical because of its interactions with other points in the system, rather than any specific inherent properties.*

- *Thus, its penetration or collapse has severe repercussions for the system as a total, often due to the avalanche or domino effect.*
- *An attack on it is likely to be far more damaging to the whole system than to the Systempunkt itself.*
- *Because of that, the real value of a 'stand-alone' Systempunkt can only be measured by the total effects of its failure or breach.*
- *It is not necessarily the most obvious or the weakest link.*
- *It is usually highly reactive to many small interactions and interventions, especially if they are aptly combined.*

Common application libraries, code repositories, centralised version control and patch management systems, SaaS, routers, switches and infrastructure protocols can make perfect Systempunkts. If data is automatically 'smeared' around the cloud without proper security checks, any point of unauthorised entry into it is a deadly Systempunkt in the waiting. As a little useful exercise, think who might make the best bipedal Systempunkts in your company or organisation from the social engineering perspective.

Identifying critical points

Figure 20 is a slight modification of the scheme on the previous Figure we have employed when discussing targets selection from the auditee perspective.

Figure 20: Where are the critical points?

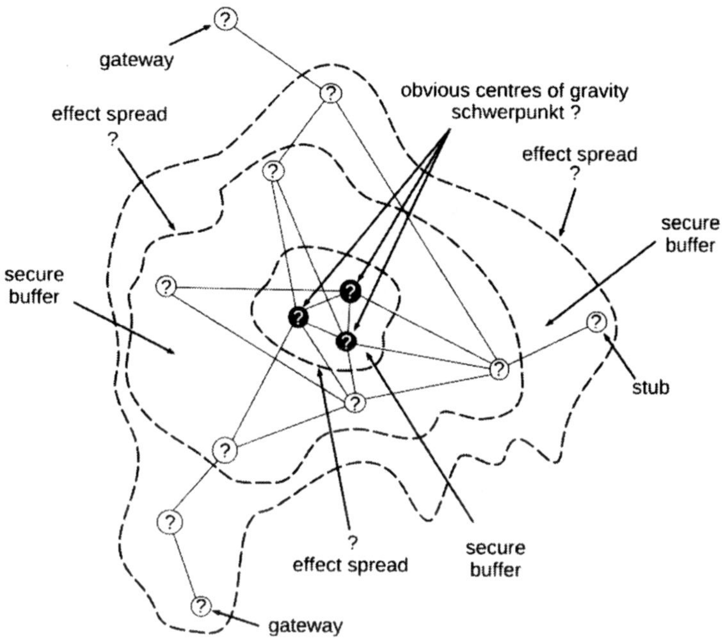

For the example's sake, this time envision this illustration as a simple computer network diagram. It has two external gateways, three nodes known to hold highly confidential data, and a single stub node. The three 'confidential' nodes are the obvious centres of gravity. No third party security assessments are required to recognise this basic fact. However, which one can be the Schwerpunkt? This would depend on many factors, including:

- *The objectives of the attack.* If all the adversaries want is disruption of the external network connectivity, then both gateways *and their uplinks* are the Schwerpunkt. If the attackers are after some specific employees, then these employees' workstations and communication channels are the most likely Schwerpunkt. Nevertheless, the three central nodes might also be targeted if they store confidential employee data. Sly internal assailants might even attack them while spoofing their victim's network address or account to frame a colleague.

- *The amount of tangible and intangible damage that can be caused by the breach.* Given the chance to protect only one of your systems storing sensitive data, which one would you go for, taking into account all known and anticipated factors? Rephrasing George Orwell, all confidential data are sensitive, but some are more sensitive than the other.
- *The attacker means*. Naturally, if the assailant is an experienced database hacker the critical node that hosts the corporate database will become the Schwerpunkt. Since the ever-present fog of war prevents us from knowing what attackers can or cannot do, it is essential that the auditors possess the needed variety of skills. Otherwise, their and the assailant's perceptions of Schwerpunkt may not match, leading to a predictable outcome when the attack takes place.

To summarise, while each of the three central nodes, or both gateways, or insufficiently protected communication channels to and from them are more likely to become the Schwerpunkt, this is not always the case. Look around. Perhaps, you can discover a network management station (or, in case of an internal audit, sniff a management protocol) that holds the keys to all critical hosts. Yet, it might be totally missed by the auditee when doing the pre-assessment gap analysis. Can such de facto network management station be one of the system administrator's laptops?

What about any possible Systempunkts on the scheme? Common sense tells that the nodes which are more interconnected should be more suitable for this role. But can the lonely stub node of Figure 20 be the Systempunkt? Envision the following scenarios:

1 The stub node is a remote workstation that has privileged access to the three central nodes or both gateways over a VPN tunnel. Although, this is more of a hidden, non-obvious Schwerpunkt case. It would be closer to a Systempunkt, though, if we look at it as a vector of malware proliferation.
2 The stub node is the only network switch to which the attackers can gain administrative access. Then they can manipulate the STP (Spanning Tree Protocol) to redirect traffic through this switch or cause a propagating network-wide denial of service with ease.
3 The nodes on the scheme are not separate hosts, but entire BGP (Border Gateway Protocol) Autonomous Systems (AS). Hackers who took over the stub AS can use wile attack methods such as *prefix hijacking* or *prefix deaggregation* to wreck large-scale, rapidly proliferating havoc. They can also try to suck in and intercept additional traffic by subverting the BGP Path Information.

Scenarios 2 and 3 demonstrate the awesome, gobsmacking power of exploiting a Systempunkt. All three scenarios show that Systempunkt, depending on the logic of the entire system's architecture and operations, could be literally anywhere. Hence, all nodes of Figure 20 are labelled with question marks. In fact, a Systempunkt may not be the actual physical node, but a link between them or, more likely, an infrastructure protocol running through these links. Besides, by plugging in a laptop and spoofing switching, routing, redundancy, address resolution and assignment, or other relevant protocols, an internal attacker actually *adds, or creates a Systempunkt*! He or she does it by joining the attacked network and effectively emulating unauthorised access to a key switch, router or server.

Can we prioritise Systempunkts and define the main one? The dash lines on Figure 20 represent how far the repercussions of hitting a Systempunkt can spread. Usually, the Systempunkt with the largest dissemination of effects is the most critical. On the example scheme, that would be the point which affects all the depicted nodes, generating the outermost dash line. In other cases, look at both the reach of the aftermath and its actual impact for every confirmed Systempunkt. *How many centres of gravity does it engulf, or even create*? Do the existing security buffers and zones restrict the pervasion of Systempunkt effects? How? Can these restrictions be bypassed? How could the defenders reinforce them?

When criticising the classical view of centres of gravity, Colonel Boyd wrote the following:

- *Clausewitz incorrectly stated: 'A centre of gravity is always found where the mass is concentrated most densely' – then argued that this is the place where the blows must be aimed and where the decision should be reached. He failed to develop an idea of generating many non-cooperative centres of gravity by striking at those vulnerable, yet critical, tendons, connections, and activities that permit a larger system to exist.*

Without explicitly naming it, John Boyd has essentially described utilising the Systempunkt concept. In our context, 'the mass' in his quote can refer to the system or data monetary or prestige value. Alternatively, it may point at the 'concentrated mass' of vulnerabilities. *Neither would make a certain Systempunkt on its own*. Subject to specific conditions and security assessment objectives, they may not even create a fully-blown Schwerpunkt! The textbook view of prioritising targets by their value as assets can be entirely correct. But taking into account all the discussed factors, it overtly looks a bit 19th Century-ish. The vulnerability-centric view typical for many auditors might also be misleading. When exploited, a system or application with the 'concentrated mass of vulnerabilities' makes a great beachhead for further attacks. This fully qualifies it as a Nebenpunkt, the focus of the supporting effort. However, to become a Schwerpunkt it still needs to cause the exposure of sensitive data and/or collapse of the assessed defences. As far as the Systempunkt goes, by definition 'it is not necessarily the most obvious or the weakest link'.

Another important part of the Systempunkt definition is '*it is usually highly reactive to many small interactions and interventions, especially if they are aptly combined*'. In practical terms, it means that low impact vulnerabilities or feeble security weaknesses can create a gaping hole when exploited in concert. If you do not think of them in such a way, they can be easily ignored or dismissed as totally unimportant. Since we have already used a few network-centric scenarios to illustrate the Systempunkt, here comes yet another one in a row:

1 There is a flaw in the network segmentation mechanism that allows unidirectional sending of traffic to a

presumably secure VLAN (Virtual Local Area Network). This is a minor vulnerability.

2 The gateway of that VLAN does not implement any egress filtering. This is not a vulnerability. It can only be viewed as a potential weakness of controls.
3 Thus, it is possible to initiate communication with external hosts on the Internet from the VLAN, but not vice versa. The VLAN address range is private and strong ingress filtering is in place. This is a feature.
4 There is a server on this VLAN which is accessed by a few highly trusted and vetted employees only. Let's say, the whole VLAN is exclusively designated for the top management use. The server has guessable log-in credentials which the senior managers are comfortable with (and try to convince them otherwise!). This is a potential vulnerability, but the outsiders can never reach it, right?

For a non-technical reader, this is what the attackers can do:

- They will use 1 to send the requests with a fake source address into the 'secure' VLAN.
- They will employ 3 to receive the replies at the external computer somewhere on the Internet.
- Thus, a bidirectional communication is effectively established, permitted by the 2.
- Now the assailants can scan the 'secure' VLAN and discover 4.
- Once it is discovered, the log-in credentials can fall to a dictionary attack.

The end result: employing a combination of a minor vulnerability, a commonly ignored security weakness, a feature and a potential vulnerability, even a junior employee or contractor can hack into the Big Bosses' accounts. We will revisit various applications of the Systempunkt and provide additional non-network centric examples when discussing synthetic risk analysis in Chapter 6. For now, it is important to state *that low impact vulnerabilities and weaknesses that could create a critical breach when fiddled with in combination, can belong to different software, systems, or even remote networks. In fact, they can have a totally different nature, some being technical, some human, and some operations and process-related.*

The strategic exploitation cycle

Armed with the knowledge of centres of gravity definitions, types and use, take a last glance at both Figures 19 and 20. How do they compare now? How profoundly different the perspectives and approaches of the auditee and the auditors (or the attacker and defender) could really be? Do you already encounter such discrepancies in everyday information security matters? Do you understand them better after the above discourse? Do you already find the notions it has introduced as valid, helpful and applicable in security auditing practice?

To summarise the possible sequential use of the strategic critical points in performing active information security assessments of all kinds, we have created the diagram depicted in Figure 21. We have called it the Strategic Exploitation Cycle.

Figure 21: The Strategic Exploitation Cycle

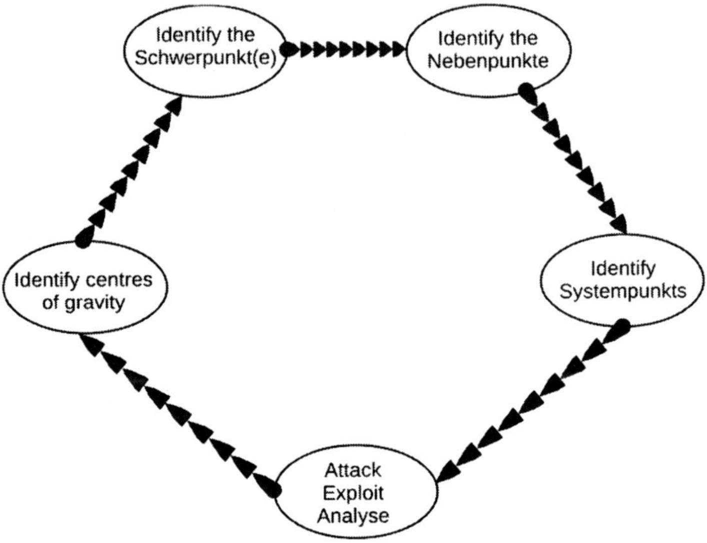

Later in the chapter, it will be supported by a tactical counterpart. The cycle builds its momentum towards increasing priority, reach, complexity and non-linearity of the assessment approach and methodologies. It is live and fluid – fiddle with it! It is entirely possible to superimpose the central OODA loop together with the loops for every strategic exploitation cycle stage, like we did with the Deming scheme in Figure 7. You can add prioritisation to, or even amid, the separate phases. It could be feasible to insert additional 'attack, exploit and analyse modules' anywhere between the cycle stages. Or add new 'recon' modules amongst them, although the operation of the whole cycle assumes continuous reconnaissance. What if you cannot pierce the fog of war and uncover the lurking Systempunkts before you begin the actual exploitation?

Which is, apropos, a form of aggressive recce. *What if the attack itself creates Systempunkts or other centres of gravity*? This is a possibility to be reckoned with. The cycle in Figure 21 can be utilised at any stage of active information security assessments – from planning the tests, to analysing risks and even compiling the audit report. It will see heavy use throughout the rest of this book.

On reconnaissance

'If you can find out the real conditions, then you will know who will prevail.'

Mei Yaochen

Reconnaissance means finding as much information about any subjects of the assessment, from any possible sources. Apart from being an essential foundation for a successful security audit, reconnaissance on its own brings great benefits to the auditee. It reduces friction and removes fog of war by discovering functionalities, whole systems, services, connections, information leaks and personnel deeds one could have hardly expected. By doing so, the recon provides a great contribution to reducing the element of (unpleasant) surprise. It is not uncommon to find a few security weaknesses, flaws and gaps during the assessment recon phase. From the reviewed critical points classification perspective, it corresponds to discovering not just the centres of gravity, but obvious Nebenpunkt, if not the Schwerpunkt, and even the elusive Systempunkts. Review Figure 21 – everything prior to the attack and exploitation stage perfectly fits a thorough, elaborate recon phase. Besides, technical reconnaissance tests frequently uncover misconfigurations that are not directly security-related. By reporting and suggesting how to rectify such problems, the auditors can assist with the overall troubleshooting and contribute to networks, systems and services stability and performance.

In the terminology we use, reconnaissance is mapping the *information security zone*. Any part of it can become a 'battlefield' if attacked. In the words of Chinese strategist Jia Lin, '*the ground means the location, the place of pitched battle – gain the advantage and you live, lose the advantage and you die*'. Knowing about the information security zone more than the assailants do is a clear advantage that allows 'getting inside their OODA loop' with ease. They still have to do their observations, but yours are already done. Your orientation is based on better intelligence data. Thus, both decision and act will be superior.

Different assessment types demand a variety of recon approaches and tactics, and also shape its scope and depth. Black box audits are the most reconnaissance-dependent. In our experience, the recon phase of a purely black box penetration test can easily take half of the time of the whole assignment. In wireless security testing the recon can be even more time and effort-consuming. Typical white box assessments require relatively little intelligence gathering, but it is still clearly needed. For example, if you are analysing application source code it is useful to know as much as possible about its SDLC (Software Development Life Cycle) and the development procedures. Was it already security tested during the development? How? What do the secure software development guidelines of the company say? If the configuration files of servers and network appliances are reviewed, find out about the people who configured them. It could turn out that some of them are internal, some are third party consultants, some are skilled, and some are evidently not. Also investigate configuration management procedures and techniques. Don't forget to consult all relevant security policies, standards and guidelines of the auditee, as they will inevitably affect the configuration peculiarities. All of these can explain and even predict many configuration discrepancies, weaknesses and flaws you see.

External technical assessment recon

In an external black box assessment all you can probe is the fuzzy borders of the information security zone. Any further investigations become possible only if successful penetration is achieved. If the external assessment is grey box, the auditors are provided an indentation in these borders to begin with. This amounts to a Nebenpunkt, and only the following hands-on tests will tell whether it is a more critical centre of gravity that presents significant risks. When the assessment is internal, the borders of the information security zone still need to be investigated. But this time, from within. For instance, the auditors can analyse egress filtering rules and gateway redundancy protocols security. If an insider can claim the role of the corporate network gateway, that's some bad news. The information security zone itself is rarely homogeneous. It will inevitably contain different security level areas within. During the recon phase of the internal assessment the auditors must determine the borders and other important characteristics of such areas prior to commencing separate systems scans.

A typical sequence of an external black box penetration test recon is shown in Figure 22.

Figure 22: External penetration test recon

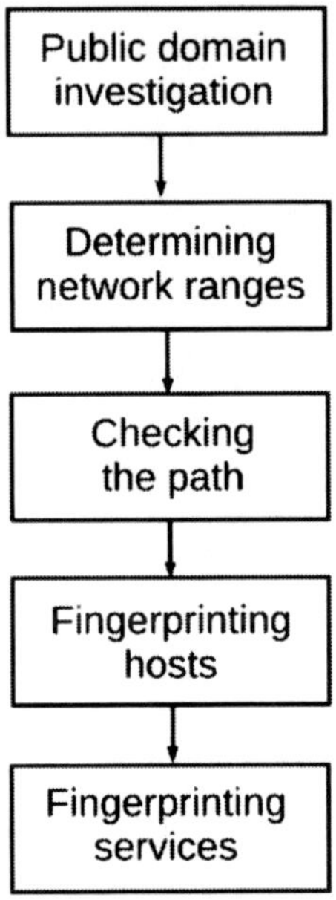

It should start with a public domain investigation aimed at finding all data pertaining to the test targets. Indeed, in our humble opinion, any security assessment must begin with thorough public domain data gathering. The difference between the audit types can only shift the focus of such investigation, directing it towards technical or human issues. When the assessment is technical, pay special attention to any questions from the auditee system administrators posted to various troubleshooting forums. In general, find all relevant public discussions in which they participate. These can reveal a wealth of information, ranging from their skill level and specific interests, to chunks of, or even the whole, configuration files. Some of them may not be properly sanitised. In a similar manner, it is sometimes possible to discover fragments of code posted by the auditee developers to programming forums for a review from their colleagues. If the auditee technical personnel participates in any online discussions and reviews of security methods and tools, these will provide valuable clues to safeguards and countermeasures deployed.

Some other interesting things you might incidentally bump into when searching the public domain for technical data pertaining to the target are:

- Their sites listed in some Googledork's (vulnerable sites that can be discovered simply by using Google) collection.
- Their sites that should be listed in a Googledork's collection, as they expose sensitive data or security weaknesses to the general public.
- Their network addresses blacklisted as sources of SPAM, malware or DDoS attacks.
- Records of previous target sites defacements.
- Phishing sites that emulate our target.
- Unauthorised websites and other services run by the auditee employees.
- Employees' e-mails and other contact details.
- Peculiarities of third parties that provide technical services to the auditee, security services included.

After you are done with the public domain investigation, determine the auditee network ranges (if not already provided). Investigate the paths to these networks. When doing so, use public looking glasses and related sites in addition to the standard tracerouting tools. If a massive network has only a single path to the Internet, or is connected through a single provider, label it as a susceptibility to Distributed Denial of Service attacks

(DDoS). In fact, redundant connections to different ISPs should belong to different BGP AS paths, to ensure proper resilience to provider shortfalls and DDoS.

Continue with enumerating and fingerprinting separate systems on the analysed networks. Determine live systems by a combination of several methods, rather than a simple ping. Consult the OSSTMM for a long checklist of system properties an auditor should try to determine. The major properties include OS type, version and patch level, system uptime, IPIDs and TCP sequence numbers. These must be listed in the assessment report. Scan for open ports using all available portscanning methods. Start from the less conspicuous ones, end with the noisy full connect scans. Use the source ports like 20 and 53 that are typically permitted by gateway access lists. Take into account the fact that there are 0 to 65,535 TCP and the same amount of UDP ports per system. Not scanning all of them might miss vulnerable services and even installed backdoors. To the contrary, trying to hit all ports of all systems on a large network, can take more time than you have to perform the entire assessment. In particular, this applies to UDP scans that can be excruciatingly slow. Thus, even such a simple and basic task as portscanning can require good judgement and experience to be performed in an effective way.

The last reconnaissance stage of a typical external penetration test is to fingerprint specific services you have discovered. A common recommendation is 'never trust the service banners'. Use a fingerprinting tool that sends probing input and analyses the responses it triggers. Use more than one such tool. If they do not produce definite results, probe the questionable services manually, employing various packet crafting utilities. Match the port number, the service response, and all network protocols this response can indicate. A protocol scan can be helpful, besides, it may identify protocols unnecessarily exposed to the outside world and assist in OS fingerprinting. Always check and map port forwarding rules using TCP tracerouting, packet sequence numbers, timestamps and other means. The ports that appear to be open on a single host can be actually forwarded to many servers behind the gateway. In contrast, multiple network nodes that look separate during preliminary scans can be virtual machines hosted on a single platform. This must be verified.

So far the penetration testing reconnaissance 101 goes. But is there more to it?

Collect all the data you have gathered together. Draw a diagram of the investigated network(s). Place all relevant information against every analysed system on the diagram. What is missing? What is unclear? Where does the fog of war still lurk? Recheck and retest where necessary to eliminate its remnants. However, don't be fanatical about it. If after several serious attempts you are still unable to identify a specific service with sufficient precision, the chances are the attackers will fail to do it too. Correct the diagram. Create a bird's eye view of the tested networks and systems in your head. Then try to think out of the box. Did you discover any VPN-related services? There must be VPN users out there. Do the conditions of the audit agreement allow including them in the testing scope? If yes, is it possible to determine their network, and even physical addresses? Are there any other trusted sites and remote access means that can be used to circumvent perimeter defences? Did the scans indicate the presence of a dial-in gateway or VOIP services? If it is deployed and running, perhaps, good old wardialing and VOIP security testing are valid options.

Finally, after you have harvested, compiled and analysed the recon data from different angles and sides, review the network diagram, as well as separate systems and services information, one more time. Recreate the bird's eye view. Is there anything that looks strange or falls out of pattern? Revisit Figure 21. Sit back and contemplate the likely centres of gravity the reconnaissance phase has uncovered. Try to identify, describe and prioritise them following the strategic exploitation cycle. Draw an attack tree or plan, if that helps. When you feel confident, select the most appropriate exploitation methodologies and prepare all relevant tools. We find this approach to be far more effective than simply trying to exploit all potential flaws one by one in a time of discovery or alphabetic order.

Social engineering recon

Social engineering-related reconnaissance is as old as the very notions of conflict and warfare are. In his infamous *Art of War,* Sun Tzu wrote: '*Whenever you want to attack an army, besiege a city, or kill a person, first you must know the identities of their defending generals, their associates, their visitors, their gatekeepers, and their chamberlains, so have your spies find out*'. Then the information about the key opponent personnel can be used to 'win the battle before it starts', employing deception, misinformation and subterfuge. More often than not, a social engineering recon would follow the sequence shown in Figure 23.

Figure 23: Social engineering recon

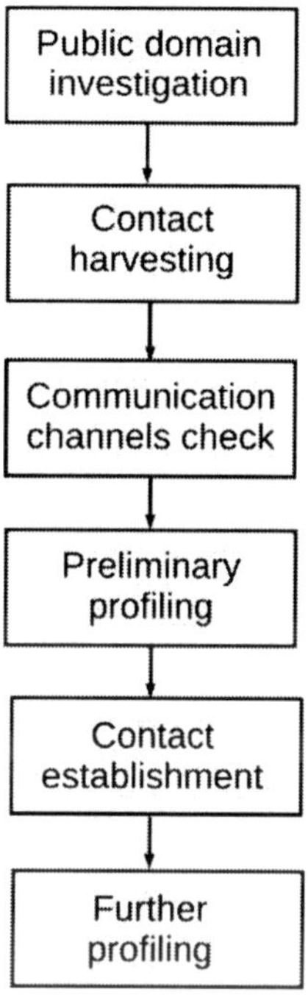

The OSSTMM template suggests gathering at least the following data on potential social engineering targets:

- Employee names and positions
- Employee place in hierarchy
- Employee personal pages
- Employee best contact methods
- Employee hobbies
- Employee Internet traces
- Employee opinions expressed
- Employee friends and relatives

- Employee history (including work history)
- Employee character traits
- Employee values and priorities
- Employee social habits
- Employee speech and speaking patterns
- Employee gestures and manners.

What is missing on this list, is the possible relations of the person to the objectives of the social engineering assessment. Does this person have access to data, premises or systems a social engineer is interested in? How privileged is this access? How often does it take place (rarely, frequently, on a daily basis)? Alternatively, does he or she know someone who has what the social engineer needs? How do they communicate? What are their relationships and level of trust? In other words, how useful is the potential target of the test for its designated aims?

A great variety of sources can be employed to harvest information about the company employees and their connections. For instance, social networks, forums and blogs are social engineers' best friends, instant messengers and chat rooms coming close second. We have heard a fable about a retired old school employee of one of the most powerful intelligence agencies who was shown a highly popular social network by his friend. After browsing it for a while, he exclaimed in total amusement: '*And they write and post it all themselves ... voluntarily and for free*?!' In the not so recent past obtaining personal information, in particular the data that allows to create someone's detailed psychological profile and contacts map, required significant effort. At times, it was even paid for in hard cash. It was necessary to observe people in different environments, approach them with care, and use various psychological tricks and techniques that sway them to expose personality traits, contacts, fragments of biography, etc. For a variety of reasons, describing which would take a book on its own, modern folk expose themselves to the public domain on their own accord. Even more, they do it regularly, elaborately, and sometimes in a great depth. This makes social engineering recon a much easier task.

However, we need to deliver a strong word of caution. When posting to open resources, people tend to exaggerate or plainly brag. Just like some 'doctor' their publicly exposed photographs to look more attractive and appealing, they can alter any displayed personal information in a similar way. For instance, they can overstate their position in the company or pretend to have access and rights they don't. They can claim to know someone important very well, while they have actually seen that person once and from a great distance. People often lie online because they think that only strangers who are very unlikely to discover the truth are watching. Unwittingly or deliberately, they provide plentiful mis- or disinformation. You can also find a variety of information about your potential targets posted by others. Naturally, it would be filtered through these poster's opinions and views. Defamatory information is particularly interesting. It may, or may not be true, however, *it clearly indicates an ongoing conflict*. So, take all data you harvest online with a bit of salt. There is always a *misinformation noise* to deal with. Also, remember that thc public information goldminc does not cancel more traditional approaches to social engineering that usually involve telephone and personal contact.

The channels through which a social engineer can obtain personal information about people could be rather unorthodox. For example, a search of peer-to-peer networks can reveal a wealth of information about their user. What does this person download or upload? Is it somehow security-relevant or related? At all accounts, it is likely to reveal personal interests, inclinations and hobbies. Does the auditee have public FTP servers or other similar resources? Which files are uploaded there, and by whom? The metadata of documents obtained from the auditee by different means can provide useful information as well. It can uncover who wrote and edited these documents, what was edited, when it was done, and who had the final word.

Frequently, the very same channels employed in gathering information about the employees are used to communicate with them during the social engineering attack. In general, the communication can be done via:

- E-mail (mind the mail lists)
- Instant messengers and chat rooms
- Blogs and social networks
- Topical message boards and professional forums
- Video and audio conferencing
- Telephone conversations and SMS
- In person
- Through a trusted third party ('the informant')
- Via written letters and documents (seldom in modern social engineering practice).

As Figure 23 states, many of these channels need to be checked to ensure that they allow effective communication with the target. Is the person prolific on that social network or forum? It makes no point trying to reach someone through a resource they visit once in a few months. Does the target use the selected communication channel at home or in the office? Can it be utilised or supervised by someone else? If the identity of the social engineer is going to be forged or concealed during the communication over the chosen channel, can the target somehow uncover it?

Prior to commencing active contact with the social engineering targets, do the preliminary profiling on the basis of information obtained from the public sources and other people. In a more traditional approach, the targets can also be physically observed without attracting their or their associates' attention. The preliminary profiling should centre on the most feasible means of establishing and maintaining the contact. For instance, it should assist in selecting the most appropriate contact avenues. These can include, but are not limited to:

- *The need to receive assistance* (present yourself as a skilled troubleshooter or someone who can get what the target wants).
- *The need to provide assistance* as a part of assigned professional duties, or to reinforce self-esteem (pretend that you desperately need it).
- *The need to co-operate* (project oneself as someone with whom the co-operation looks fruitful).
- *Common ground* (emerge as someone who strongly shares opinions, values, inclinations, interests and hobbies with the target. If possible, also claim that you are facing similar difficulties or opposition to generate sympathy).
- *Part of the routine* (appear as someone expected in due course, or in the regular course of business, and you won't raise any eyebrows. This is the common way of penetrating physical premises security).

Note, that these contact avenues can be related to both professional and private activities of individuals. Besides, they can be combined to achieve the best result.

Do not perform the 'strategic analysis' of weaknesses and centres of gravity yet. The actual contact with the target may introduce significant correctives to the picture a social engineer has already started to create. The reality could be quite different from what people write about themselves or what is said about them by others. Besides, a personal contact, or even a telephone conversation, will provide plentiful non-verbal information that cannot be obtained otherwise. Unless we are talking about a one-time contact assignment like bypassing physical premises controls, the first contact (or even a few initial contacts) is usually non-aggressive and non-committal. Otherwise, it can reveal the social engineer's intent and trigger unnecessary suspicions. It is still more of a reconnaissance than the actual attack, as Figure 23 attests.

Only when a sufficient volume of information about the targets is obtained from the public sources, other people, and by communicating with the targets themselves, can the 'strategic analysis' be done. First, try to dispel the fog of war by eliminating clear misinformation. In this process of elimination think why and how did it appear in the first place? Can it be a sign of a weakness? *People frequently lie to conceal something a social engineer can use*. Then, if applicable, build a 'human diagram' showing connections between the auditee personnel involved. Label it. Create profiles of key persons where necessary. Who knows what? Who has relevant access privileges and where? Who can be reached through whom? Which connections are stronger or weaker? Are there any personality traits or specific facts that clearly strike the eye? What about apparent human weaknesses that can be exploited (we will address some of these in the next section of this chapter)? In a given situation, how is it possible to reduce suspicion, conceal your intentions and build the necessary level of trust?

Generate the bird's eye view. Contemplate the likely centres of gravity the reconnaissance phase has uncovered. Try to identify, describe and prioritise them following the strategic exploitation cycle. What can be the Schwerpunkte, Nebenpunkte and Systempunkts of the 'human network' you need to assess? How about the separate key person(s)? The individual human *situation and psyche* can be effectively subjected to the strategic exploitation cycle of Figure 21. Hereupon, you should be able to execute social engineering tests in a more accurate and efficient way.

Internal technical assessment recon

Internal penetration tests are significantly different from their external counterparts. The main distinction that affects the reconnaissance phase operations and sequence is auditors having access to the internal network traffic flows. Thus, they should be analysed in a great detail prior to performing further scans of separate systems. In essence, this means that additional investigations as shown in Figure 24 are necessary.

Figure 24: Internal penetration test recon

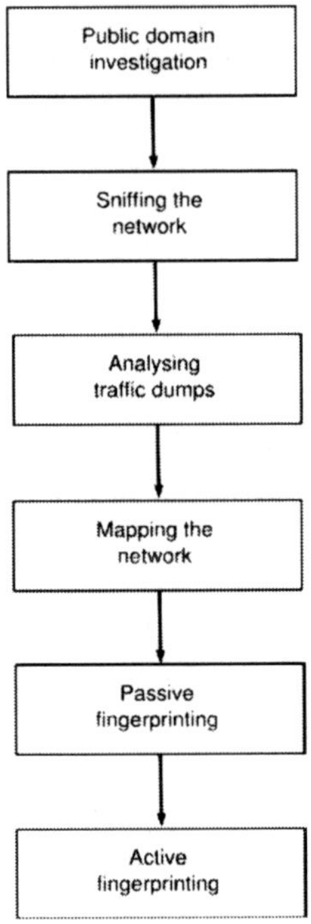

Depending on the conditions of the assessment, the auditors might have network diagrams and schemes supplied by auditee contacts prior to the tests. This will make the audit closer to a grey hat variety. If such is the case, analyse these diagrams to determine the likely centres of gravity. Perhaps you can also gather some helpful data by searching public resources in a similar way to external audits. The auditors should aspire to connect their laptops or other testing equipment as close to the potential centres of gravity as possible. In contrast, if the assessment is fully black box, it might be possible to persuade the auditees to provide different connection ports after all network mapping is done and likely centres of gravity are identified.

Start testing from sniffing the network(s) at a variety of accessible points. In a grey hat test the auditors should be allowed to use special monitoring ports or VLANs for traffic interception. Sniff for 30-something minutes, as several critical infrastructure protocols use the half an hour interval to send regular updates you would want to catch. Keep in mind that the traffic dumps are going to be large – have sufficient available space at hand. Then perform an in-depth analysis of all collected data using your favourite sniffer's regular expressions and appropriate custom scripts. In the majority of cases, you can already build preliminary network maps based on the results of this dissection. Frequently, it is also possible to identify security weaknesses or even outright vulnerabilities of network protocols settings. Keep an eye open for any activities that clearly contradict the auditee security policies, like peer-to-peer and illicit sites traffic.

The collected traffic dumps can also be used to perform passive fingerprinting of separate hosts. For a non-technical reader, passive fingerprinting refers to determining the character of systems and their services without sending any data to them. It is the least intrusive fingerprinting approach that will not set off any intrusion detection alarms. Alternatively, passive fingerprinting can be done on live traffic in the process of sniffing. After all these internal audit-specific reconnaissance procedures are performed, the assessors can continue with the 'traditional' active scans. These are done in exactly the same manner as described when discussing systems and services enumeration and fingerprinting in external penetration tests.

The wireless penetration tests recon phase is similar to its internal black box assessment counterpart. Although, there are a few peculiarities that warrant it as a distinct sequence scheme (Figure 25).

Figure 25: Wireless penetration test recon

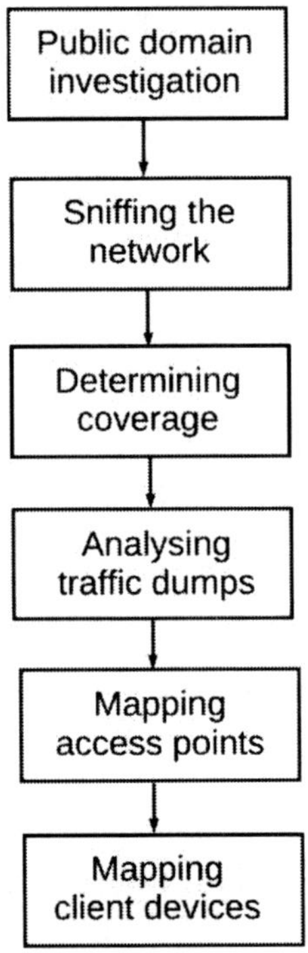

Initially do a wireless survey of the area to determine:

- How far the network signal spreads
- Other wireless networks and devices presence
- Sources of radio interference.

This shall assist in estimating the potential attacker's position, discovering rogue devices and troubleshooting wireless connectivity. Do a thorough analysis of wireless traffic dumps. Even if the data traffic is encrypted, the management and control frames are not. They can provide plentiful data about the evaluated networks, like the encryption, authentication and quality of service (QoS) mechanisms in use. Are there any abnormal frames, or abnormal quantities of some specific frame type? Which network misconfigurations or weaknesses do they indicate? By looking at wireless network card's addresses in the harvested packet dumps, you can usually tell their vendors. It is even possible to guess some of the running encrypted infrastructure protocols, if the specific multicast MAC (Media Access Control) addresses they use are seen, and the intervals between packets sent to these addresses, are clearly defined.

List all wireless access points. Flag those that fall out of the observed configuration and manufacturer pattern as misconfigured or rogue. How many clients are associated to all access points you have discovered? Do they roam? Are wireless nodes or wired hosts sending traffic to the wireless network? Do all wireless hosts appear to use the same encryption and authentication means? If not, what could be an explanation for the discrepancies observed? Are there any client devices that are not associated and actively scan for available wireless networks? Are they likely to belong to the auditee employees? Which networks do they search for? Do they leak any other interesting data you can ferret out? All these considerations are 802.11 standard-based. However, when assessing other types of wireless networks a similar approach can be applied.

Just like with the external penetration and social engineering tests, finish their internal and wireless recon counterparts with assembling the grand view, re-checking unclear facts, drawing appropriate schemes and performing the strategic analysis as per Figure 21. Since the reconnaissance in application security testing goes in parallel with the actual vulnerability search, it will be reviewed in the upcoming section of this chapter when application assessments are addressed.

On evaluating vulnerabilities and gaps

'Invincibility is a matter of self-defence; vulnerability is simply a matter of having gaps.'

Wang Xi

Armed with the reconnaissance data and its thorough analysis, the auditors can begin determining vulnerabilities and gaps. A passive security assessment will typically stop at producing a list of potential flaws generated by an automatic scanning tool, hence the vulnerability scanning. Its social engineering counterpart will throw a pre-defined set of basic attacks at its targets and evaluate their outcome. An active security assessment, whether technical or human, will carry on with exploiting the discovered vulnerabilities until the assessment time or exploitation possibilities are exhausted. To emphasise the nature of active security assessments one more time, '*we must try to see ourselves through our enemy's eyes in order to identify our own vulnerabilities that he may attack and to anticipate what he will try to do so that we can counteract him*' (MCDP 1 *Warfighting*).

Technical vulnerability discovery process

A typical vulnerability search in external penetration testing is summarised in Figure 26.

Figure 26: 101 of external penetration vulnerability discovery

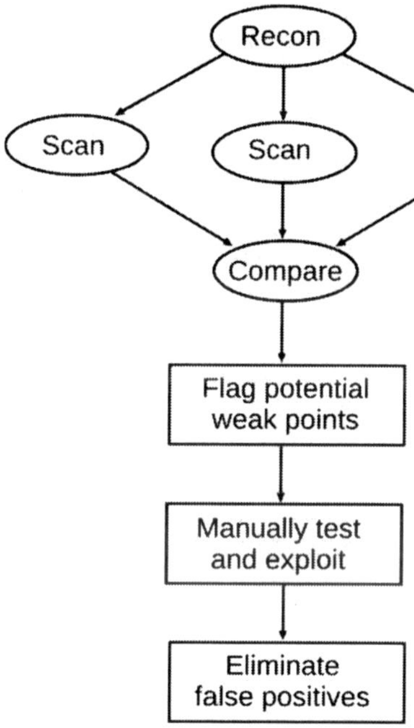

The three repeated 'Scan' entries on the scheme symbolise utilising more than a single vulnerability scanning tool. The more vulnerability scanners the auditors use – the better. Binding oneself to a single vulnerability scanner is a cardinal sin that goes beyond the vendor dependence. In our humble opinion, even the passive security scanning should employ several vulnerability scanners at once. These important tools are not the same, and one scanner can discover gaps the others do not detect. Some vulnerability scanners are highly specialised to address certain vulnerability classes and types. For instance, there are Web application and database scanning tools that do more profound work on uncovering such vulnerabilities than their general purpose siblings. Specialised scanners must be used where applicable. In the case of Web applications security, this probably amounts to more than 90% of all modern external penetration tests.

Compare the scan results of all vulnerability discovery tools you have employed. Where do they match? Where do they differ? How large are these differences? What can explain them? Mark all potential weaknesses and gaps. The vulnerabilities shown by several security scanners at once make the most obvious candidates. If something is unclear, or you suspect that at some point scanning was interrupted by connectivity or other problems, rescan. Then, you can subject the detected issues to the strategic analysis cycle, just as you did during the reconnaissance phase. Indeed, vulnerability scanning can be viewed as a 'battlefield recon', or recon-in-depth. After all the priorities are sorted, begin manual exploitation of the uncovered flaws in a logically defined order of importance. This will eliminate false positives and hopefully provide a foothold for further exploitation. Such is the bird's eye view of the vulnerability discovery process.

Figure 27 presents a more in-depth perspective of the same.

Figure 27: Vulnerability discovery explained

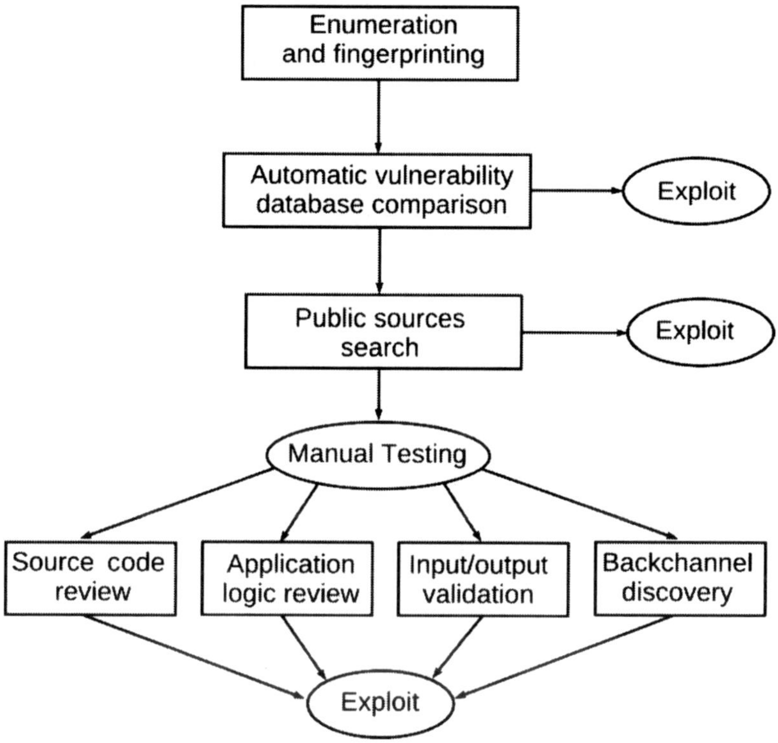

The first stage of exploitation is trying to break in at the conclusion of vulnerability scanning results. There are vulnerability scanning tools that also perform automated exploitation. In our practice, they were efficient at doing so only when used in internal security audits. This is a classical consequence of the 'Maginot Line mentality': behind the hardened network perimeter lays a soft, vulnerable underbelly. Defence-in-depth is clearly out of the question. Overall, if a system can be broken into by vulnerability scanning results alone, or even by automated tool exploitation, its security level is abhorrent. If this happens during an external test, it is plain disastrous. Stop the assessment, call the auditee contacts, explain the situation and wait until the flaw is fixed before continuing.

The second stage of exploitation is trying to break in after investigating all available sources relevant to the suspected vulnerability. These often provide important clues to how the issue can be successfully exploited. You can look at other similar vulnerabilities to gain the needed insight. At times, a public exploit is available for the same issue, but is applicable to a different service version or platform on which it is running. The auditors can then modify this exploit to accommodate for the differences. Nowadays, easy to use utilities designed to do just that are freely available online. Thus, one does not have to be a dedicated programmer to accomplish this task. Generally, if a system can be broken into at this stage, it is vulnerable to medium skill level opponents, who have sufficient determination to do some research.

The third stage of exploitation is trying to gain access utilising manual testing. More often than not it involves breaking the software application involved. Hence, Figure 27 provides an application testing example as a part of this phase. However, intelligent password guessing based on custom lists generated for the specific situation on the basis of recon data, would also amount to manual testing. The same applies to hand-crafting malicious packets in network protocols security tests. If a system or network can be broken into at this stage, it is vulnerable to skilled and determined assailants.

On application security testing methods

The four modules of hands-on application security assessment shown in Figure 27 are by no means all-inclusive. However, they are commonly applied. A general and rather basic checklist of application security tests is provided by the OSSTMM. The OWASP Testing Guide is a great free resource on performing in-depth Web applications security tests. Numerous approaches and techniques it describes are evidently workable beyond Web application audits only. Some of the authentication mechanisms, buffer overflow and denial of service tests provide good examples of these. We do not feel the need to repeat the recommendations of OSSTMM, OWASP and other relevant guides in this book. They are widely available and are regularly updated. With the next update some of the information these sources supply will inevitably become obsolete. Nevertheless, a few words about the general application testing methodologies listed in Figure 27 should be said.

Source code reviews are probably the most traditional way of assessing application security. There are multiple automated utilities and tools designed to assist in them. However, at the end of the day it all comes down to the skills and 'try to break everything we can break' mindset of the programmers performing the review. The problem, as stated earlier in this book, is that often the source code of the application is proprietary and not available for analysis. At the same time, employing reverse engineering techniques to reveal the application structure and weak points is likely to be illegal. This, of course, won't stop malicious hackers using them in vulnerability discovery. To counter it, source code security reviews by proprietary software vendors should be supplemented with reverse engineering tests. The latter can be done by an authorised specialist third party.

Application logic analysis is instrumental in any relevant security assessments. It has a very strong element of recon. First, the application must be understood. Study all available documentation, such as manuals, requirements, functional specifications and use (or breach!) cases. Learn the application workflows, business and operations logic, user roles, privileges and access rights, acceptable and unacceptable use scenarios. Contemplate the application dependencies, any files it creates, modifies or deletes, communication protocols it employs (if networked), the environment in which it operates. When all these matters become crystal clear, determine and analyse centres of gravity and the likely security threats. Again, the strategic exploitation cycle (Figure 21) can come in handy. Finally, design and execute appropriate logical tests.

Application input/output validation is probably the most common contemporary method utilised in black and grey box assessments. Its logic is very simple. Supply a variety of expected and unexpected input and analyse the output using application and system logs, debuggers, network sniffers, or other suitable means. The application might crash or otherwise misbehave, indicating a potentially exploitable flaw. In essence, this is the 'if then' or 'fiddle until it smashes' approach incarnate. As such, it could discover the target Systempunkts. If 1,000 crashes result from a single flaw, it is a Schwerpunkt, Systempunkt or both. When properly automated, this methodology is referred to as 'fuzzing'. Due to the aforementioned facts, fuzzing production systems is not a brilliant idea. This type of application security evaluation is better done against a testing set-up.

Fuzzing comes in two main varieties. Mutation fuzzing is the dumber 'everything but the kitchen sink' type. Flip the bits, add or subtract them, and throw the resulting data at the application *attack surface*. *Generation fuzzing* is far more creative. Learn about the application logic, protocol and file formats it accepts, etc. In a nutshell, do a decent recon. Then select, modify or create a fuzzer tool that will take this vital information into account when producing the input for the tests. As a result, their performance and effectiveness will be optimised. A promising avenue is evolutionary fuzzing, that combines both approaches in a sequence. To be considered as truly evolutionary, a fuzzer should start as a mutation tool and employ artificial intelligence to teach itself the generation methodologies. Nevertheless, no matter how sophisticated the fuzzing technique could be, the supreme art is not in producing the needed input. It is in detecting the errors caused by this input and determining which vulnerabilities such faults signify and how to exploit them.

It is interesting to note that the logic and elements of the fuzzing approach can be applied to different areas of information security outside hands-on software testing. When discussing security assessments of processes using the access management example, we have already utilised a fuzzing-like methodology to analyse this sample process. There are many things you can fuzz. It can even apply to security policies, standards, guidelines and other relevant documentation. Envision how applicable their statements, rules and recommendations could be in a variety of changing conditions. Which alterations of the environment, whether business, operational, technical or human, will make them irrelevant or flawed? Are these situations likely? If yes, is it possible to implement sufficient resilience to them in the existing security documentation and processes?

By subjecting people to batteries of different tests and analysing their output, a psychologist effectively fuzzes human consciousness and mind. This allows one to establish personality problems and traits, predict and even modify human reactions and behaviour. But is it not what a social engineer wants, alas with a more sinister end goal? So, generation fuzzing or even, to a certain extent, mild evolutionary fuzzing, can be utilised to reach social engineering aims. Indeed, the tests used by professional psychologists provide a great example of the generation fuzzing input. Think what could be their social engineering equivalents. Borrow the psychologist's tricks to make people talk and gain their trust. Carefully probe the auditee employees and their relationships, fiddling until the exploitable human weaknesses become evident.

The last application security methodology of Figure 27 is checking for backchannels or backdoors left by its developers. This can be done by various means, such as looking for and analysing plaintext strings within the application binaries, or applying various log-in methods to the application attack surface. Common sense dictates that if a backdoor is present, it will eventually be discovered and abused by someone other than the developers who did not remove it. It also raises doubts about the developer's true intent. Can it be deliberate rather than simply forgetting about a temporary feature created for testing purposes? Note, that the backchannels could be present in any close source software, from Web applications to device drivers. Thus, searching for them is relevant for literally any system security checks. We can recall a few examples of entire operating systems having in-built administrative backdoor accounts left by their creators for whatever the reasons could be.

Assessing network protocols security flaws

Similarly to the recon phase, vulnerability discovery and exploitation in internal penetration testing includes an additional preliminary stage centred on network protocols security. Its sequence is reflected in Figure 28.

Figure 28: Protocols vulnerability testing

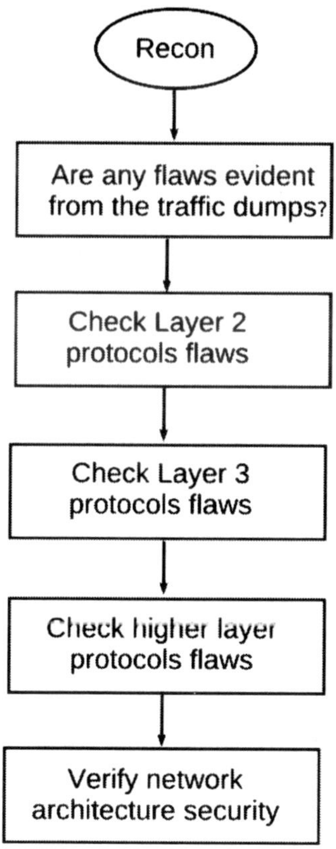

During the reconnaissance you have collected plentiful samples of network traffic. Analyse them, searching for the obvious flaws, like important infrastructure or management protocols lacking strong authentication. Then perform active checks which would involve crafting custom packets to exploit the detected security weaknesses. The end results of effective network protocols exploitation could be:

- Diverting traffic to the attacker's host for interception and modification.
- Successful man-in-the-middle and session hijacking attacks.
- Bypassing the existing network segmentation boundaries and separation of data streams.
- Gaining access to network appliances and other systems, via insecure management protocols.
- System-specific or network-wide denial of service.

Thus, this type of security evaluation is likely to cause severe availability problems for separate systems or even the whole network. At the same time, it is not realistic to mirror the entire internal network for security testing purposes. So, a thorough network protocols security verification should be done during the off-hours, such as at weekends.

To keep the protocols testing structured and organised, Figure 28 suggests performing it in a bottom-up fashion. Start with the OSI model Layer 2, or data link protocols security. Assess whether the spanning tree can be abused, VLAN boundaries can be circumvented, 802.1x-based authentication can be cracked, etc. Then, test security of the OSI Layer 3. In practice this usually means assessing vulnerabilities of routing and gateway redundancy protocols. In *Hacking Exposed: Cisco Networks*, we have covered the relevant Layer 2 and 3 testing methods in detail. Despite the time passed since, they still hold relevant for the modern networks and there is no point in reiterating them here in detail. Finally, check security of higher layer protocols, centring on the management ones. Using SNMP versions below 3 is still common, and so is employing insecure Telnet and HTTP for network appliance access. These are typical security weaknesses that can be easily exploited by insiders.

A few words should be said about the 'traditional' network attacks like switch CAM (Content Addressable Memory) table flooding and ARP (Address Resolution Protocol) spoofing. By their very nature all IP networks are susceptible to these old attacks. A similar issue exists with higher layer protocols like DHCP and DNS. ARP and DNS spoofing against stand-alone systems can be used to assist in other man-in-the-middle attacks resilience testing. For example, it comes in handy in SSL/TLS vulnerability evaluation. At the same time, launching CAM flooding or DHCP spoofing attacks on their own will severely disrupt connectivity to prove quite the obvious. Thus, such tests are not compulsory. They should be applied in agreement with the auditee only if the real need exists. By the 'real need' we mean assessing the deployed countermeasures that thwart such attacks.

The last stage of the network protocols security assessment is gathering all test results together and generating the overall network security state view. The latter should reflect all uncovered vulnerabilities and possible relationships between them. Are they incidental misconfigurations that can be easily corrected? Or, could it be, that the network architecture itself is fundamentally flawed and all security problems you see are only the tip of an iceberg? On several occasions we had to recommend the auditee to rebuild large network segments or undergo significant equipment upgrades. When these important matters are thoroughly evaluated and addressed, the auditors can continue with systems and services exploitation in a manner identical with the external penetration tests.

Wireless vulnerability assessments are expectedly akin to their internal audit counterparts. Even the vulnerability subsets of both can intersect. Reasonably common wireless-specific security gaps the auditors should look for include:

- Flaws of authentication mechanisms and protocols.
- Weaknesses of network discovery and association mechanisms (in wireless client security testing).
- Rogue or obsolete devices that provide excellent wireless entry points.
- Lack of secure separation between wireless and wired networks.
- Device drivers vulnerable to buffer overflow attacks.
- High susceptibility to Layer 2 denial of service attacks.

When talking about the latter, it makes no sense to evaluate denial of service conditions no one can protect against. A radio signal can be jammed, and that's that. In contrast, all DoS threats that have valid countermeasures must be assessed. By the way, when performing wireless security testing and actively poking at the network, observe whether a wireless IPS will manifest itself. If the active defence is on, it might try to kick the auditors off. Analyse all packets the IPS sends. What is it possible to tell about it? Can it be tricked? Or even have known vulnerabilities?

A brief on human vulnerabilities

What about social engineering? Social engineering vulnerability checks are highly situational and flexible. Typically, they require plenty of improvisation and are hard to systematise and methodise. Nevertheless, it is feasible to list major 'human vulnerabilities' that can be exploited to gain access to data, systems, networks and premises. An attempt to summarise them is presented in Table 4.

Table 4: Common human security flaws

Human weakness	Notes
Lack of security awareness	It can be revealed by rather simple tests. 'Click on this link', 'open the attachment', or 'please change your password' are the textbook examples of these.
Naivety	Tread carefully, especially if dealing with other security specialists. It could easily be a disguise. All truly intelligent people have learned the old trick of playing the fool.
Dissatisfaction and disaffection	Disaffected employees are obvious targets. At times, they can look to pass sensitive data to outsiders themselves. Boredom and lack of interest in the surroundings are signs of disaffection. They diminish vigilance and suspicion. Dissatisfaction often results from rigid command, misplacement, work and peer pressure.

Desperation	Desperate people can provide great boons for little help or simple compassion.
Conflicts	Both sides of a conflict tend to leak valuable information when slagging off their foe. By taking sides or expressing sympathy to one side's cause, you can gain immediate trust since 'an enemy of my enemy is my friend'.
Overblown ego	Napoleonic ambitions, galaxy-sized ego and overblown self-esteem are exploited with ease since the ancient times. Flattery is the key.
Obsessions	Obsessions can be shared to gain rapport and trust. Even a little satisfaction of someone's personal obsession can bring hefty rewards. Besides, obsessions often contribute to 'tunnel vision' which decreases vigilance.
Fear	Fear of being dismissed, held responsible or becoming socially denigrated opens many gates. A typical 'we have found a virus on your system, please install our virus removal tool' online scam exploits fears of being hacked. A social engineer can play disaffected customer or partner to abuse responsibility fears.

Notice that many of the weaknesses listed in Table 4 are closely related to contact avenues outlined in the recon section. Exploiting them is these contact avenues carried forward and amplified. For instance, the need to receive assistance, the need to co-operate and common ground can be efficiently combined to exploit both human conflicts and obsessions. The need to provide assistance and common ground go well towards the overblown ego. Replace common ground by the part of the routine and the approach becomes suitable for playing the work responsibility fears.

Also, a great deal of social engineering vulnerabilities are related to processes and procedures, rather than actual human weaknesses. A classical example is lack of proper identity verification within the access management process. Insufficient employee background checks and vetting procedures generate multiple gaps social engineers can exploit. Lack of communication between company departments, branches or teams, as well as with partners, customers and suppliers can allow effective impostor attacks. Skilled social engineers will weave together a variety of human and process weaknesses and gaps to develop the most fruitful approach to accomplishing their tasks. When the appropriate use of relevant technologies is added to the concoction, they can become virtually unstoppable.

The tactical exploitation cycle

For now we assume that by applying technical or human-centric approaches discussed, the auditors managed to uncover and exploit a few important vulnerabilities. At this point, many information security assessments would stop. The halt could be justified by specific limits imposed on the audit scope by its contract conditions. Otherwise, it amounts to breaching the defence line without following up the advantage. From the military strategy viewpoint it is a major, egregious mistake. The exploitation must continue, penetrating the remaining defences deeper and deeper until all valid opportunities are exhausted. It should follow a cyclic pattern as shown in Figure 29.

Figure 29: The tactical exploitation cycle

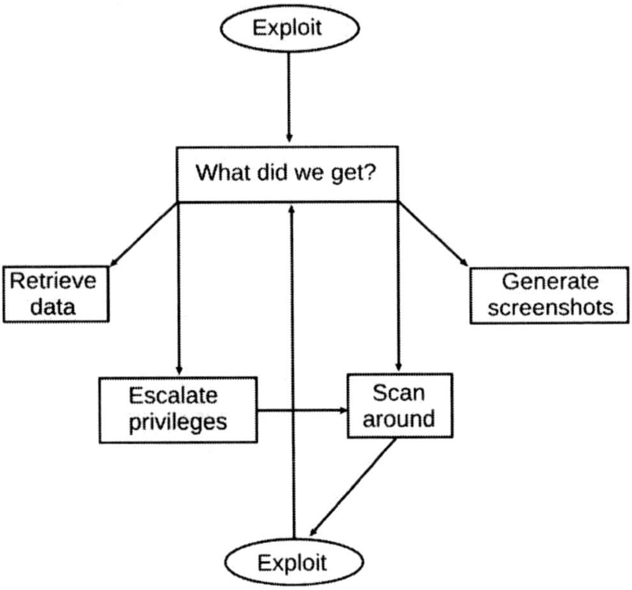

After the initial breach is achieved, look around and analyse its consequences. Where did we get? What did we get? Which data can we now retrieve? Is it sensitive? Does it provide any clear opportunities for further attacks? If the data are interesting, retrieve it. It should be submitted to the auditee, together with the final assessment report, all confidentiality preserved. If the audit is technical, generate illustrative screenshots of the accessed data and broken systems interfaces. Proving the actual significance of all uncovered vulnerabilities to the auditee is just as important as getting in.

Is there a need to escalate privileges? Study the accessed system well. Which other security flaws can be identified? Attempt the escalation. Scan all surrounding systems and sniff the network. If it is a social engineering attack, think what else can be gained from the person who fell prey to it, unless the alarms were triggered and it is time to retreat. Can this person's trust and access rights (if obtained) be used to social engineer other interlinked employees? Execute the strategic analysis (Figure 21) of newly acquired targets, data and opportunities, if you feel the need. Or, at least, spin the full OODA loop with proper 'OO' to begin with. Then perform further tests. Exploit all potential vulnerabilities and gaps. Repeat the Figure 29 cycle.

The real-life adversaries are unlikely to halt when they have achieved the primary foothold. They will expand it by pushing forward and abusing the connectivity and trust the exploited systems or people possess. The risks presented by a vulnerability are not limited to the immediate exposure, corruption, or loss of sensitive data it allows. They also include all the opportunities that the exploited flaw opens up. Is it a barren cul-de-sac, or does it lead directly to the treasure chests? Can it cause any additional deterioration of the auditee defences? What if by not exploiting it any further the auditors have missed a critical Systempunkt, as they did not initiate a cascade of events that can follow the initial breach? Understanding these matters is absolutely essential in estimating the genuine security risks. Without evaluating them the risk assessment will be incomplete.

The operational art of vulnerability assessment

'General Arroyo told him that the Federal army, whose officers had studied in the French Military Academy, were waiting to engage them in formal combat, where they knew all the rules and the guerrillas didn't. "They are like virgins," said the young Mexican general, hard and dark as a glazed pot. "They want to follow the rules. I want to make them".'

Carlos Fuentes, *The Old Gringo*

We began this chapter observing the strategic matters. Then the discussion inevitably slipped into the more tactical realm. It is time to take a step back and stand in-between. This allows us to contemplate on subjects that frequently go amiss, becoming the source of common errors that plague numerous information security assessments. One such important subject is whether the auditors should seek to approach their targets laterally, frontally, or both. Sometimes, they are given a precise list of targets that must be tested. However, on other occasions the scope of a black box assessment is not clearly defined. The aim is to clarify the borders of the auditee information security zone and get in by any possible means.

Front, flank, simple, complex

Recall the external reconnaissance section discourse on discovering lateral exploitation paths, like remote trusted users and sites, or out-of-band channels of access. If these are present, where should they be on the assessment's priority list? Logically, the answer has to depend on the ease with which such lateral elements can be discovered. If they are easy to find, they should be tested, together with the obvious network perimeter hosts. If it takes quite an effort to detect them, their assessment can be postponed. Nevertheless, this approach does not take into account indiscriminate attacks. For instance, a trusted remote network can be infected with a worm which will then spread to the target net. Or, a wardriver can find an insecure wireless network in a telecommuter's home and use it as a foothold to penetrate the corporate LAN. These scenarios are far from being unrealistic.

The solution we propose is reflected in Figure 30.

Figure 30: Frontal versus lateral tests

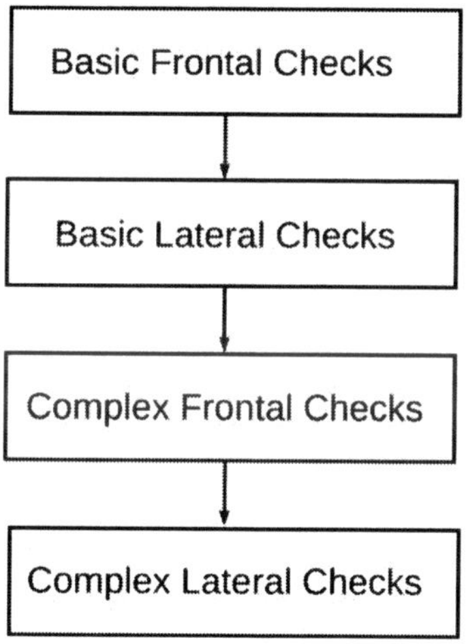

First, assess the most obvious attack surfacc, using thc basic evaluation means. By 'basic evaluation means' we imply:

- Automated security scanning
- Non-specific dictionary attacks
- Spidering for sensitive data leaks

- Evaluating guest and anonymous log-ins
- Running simple social engineering checks.

There are security auditors who take great pride in their skills that allow them to discover new vulnerabilities and write 0-day exploits. This pride is entirely justified. At the same time, such experts can ignore the checks for low hanging fruit that look boring and uncreative. Indeed, they are. However, they also address the greatest risks the auditee company or organisation is facing. As Bruce Schneier pointed out, '*insecurity is the norm*'. Figure 27 and the discussion it triggers, attest that more sophisticated tests should stay lower in the priority list. The auditors should aspire to reach their objectives employing the simplest well-known methods before their advanced counterparts are called in. Take no shame in it. Even Sun Tzu proclaimed, that '*in ancient times those known as good warriors prevailed when it was easy to prevail*'.

Next, apply similar basic checks to the potential lateral entry points, if present. This addresses the issue of indiscriminate or incidental attacks these points can be exposed to. Also, the attackers who failed to get across the frontal line of defence the easy way, face a simple dilemma:

1 Find and exploit a new or unorthodox vulnerability of the frontal surface (easy recon, difficult attack).
2 Outflank it (harder recon, easy attack).

Guess which one many of them are going to select? Indeed, if the attackers are not skilled in novel vulnerabilities discovery and exploitation, they are left with a rather simple choice. Cao Cao, a dedicated disciple of Sun Tzu, supplied the following sound advice:

- *Find out the subtle points over which it is easy to prevail, attack what can be overcome, do not attack what cannot be overcome.*
- *Appear where there is an opening and strike at a gap; avoid where they are guarding, hit where they are not expecting it.*

These suggestions are clearly applicable to the aforementioned situation.

Then, when you have finally arrived at the complex and demanding assessment methodologies, return to the frontal defences first. This corresponds to point 1 above: 'easy recon, difficult attack'. Even if this does not succeed, the only option left is 'hard recon and hard attack', which is the final Figure 30 stage. In our experience, in the majority of cases successful penetration happens before it is reached.

The strategies of creating gaps

The MCDP 1 *Warfighting* declares that '*whenever possible, we exploit existing gaps. Failing that, we create gaps*'. In the context of technical information security assessments, this astute statement can apply to two things:

1. Discovering and exploiting novel vulnerabilities (that evil 0-day).
2. Combining several non-critical vulnerabilities to achieve a much greater result (see the previous Systempunkt descriptions).

In social engineering, creating gaps might correspond to:

1. Bringing otherwise stable, reliable and apparently (information security-wise) flawless people out of balance.

2 Disrupting the intended flow of a relevant security process, so that its friction exceeds the safety limits.

Alas, the Systempunkt principle application, similar to the technical gap creating point 2 above, can also apply.

Gaps can be created through depth, and gaps can be created through breadth. Creating gaps through depth means dedicated effort and research applied to a highly specific point. This is clearly at work when novel vulnerabilities are discovered and corresponding exploits are written. Hard manual testing, similar to that shown in Figure 27, is absolutely required. In different situations it may also involve reverse engineering, applied cryptanalysis and other advanced attack means. For the auditors that do not possess such knowledge and skills, this avenue is completely closed. Automatic vulnerability scanning cannot bring them any further than Figure 30's second stage. Hence, the natural limitations of this method. Notice, that the similar depth-centric approach can be utilised in social engineering. If enough directed effort and wit are expended, anyone can be placed in a staged tricky Catch 22 situation, in which people typically become vulnerable. If human weaknesses, listed in Table 4, are not manifested, some of them can be successfully cultivated given sufficient time.

Creating gaps through breadth frequently means using the *combined arms* approach. We have already touched it when addressing social engineering vulnerability evaluation. Mix technical and social engineering means. Fiddle with applications, services, systems, network protocols, operational processes and people simultaneously and from various angles. Recall that the minor weaknesses that can create a greater flaw can belong to different applications, systems, networks, people, processes, classes, types or entire levels of abstraction. The sample Systempunkt scenario we have employed when outlining this vital concept consisted of the following elements:

- Flaws of a network switch configuration (technical, network appliance).
- Permitting features of the gateway or firewall (technical, network appliance).
- A service that uses weak authentication mechanism (technical, service).
- Weak log-in credentials (human, policy or guideline).

Thus, it can serve as a reasonable illustration of utilising *combined arms*. Basic social engineering could have being used to assist in guessing the log-in credentials or obtaining the network scheme from a system administrator. Indeed, a single over-the-shoulder glance at the scheme would have sufficed.

A powerful mix-and-match technique that can apply to breadth, but also depth-centric ways of creating security gaps, is merging what is considered as orthodox and unorthodox. As Sun Tzu wrote, '*making the armies able to take on opponents without being defeated is a matter of unorthodox and orthodox methods*'. In truth, this is more of a psychological exercise for the auditors, to enable strategic vision and train lateral ways of thinking. Wardialing was orthodox in the past and is unorthodox now. Only a decade ago, wireless hacking was viewed as unorthodox. For a social engineer, using an RFID hack to gain unauthorised premises entry is unorthodox, at least, for now. In contrast, to a purely technical hacker common social engineering methods can be non-trivial. '*Various people have different explanations of what is orthodox and what is unorthodox.*

Orthodoxy and unorthodoxy are not fixed, but are like a cycle' (Ho Yanxi).

As an illustration, consider that a plain frontal attack against a firewall, or a social engineering attempt aimed at the company CISO, can bear fruits. For the proponents of a 'smart' lateral approach, this is blasphemy. Yet, we have discovered industry standard firewall security flaws in the past. '*Striking an open gap does not only mean where the opponent has no defence*' (Chen Hao). Besides, the scope of penetration tests often includes (and should do so!) the assessment of various countermeasures and safeguards. If these are not evaluated in sufficient depth, they can become the sources of a false sense of security, or even the bearers of fatal gaps. At the same time, information security audits are the perfect time to put one's monitoring, intrusion detection, logging and alarm systems on test. The real assailants would not debrief on their techniques or tell when exactly the attack begins.

Review the following scenario we call a 'clock trick':

1 All system's clocks on the network are synchronised with a central time server. This is a good practice.
2 This server gets its time from reliable sources on the Internet. This is also highly recommended.
3 However, the NTP (Network Time Protocol) is not authenticated. This would be classified as a minor security flaw.
4 The access lists do not block access to the NTP service from unauthorised sources. This is a minor security weakness.

A wile attacker floods the time service with incorrect updates. The 'echo' of these updates spreads across the entire network, altering all systems time. The hacker checks that the trick is successful by verifying systems uptime with a basic scan. What could be the outcome?

1 As the time of systems is now altered, security updates can fail. The licenses of anti-virus, or other protective software, are now officially expired. It stops working properly.
2 The timestamps of logs are now incorrect, making the logs useless. Who would take such laterally tampered logs as a proof?

The first ramification means that malware can now be pushed through, or potentially vulnerable services remain unpatched. The second allows the assailants to utilise more intrusive, aggressive and effective attack means (like application fuzzing or log-in credentials bruteforcing) without fear of persecution. This can enable discovery or even creation of new gaps through depth. All of it is achieved via two minor security flaws using rather simple methods. On its own, it is a typical Nebenpunkt that softens the opponent's defences. If the overall attack succeeds, and the 'clock trick' has clearly contributed to this success, it becomes a part of a Systempunkt. Is it really orthodox or unorthodox? Depends on a point of view. By the way, externally exposed unauthenticated NTP service can be easily running on the otherwise secure firewall!

To summarise this vital discourse on a strategic note:

- *Creating gaps through depth is the Schwerpunkt principle at work.*
- *Creating gaps through breadth is the Systempunkt principle at work.*
- *Merging both principles together is the pinnacle of exploitation science and art.*

In real-life situations it is also possible to 'create' gaps *through time*. Wait and observe for long enough, and due to inevitable *fluctuations of friction,* a security gap can surface. However, the passive 'good things come to those who wait' approach is not highly feasible for information security audits which have timetables, schedules and deadlines. Nevertheless, it can still be used by dedicated, focused assailants.

We would like to end this key chapter with a lengthy excerpt from MCDP 1 *Warfighting*. It provides a perfect extraneous independent summary to many of the issues we have just discussed. Indeed, there is little in it for the 'substitution exercise', and nothing for us to add.

- *When identification of enemy critical vulnerabilities is particularly difficult, the commander may have no choice but to exploit any and all vulnerabilities until action uncovers a decisive opportunity. By exploiting opportunities, we create in increasing numbers more opportunities for exploitation.*

Furthermore,

- *We should try to understand the enemy system in terms of a relatively few centres of gravity or critical vulnerabilities because this allows us to focus our own efforts. The more we can narrow it down, the more easily we can focus. However, we should recognise that most enemy systems will not have a single centre of gravity on which everything else depends, or if they do, that centre of gravity will be well protected. It will often be necessary to attack several lesser centres of gravity or critical vulnerabilities simultaneously or in sequence to have the desired effect. A critical vulnerability is a pathway to attacking a centre of gravity. Both have the same underlying purpose: to target our actions in such a way as to have the greatest effect on the enemy.*

CHAPTER 6: SYNTHETIC EVALUATION OF RISKS

'What is required of an officer is a certain power of discrimination, which only knowledge of men and things and good judgement can give. ***The law of probability must be his guide.'***

Carl von Clausewitz

Discovering and evaluating vulnerabilities and gaps without the thorough analysis of risks they introduce, is as good as doing recon without using its results. In fact, for the risk analysis phase, all previous security audit stages are nothing more than the necessary reconnaissance. One of the fundamental principles of Chapter 1 states that '*information security assessment always operates with probabilities*'. Gauging these probabilities is a fine science and art that has to be fully mastered by at least a single member of the auditing team. It is absolutely essential for success of both the assessment and its follow-up acts. For the latter, the evaluation of risks represents the 'OO' in its overall OODA loop.

Numerous information security-specific risk assessment methodologies and frameworks exist. The most commonly referenced examples are probably:

- NIST Special Publication 800-30 Risk Management Guide for Information Technology Systems.
- OCTAVE (Operationally Critical Threat, Asset, and Vulnerability Evaluation) from SEI (Software Engineering Institute) and CERT (Computer Emergency Response Team).

- FRAP (Facilitated Risk Assessment Process) by Peltier et al.
- SRMD (Security Risk Management Discipline) from Microsoft.

ISO is developing a family of risk management standards designated as ISO31000, which is to include the IEC31010: Risk Management – Risk Assessment Techniques guidelines. Knowing these and other relevant published methodologies and recommendations can come in handy when performing the risk evaluation phase of an information security assessment. However, trying to absorb all available sources on methods and techniques of weighting and prioritising information security risks could easily lead to confusion. Reviewing many such publications creates a strong impression that anyone who dedicated enough time to the subject eventually came up with their own specific methodology, which was consequently given a fancy abbreviation name.

In adherence with the general approach professed in this book, we divide the evaluation of risks into three levels: strategic, operational and tactical. The tactical plane refers to analysing risks introduced by separate vulnerabilities and gaps. The strategic level refers to assessing the overall auditee risk posture, which is a non-linear sum of its segregate components. The operational level connects the other two, by dissecting possible links between different security risks, addressing the whole affected processes, and transcending the boundaries between what is perceived as technical, human, procedural and policy flaws. When all three levels work in harmony and concert, a realistic picture of various risks faced by the auditee company or organisation can be established. Hence, the synthetic evaluation of information security risks and its core element – the synthetic risk analysis.

On applicable epistemology of risk

'Take calculated risks. That is quite different from being rash.'

Gen. George S. Patton

In all its complexity, the assessment of risks is but a part of a much larger and all-encompassing risk management process. The split of this process between the security audit and its after-effects is nothing more than the division between *risk evaluation* and *risk control* (Figure 31).

Figure 31: Risk management process and information security assessments

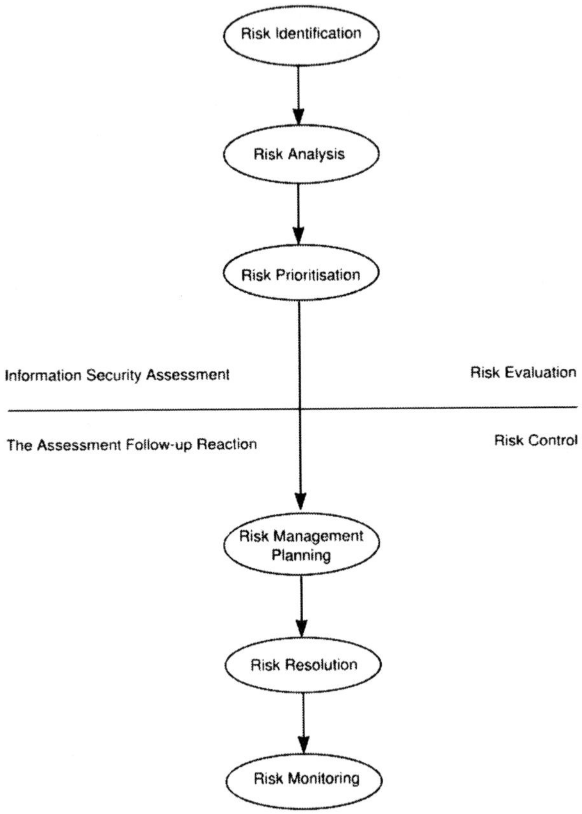

In this chapter, we are mainly concerned with the upper risk evaluation half of the scheme. Which practical approaches to it could be the most feasible for information security auditors? Are there any complications and traps they should be aware of?

First of all, there is a need to select a suitable definition of what is actually assessed. There are numerous ways of defining what information security risk is. Usually, they come down to explaining some variety of the *Risk Severity* = (*probability of the event*) x (*impact of the event*) formula. A definition of risk as provided by the NIST Special Publication 800-30 is:

- *Risk is a function of the likelihood of a given threat-source's exercising a particular potential vulnerability, and the resulting impact of that adverse event on the organisation.*

Thus, a risk is estimated by how likely a security incident is to occur and how severe its aftermath would be. We are going to utilise the NIST definition of risk as highly applicable for this discussion's purpose.

Risk, uncertainty and ugly 'black swans'

A sensitive issue is distinguishing between risk and uncertainty proper, as sometimes they are mistaken for each other. The Boston Consulting Group Strategy Institute *Clausewitz on Strategy* book, provides a perfect summary that deals with this problem:

- *American economist Frank H. Knight (1885-1972), who is considered to be among the most influential economic thinkers of the 20th Century and is a founder of the Chicago School of Economics, broke new ground by distinguishing between risk, where outcomes can be identified and their probabilities gauged, and uncertainty proper, where outcomes and their probabilities elude analysis. Risk can be insured; uncertainty cannot. In his seminal work, 'Risk, Uncertainty, and Profit' (Boston: Riverside Press, 1921), he attributed entrepreneurial profit to successful engagement with uncertainty proper.*

In practical terms, *there are certain limits by which a security audit can diminish the auditee friction*. After all, as one of the cornerstone Chapter 1 statements declares, *an information security assessment is never complete*. However, not all of the limitations are related to the expected restrictions imposed upon audits by budget, time, or the assessor's skills and tools. One of the key factors that contribute to friction is pure chance. No security audit can eliminate the possibility of its intervention. Nonetheless, *the auditors can address auditee capabilities of adapting to chance*. For instance, they can do it by pointing out risks related to insufficient redundancy and resilience measures implemented. Thus, apart from reducing *self-induced friction*, thorough information security assessments can actually assist with the '*successful engagement with uncertainty proper*'.

An interesting spin-off of this discourse on uncertainty and risk is dealing with the so-called '*black swan events*'. The term comes from the popular book by Nassim Nicholas Taleb, *The Black Swan: The Impact of the Highly Improbable*. A 'black swan' event is considered to possess the following characteristics:

- It is highly unpredictable
- It has a massive impact
- It is rationalised to look more predictable afterwards.

To quote Taleb, '*before the discovery of Australia, people in the Old World were convinced that all swans were white, an unassailable belief as it seemed completely confirmed by empirical evidence. The sighting of the first black swan might have been an interesting surprise for a few ornithologists (and others extremely concerned with the colouring of birds), but that is not where the significance of the story lies. It illustrates a severe limitation to our learning from observations or experience and the fragility of our knowledge. One single observation can invalidate a general statement derived from millennia of confirmatory sightings of millions of white swans. All you need is one single (and, I am told, quite ugly) black bird.*'

In technical information security, a completely novel and highly effective way of exploitation or totally overlooked giant gap in abundant implementation, are examples of the 'black swan'. Note, that there could also be beneficial 'black swans' in the shape of discovering potent unorthodox defensive means. Zero day vulnerabilities and exploits could be 'black swans'. The Morris worm surely was. The majority of current '0-day birds' belong to the shades of grey. It is often possible to predict a 0-day or, at least, be wary of the heightened probability of its emergence. The threat of buffer overflows was outlined back in 1972, 16 years prior to the earliest documented malicious buffer overflow utilisation. 'Bloatware' (bloated and bulky software) and highly complex network protocols are more likely to be insecure: complexity breeds potentially vulnerable points and increases the attack surface. Besides, it is possible to look at the security history of the investigated application or other target to draw useful forecasts. There are known network services that were hit by a 0-day, patched, then hit afresh, patched again and so forth. Although history records could be deceiving. Sometimes people repeat the same mistakes over and over again. But some learn a lot from them, and do it well. The same applies to social engineering and human security issues.

How can information security assessments and their risk evaluation phase address the 'black swan' problem? If the auditors discover a novel vulnerability or method of attack before the bad guys do, our bird is painted snow-white. This was referred to as 'getting inside the opponent's OODA loop' earlier in this book. Notice that the mutation fuzzing is a direct hands-on approach to tackling the 'black swan'. By applying unexpected and outright random input, this type of testing can produce a similarly unexpected outcome. When its results are analysed, and corresponding potential risks are gauged, the bird changes its colour. These are some of the tactical means applicable to dealing with the 'black swan' issue. What about their strategic counterparts?

In his principal work, Nassim Taleb has suggested that humans are prone to concentrate on specifics when they should focus on generalities. This trend strongly aggravates vulnerability to 'black swan' events. By uncovering and addressing *strategic level risks*, such as those introduced by lack of defence-in-depth or prevalence of the 'autocratic control and drill-machine approach', security audits evaluate adaptability. Which is, according to military strategists, from Sun Tzu to John Boyd, the proper answer to uncertainty. The absence of strategic failures will not prevent assailants from *creating a gap* employing a 'black swan attack'. However, it will enable robust *containment* of the attack's impact, as well as effective incident response and recovery reactions. In Taleb's own words, '*you are exposed to the improbable only if you let it control you*'. This shall conclude the brief uncertainty, the unknown and harmful unpredictability interlude.

On suitable risk analysis methodologies

The next step is to choose a general risk analysis approach. Risk analysis methods can be quantitative or qualitative. The quantitative variety strives to assign independently objective monetary values to different objects of the risk evaluation and to the estimates of the potential loss. In contrast, qualitative risk analysis is typically scenario-based. Information security assessments address, or even emulate, active and passive security incident scenarios and their outcomes. Thus, the data they produce fits the qualitative, rather than quantitative approach. Besides, even the in-house security auditor teams are usually not supplied with sufficient details regarding their target's monetary values. Together with the previous observations on the role of intangibles and difficulties in estimating the value of data, this tilts the balance towards employing the qualitative risk analysis means. At the same time, *the results of such qualitative evaluation should be presented in a quantified way*. This helps to prioritise weighted risks and clearly explain their significance (or lack of thereof) within the security assessment report.

Then we need to select the parameters convenient for estimating risks in accordance with the aforementioned risk definition and the corresponding formula. Which is, to remind, *Risk Severity = (probability of the event) x (impact of the event)*. What the auditors could see from the results of the performed tests is:

1 Various security weaknesses, vulnerabilities and gaps, and how easy or difficult it is to discover and exploit them.

2 The consequences of such exploitation (exposure of sensitive data, gaining unauthorised access, disrupting availability, etc.).
3 The efficacy of the auditee defences.

The data which contributes to assessing the impact (mainly point 2 of the above) is more tangible and objective, as compared to its probability gauging counterparts. It could be hard to evaluate the overall end effects of a successful security breach. However, it is not difficult to spot where and which level of access was obtained, and what kind of data became disclosed, or, to detect any significant service or network availability disruptions. Thus, weighting the vulnerability impact is the easier half. The next section of this chapter will provide examples of numerous parameters that can be utilised for this important task.

Measuring the probability of the event can be tricky. If the auditors are looking at *passive* incidents only, relevant security history statistics come in very handy. Unfortunately, such statistical data is frequently unavailable. Does your company or organisation keep track of all accidental sensitive data losses and their frequency? What about availability shortfalls? However, it is the active security incidents that make the matter truly complicated.

As discussed in the Introduction, they involve the clash of wills. It is possible to contemplate different attacker types and their traits, and make reasonable guesses about the opponents one is more likely to encounter. This could be advantageous when doing preliminary planning for an upcoming security audit, hence discussed in Chapter 4 when covering threat profiles. Nevertheless, trying to predict motivations, aims and means of complete strangers (or even someone you think you know) can easily become an unrewarding business. At the end of the day, it is nothing more than creative guesswork. Estimating the likelihood of attacks on such shaky grounds, during the risk evaluation phase of an audit, is clearly far-fetched. The security assessment is expected to decrease the fog of war covering its targets and their close surroundings. Away from the assessment scope the dense fog persists. As ancient Chinese strategist Du Mu pointed out, '*you can only know if your own strength is sufficient to overcome an opponent; you cannot force the opponent to slack off to your advantage*'.

Thus, a different approach should be adapted instead. Assume that sooner or later the attack will take place. Then, estimate the likelihood of its *success* by gauging points 1 and 3 of previously listed assessment results. That is, the ease of vulnerability discovery and exploitation combined with feasibility of bypassing deployed countermeasures and safeguards. In practice this comes down to estimating attacker skills necessary to find and abuse the discovered vulnerabilities, security weaknesses and gaps. If the skill and effort bar is high, the probability of successful attack is low, and vice versa. This is a simple, yet highly effective method of dealing with the attack likelihood issue.

The final set of parameters that cannot be ignored when assessing security risks relates to the rectifying action. The situation in which a workable and reliable remedy for the evaluated vulnerability is readily available is dramatically different from its opposite. The absence, inapplicability or demanding complexity of the fix significantly increases the risk the vulnerability presents. Thus, the basic formula for evaluating per vulnerability risk in hands-on security assessment practice would be:

- *Risk Severity = f (vulnerability impact, attacker effort/skill, suitable remedy availability).*

Armed with this knowledge, the auditors can now commence the synthetic analysis of risks described in detail in the remaining sections of this chapter. Its results will allow effective prioritisation of risks that harmonises future remedial acts.

On treatment of information security risks

Various activities that address the evaluated risks, also referred to as risk treatments, are divided into four major categories:

1 Avoidance, or complete elimination of risk. This is desirable, but rarely applicable in practice, outside disabling what is not needed anyway. If you don't use a feature, system or service the related risks are gone. However, if it is there in the first place, it is probably required for business operations.
2 Reduction, or mitigation of risk. This is the most sensible and commonly utilised approach of dealing with risks. Patch the hole. Replace the component by its more secure equivalent. Introduce appropriate safeguards. Improve security of processes. Tighten policies, standards and guidelines. Provide relevant security training. Some risk will inevitably remain, but presumably at a much lower level.
3 Transfer. Risks can be outsourced or insured against. For example, an appropriate SLA with a third party like hosting, data storage, cloud or SaaS provider, can transfer some risks to such an entity. Currently, insurance against information security-specific risks is

uncommon. As time passes, this situation is likely to change.

4 Retention, or risk acceptance. Sometimes a risk can be retained. This happens when it occupies the very bottom of the priority list, or its mitigation can introduce more problems than the original risk itself. Risk retention can be accompanied by suitable budgeting arrangements that cover the estimated acceptable loss.

Risk acceptance is the most controversial and arguable point on the list. Many security specialists feel uncomfortable with retaining even the minimal risks, which they perceive as inaction. It is almost like being silenced or pushed down by financial or political considerations. It offends the perfectionist attitude. However, accepting risks on the basis of their detailed assessment by experts is not the same as ignoring them. The MCDP 1 *Warfighting* made a great observation highly relevant to this subject:

- *By its nature, uncertainty invariably involves the estimation and acceptance of risk ... Risk is equally common to action and inaction. Risk may be related to gain; greater potential gain often requires greater risk. However, we should clearly understand that the acceptance of risk does not equate to the imprudent willingness to gamble the entire likelihood of success on a single improbable event.*

Note the correlation of the last statement with the 'black swan intermezzo'. Also, the excerpt above underlines that acceptance of risks is not a gamble. It should never become one. In his bestseller *The 33 Strategies of War,* Robert Greene draws a clear line between gambling and taking measured risks:

- *Both cases involve an action with only a chance of success, a chance that is heightened by acting with boldness. The difference is that with a risk, if you lose, you can recover: your reputation will suffer no long-term damage, your resources will not be depleted, and you can return to your original position with acceptable losses. With a gamble, on the other hand, defeat can lead to a slew of problems that are likely to spiral out of control.*

When the logic of both *Warfighting* and Robert Greene discourses are combined, the consequent conclusion can be derived:

- *When the acceptance of risk is gauged, not the likelihood of the event, but its actual impact should be favoured as the basis for the final decision.*

The impact is more straightforward to judge. It is predominantly intrinsic to the auditee. In contrast, the probability depends on a multitude of external factors concealed by the ever-present fog of war.

Envision a high attacker skill, high impact technical vulnerability that requires in-depth analysis of the target with subsequent creation of exploit code in order to be abused. For now, its exploitation appears to be unlikely, thus strongly reducing the associated risk. However, there is no guarantee that tomorrow the exploit would not be released. Or, that the relevant exploitation technique would not be sufficiently simplified. Are you going to gamble leaving such vulnerability unfixed? The human factor security bears its own burden of the risk acceptance issue. A highly trusted and loyal person holds the keys to confidential data and privileged access. This is acceptable risk. However, tomorrow the situation might change. For instance, this person may suffer a mental breakdown that opens opportunities for successful social engineering attacks. A common sense answer is 'trust, but monitor'. As soon as any reasons for suspicion appear, remove the trust.

When evaluating risks and contemplating appropriate risk treatments, the concepts we have borrowed from military science can offer vital insights. Spin the strategic exploitation cycle (Figure 21) the last time, feeding into it all security testing results at hand. Ideally, at this assessment stage all centres of gravity should be identified, studied and categorised. If breaching the determined Schwerpunkt or Systempunkt is possible, but requires high attacker effort and skill, not defending it any further is a gamble. This can apply to the above examples of the critical vulnerability which is hard to exploit, or the highly trusted and loyal employee that should still be monitored. However, if the risk is not:

- Related to any established centres of gravity
- Evidently a part of a Systempunkt or
- Could be a useful Nebenpunkt ...

it can be safely retained in order to dedicate effort and time to more critical security issues.

Analysing individual vulnerability risks

'So the rule of military operations is not to count on opponents not coming, but to rely on having ways of dealing with them; not to count on opponents not attacking, but to rely on having what cannot be attacked.'

Sun Tzu

Risks introduced by separate vulnerabilities are the building blocks of the entire information security risk state of the auditee. If one of the blocks is defective or goes amiss, the whole structure might collapse. The devil is in the details. Precise measurement of risks for every assessed security weakness, vulnerability or gap, is the key to a successful risk evaluation phase of any information security audit. Yet, we are employing the qualitative, and not quantitative method. How is it possible to maximise its precision? The likely answer is to take into account as many details as you can while keeping in mind their relevance and criticality for the specific situation.

Relevant vulnerability categories

Prior to reviewing practical assessment of vulnerabilities impact and exploitation likelihood, it is sensible to revisit their classifications. There are many ways of categorising security flaws of various nature. Not all of them are suitable for evaluating risks these vulnerabilities present. Thus, only the pertinent taxonomies that closely reflect our previous discussions will be examined.

A handy methodology is to sort vulnerabilities by their specific discovery means. In accordance with the general assessment categories, it is possible to split all security issues into *uncovered by black, grey or white box testing.*

All flaws detected and exploited during black box tests can be abused by anyone. If the test is internal, the 'anyone' amounts to any insider. Their grey box equivalents require an additional exploitation step – getting the needed unprivileged access. Vulnerabilities that can be uncovered via white box assessments only are usually the hardest to detect and abuse.

It is also feasible to classify vulnerabilities as discovered via:

- Frontal recon and exploitation
- Lateral recon and exploitation
- The combination of both approaches.

Revisit Figure 30 and the corresponding discourse if you feel the need to refresh your memory. Vulnerabilities that require lateral reconnaissance and exploitation means are usually more difficult to attack, although some peculiar exceptions do exist.

Besides, it is useful to categorise vulnerabilities as *discovered by intrusive or non-intrusive techniques.* Intrusive methods are more likely to trigger alarms. In social engineering it corresponds to arousing suspicion, doubt and mistrust. In technical attacks – to setting off intrusion detection, monitoring and prevention systems. Intrusive technical testing is also likely to cause denial of service conditions that can prevent further exploitation. To summarise, vulnerabilities that demand the intrusive approach are harder to exploit, especially if appropriate safeguards are in place.

Finally, note how accessible the vulnerability is. It could be:

- Remote

- Local – network
- Local – system or application.

Remote vulnerabilities can be reached from any position providing that connectivity exists. Local – network vulnerabilities are accessible from the same network. Local system or application vulnerabilities require some form of unprivileged access to the target. This is a purely technical classification. In social engineering, it is possible to create an equivalent by looking at communication channels that were employed to reach the assessment goal. Did it require personal contact, telephone conversations, or were the online communications sufficient? Also, did the one-time contact suffice, or were multiple contacts with the target(s) necessary?

Gauging attacker skill

The classifications outlined above clearly relate to the exploitation likelihood, rather than the vulnerability impact. If you look at them more closely, it will become apparent that the pivotal point is, indeed, the attacker's skill and respective effort. How to get a foothold to enable grey box tests? How to outflank strong frontal defences and discover what is hidden? How to employ highly effective, but intrusive techniques without crashing (or scaring away) the target and sounding the alarm bells? How to reach the soft vulnerable underbelly?

When discussing the tactics of assessing vulnerabilities and gaps, we have noted that security problems discovered earlier in the audit process tend to be less skill-demanding. Figure 27 was used as an illustration of the three typical exploitation stages which correspond to a gradual increase of required attacker proficiency and effort. In a nutshell, this divides technical attacker skill levels according to the testing methods employed:

- Low level – automated scanning only
- Medium level – semi-automated testing
- High level – manual testing.

Shifting further to the next 'operational' section of Chapter 5, it is reasonable to draw a similar categorisation on the basis of ability to utilise security gaps:

- Low level – exploiting well-known gaps
- Medium level – exploiting little-known gaps
- High level – creating gaps at will.

The attacker skill level classification we use in actual penetration testing reports is represented in Table 5.

Table 5: Categorising technical attacker skills

Skill level	Description
user	The *user* skill level attack can be easily performed employing well-known techniques and 'canned' tools that are freely available on the Internet. No specialist knowledge of the attacked application, system or network protocol is needed.
administrator	The *administrator* skill level attack would usually require using several methods and tools in a specific sequence, or employing a sophisticated attack tool with complex command line syntax. Good knowledge of the targeted application logic, system structure, configuration and commands, or network protocols operations, is necessary.
expert	The *expert* skill level attack would typically require writing a new hacking tool from scratch or heavily modifying the existing tools to address a specific vulnerability. Discovering novel security flaws and attack techniques, producing zero-day exploits, performing reverse engineering or cryptanalysis, belong to this skill level.

The 'administrator' designation in the table reflects the fact that at this particular level attackers should be able to manage what they are able to breach. Or, at least, possess the same degree of competence as the system or network administrators they confront do. Note, that more often than not passive security incidents could be judged as having 'User' attacker skill level. Picking up what was incidentally exposed anyway should not require a high degree of labour or proficiency.

Social engineering is a highly fluid and agile sphere of action where the levels of attacker effort and skill are harder to formalise. The following classification, similar to its technical counterpart above, can be used as a model for further pondering:

1 Amateur. Just like its technical equivalent, the 'script kiddie', an amateur social engineer relies on the application of simple and well-known methods en masse. The ruling principle is 'you are unlikely to kill two birds with one stone, but throwing a million stones will smash a sitting duck or two'.
2 Conman. At this level social engineers can employ inventive or cunning attack plots, consisting of several co-ordinated moves. They can also make active use of the Nebenpunkt concept. Unlike the amateurs who mainly operate online, a conman attack can involve telephone conversations and personal contacts.
3 Spy-master. Highly skilled social engineers can handle complex far-reaching schemes that involve numerous people, connections and communication channels. They are able to create gaps in apparently well-protected lines of defence. The analogy supplied by modern chaos theory is the one of the strange attractor influencing complex dynamic systems via a variety of variables while being difficult to take notice of.

Highly skilled social engineers are also more likely to apply the interdisciplinary approach, by utilising suitable technical means to assist in the human factor exploitation.

The descriptions in Table 5 were attuned to reflect diverse attacker skill-related categories we have previously discussed. However, they could not fully absorb all relevant taxonomies and factors. For instance, the table does not explicitly state whether the lateral approach had to be taken, or highly intrusive techniques have been successfully used. The criteria that did not fit into the table can still be utilised as modifiers, when the decision on assigning the attacker skill level to the evaluated vulnerability is made. This can be of great assistance when making this decision is not straightforward. In other words, when in doubt, check them out. As for the listed accessibility categories, we routinely reference whether a vulnerability is local, local-network or remote, in a separate line of its description.

Weighting vulnerability impact

There are plentiful classifications that directly pertain to gauging vulnerability impact. A successful exploitation of a security flaw carries a multitude of tangible and intangible negative repercussions. These effects can be thoroughly categorised so that the actual impact can be measured with a good degree of certainty.

Vulnerability impact can be estimated in monetary terms, causing:

- High loss
- Medium loss
- Minimal or no loss.

As compared to quantitative risk analysis calculations, such estimates are highly subjective. They would depend on what is perceived as high, medium or minimal loss by the auditee, which is something third party auditors are unlikely to be well-familiar with. Thus, it is rarely used. However, in some specific cases, like trade secret or customer database exposure, monetary considerations may become predominant. This is even more so when the impact of vulnerability on the availability of services is judged for online traders, casinos or betting shops.

Since everything is a part of some process or, more likely several processes at once, the impact can be weighted by its operational effects. It can:

- Disrupt a process (or a few processes)
- Impair a process (or a few processes) or
- Have minimal or no process-related effects.

This categorisation strongly depends on the criticality of the affected processes for the auditee business operations. Which again lies beyond the auditor team competence in numerous, but not all cases.

A common, and evidently fruitful way of gauging vulnerability impact, is by looking at the effects the security breach has on the CIA triad:

Confidentiality

- Exposure of highly confidential data
- Exposure of confidential, but not critical data
- Exposure of private non-confidential data
- No sensitive data disclosure.

Integrity

- Modification of highly confidential data
- Modification of confidential, but not highly critical data
- Modification of private non-confidential data
- No sensitive data alterations.

Availability

- Severe disruption of availability
- Tolerable reduction of availability
- No or minimal effects on availability.

To remove any doubts, the auditors can contact the auditee while being engrossed in the process of risk evaluation, and ask to provide the existing data classification standards, policies and guidelines. Responding to such a request in a positive and rapid manner is clearly in the auditee interest.

Technical vulnerabilities impact can be weighted by the levels of unauthorised access to systems and applications their successful exploitation provides. These reduce to:

- Highly privileged access (root, administrator, etc.)
- Unprivileged user access
- No or negligible unauthorised access.

The same classification can apply to some of the social engineering-related security flaws. When physical premises access is the social engineering test's aim, a similar approach can be used by categorising criticality of the penetrated premises.

The military science concepts that saw heavy use in this work could also be utilised to estimate the impact of assessed vulnerabilities, security weaknesses and gaps. In more general terms, a security issue can:

- Belong to a centre of gravity
- Lead to a centre of gravity
- Be unrelated to a centre of gravity.

Coming down to the strategic contemplations of specific critical points, the analysed issue can constitute, or be inseparable from:

- A Schwerpunkt
- A (part of a) Systempunkt
- A Nebenpunkt
- None of the above.

The most critical vulnerabilities, weaknesses and gaps pertain to determined Schwerpunkte or Systempunkts. When reflecting on the decisive moments of military conflict, Clausewitz wrote that '*no battle is decided in a single moment, although in every battle there are moments of great importance, which chiefly bring about the result. The loss of a battle is, therefore, a gradual falling of the scale. But there is in every combat a point of time when it may be regarded as decided, in such a way that the renewal of the fight would be a new battle, not a continuation of the old one*'. Think which particular flaws 'chiefly brought about' the security assessment result and at which point of time and specific testing sequence it was decided. These are the key vulnerabilities that have the highest impact.

In fact, even the 'FUD game' described in the Introduction might be utilised to contemplate the most intangible, psychological or moral effects a security breach can produce. As previously discussed, it may end up with the following outcomes:

- Attacker wins the FUD game
- A draw-like condition (which favours the defender)
- Defender wins the FUD game.

Would a successful vulnerability exploitation push the auditee friction to the point of causing disorder, disarray or even panic? When performing the security assessment, watch all auditee reactions with utmost attention. You might get a call with an agitated voice on the other end telling something like: 'Oh, my God! Our critical database has got new entries saying "penetrated by Bob the security tester. We can modify all stored data at will". What should we do?! Do we have to stop all tests ASAP and try to close the hole whatever it is?' If an actual malicious database attack took place, guess who would become the undisputed FUD game champion? Whose will would be shattered in the never-ending attacker-defender conflict of wills?

This brings into the spotlight a rather subjective, but nonetheless potentially handy way of judging vulnerability impact by gauging it against the expected assailant goals. As a result of the specific vulnerability exploitation, the attacker aims can be:

- Fully realised
- Partially achieved
- Not reached.

A decent preliminary threat model can make at least some of the attacker goals predictable, e.g. 'gain access to the credit card database' or 'abuse the shopping card application to reduce prices of goods'.

Table 6 provides an example of vulnerability impact classification we utilise when performing analysis of risks in the course of penetration tests.

Table 6: Categorising vulnerability impact

Impact level	Description
severe	The *severe* impact level vulnerability usually leads to full takeover of the targeted system or critical application and/or exposure of sensitive information to attackers. Malicious hackers can utilise this vulnerability in order to gain privileged access to the system, copy, alter or delete sensitive data, or capture and modify confidential or otherwise security-critical information passing through communication channels.
considerable	The *considerable* impact level vulnerability typically allows limited unauthorised access to data, application, service, system or network. Attackers can utilise this flaw in order to gain unprivileged user level access to non-critical data. Denial of service (DoS) attacks belong to this category in the majority of cases, since they do not provide access to systems or confidential data, but can severely disrupt service or network operations. However, if the availability of affected resources is business-critical (online trading, betting, news services, SaaS, etc.) the impact of non-generic DoS can be classified as *severe*.
limited	The *limited* impact level vulnerability commonly leads to non-critical alterations in systems behaviour or non-confidential private data disclosure to attackers. It is often considered as opportunistic, thus requiring a specific set of circumstances in order for attackers to benefit from it. A typical example of a low level vulnerability is leaking additional information about networks or systems, which allows attackers to map the network topology or server directory structure with precision. Often, low impact level vulnerabilities are auxiliary to their medium and high impact counterparts, and are abused by assailants to increase their attacks efficacy or stealth.

It is founded upon the most objective and tangible (from the auditor's point of view!) repercussions related to the CIA triad and levels of unauthorised access. Some conceptual strategic overtones are also present. Similarly to the case of evaluating attacker's effort and skill, the rest of the relevant categories discussed can serve as applicable modifiers in the decision-making process. A very similar classification can be developed for estimating the impact of social engineering attacks.

Contemplating the vulnerability remedy

The remaining element of our per vulnerability risk evaluation formula is the remedy. It might fully *eliminate or mitigate* the risk. It can be *complex, of average complexity, or simple*. The complexity of the fix is usually correlated with its costs in terms of money, time and effort spent. A remedy can also have a different application scope. It can be *separate security flaw-specific or generic in nature*. In theory, the generic remedy is preferable, since it addresses many facets of the issue, or even multiple issues at once. It is also a good indicator that the root of the uncovered security problem has been firmly established. However, in practice the combination of specific and generic remedial actions is often the most sensible approach. For instance, a vulnerable critical service must be patched ASAP (a specific remedy), while the entire patch management process and the corresponding guidelines are appropriately improved (its generic counterpart).

The most important criteria in evaluating the remedial action is whether a suitable solution is readily available or not. Table 7 represents our practical take on this issue.

Table 7: Categorising vulnerability remedies

Remedy	Description
Non-existent	There is no permanent or acceptable temporary fix for this vulnerability. Until an appropriate remedy is discovered and produced, the affected application, service, system or network protocol must be disabled or disconnected from the network, to be replaced by a sufficiently secure equivalent.
Temporary	The fix is indirect, does not mitigate the issue in full or address its real cause, and might partially impair the functionality of the affected application, service, system, or network protocol.
Available	The adequate security fix is readily available from the system or application developer or vendor. Alternatively, the remedy involves easy-to-perform and straightforward changes of the affected target's configuration.

An example of temporary, or partial remedy, could be restricting access to a vulnerable service or application to highly trusted and monitored systems or users only. The risk is reduced, but as soon as the fully-fledged fix is available it must be applied. Since social engineering attacks rely upon basic principles known since the ancient times, situations in which appropriate remedies are non-existent are seldom. The majority of human security issues can be solved with relevant training. However, at times all access of vulnerable persons to critical data and systems must be completely removed until suitable replacements are found. This corresponds to the temporary remedial action. Keep in mind that many social engineering-related headaches can be effectively addressed through technical, operational and policy means.

Defining vulnerability risk level

After the vulnerability impact, attacker skill and remedial action levels are assigned, a consolidated per vulnerability risk value can be produced. Table 8 demonstrates a possible way of generating this value for all assessed vulnerabilities, security weaknesses and gaps. This is the approach we currently use in routine security auditing practice.

Table 8: Per-vulnerability risk level estimation

Impact	Attacker skill	Remedy	Per-vulnerability risk level	
			Level	Description notes
Limited (+1)	Expert (+1)	Available (+1)	Low (= 3-5)	The risk is limited and easy to mitigate. Elimination of such flaws can be safely placed at the bottom of the remedial priority list. A possible exception is when other uncovered issues are at the same Low level of risk and the Impact of the particular flaw is estimated as Considerable. Limited Impact Expert skill level flaws with no available fix (risk level 5) can be safely retained.
Considerable (+2)	Administrator (+2)	Temporary (+2)	Medium (= 5-7)	The actual risk often relies on multiple factors, thus an individual judgement of Medium risk level issues is crucial. The differences between the lowest (5) and highest (7) ends of the medium risk interval can be highly significant: compare a Limited Impact Expert attacker skill level flaw with no

				available fix (risk level 5) and Severe Impact User attacker level skill flaw with a readily available fix (risk level 7). It is evident which one has to be addressed at the first place.
Severe (+3)	User (+3)	Non-existent (+3)	High (= 7-9)	The vulnerability presents a grave threat. It must be dealt with ASAP and by all means possible, even if the level of Impact is judged as Considerable rather than Severe. If its elimination is going to involve disabling the affected application, service or system functions or network connectivity, it must still be done until this serious security issue is fully resolved.

The risk summary for individual vulnerabilities is quantified by simply adding up the points assigned to three major risk-defining criteria as shown in Table 8. By adding them up, it is possible to obtain the summary values ranging from 3 (the lowest level of risk) to 9 (the highest level of risk).

Notice that the borders between Low, Medium and High risk summary levels are 'fuzzy': a vulnerability ranked as 5 can be labelled as low risk or medium risk, while a vulnerability ranked as 7 can be marked as medium or high. This is done on purpose and aims at providing the auditors with additional manoeuvring space in judging the risks presented by the examined security issue. It can be done on the basis of personal experience and specific situations that pertain to the particular assessment. At this point, various modifiers we have outlined can be recalled to assist with the decision.

For example, a Severe impact (3) vulnerability that is easy to exploit ('User' attacker skill, 3), but is also very straightforward to fix ('Available' suitable remedy, 1) would sum up as risk level 7. It could be marked as presenting Medium risk if the auditee has a proven rapid remedial reaction record and eliminates the flaw as soon as it is found and reported. Otherwise, the risk presented by such a vulnerability should be judged as 'High'. In particular, this applies to situations where numerous uncovered security issues have 'available' remedies, indicating that the relevant mitigation procedures within the auditee are ineffective (if present at all). Thus, we have already arrived at the point when the *synthetic overall risk state* is taken into account.

Risks synthesis, summary and its breakdown

'... war is an indivisible whole, the parts of which (the subordinate results) have no value except in their relation to this whole.'

Carl von Clausewitz

Synthesising all individual risks to create the summary that demonstrates the overall risk state, provides numerous eloquent advantages. The majority of them originate from being able to:

1 Generate, analyse and streamline the strategic view of the information security state.
2 Deduce important details that cannot be seen without assembling the whole picture.

The first point enables creation of a risk reduction plan aimed at strategic organisation-wide risk treatment. This goes hand in hand with recommendations of the OCTAVE process Phase 3: 'Develop Security Strategy and Plans' using a common evaluation basis. Instead of merely selecting tactical responses to individual risks, OCTAVE risk assessment methodologies aim at establishing a protection strategy for the critical assets of the entire auditee company or organisation. Alas, the approaches to identifying critical assets we have previously described are different from the corresponding OCTAVE Phase 1 ('Build Asset-Based Threat Profiles'). Besides, the OCTAVE process Phase 2 ('Identify Infrastructure Vulnerabilities') does not appear to go any further than automated vulnerability scanning.

As the strategic concepts-based illustration of the second point above, the process of producing the total summary of risks can assist in determining Systempunkts. In fact, current risk assessment theories have a concept *similar, but not identical,* to the Systempunkt – the so-called *compound risks*. A compound risk is usually described as a '*dependent combination of risks*', and is considered to be one of the most troublesome issues of risk analysis. A textbook advice for dealing with the compound risk is to reduce it to a non-compound one where feasible. This echoes the centuries old recommendation of Clausewitz to curtail several determined centres of gravity to one. However, it is practically impossible to do with the ¬Systempunkt proper. The great Prussian strategist was totally unaware of this modern concept. In contrast, the MCDP 1 *Warfighting* quote that closed the previous chapter, outlines the current productive approach to the problem. To conclude:

- *All Systempunkts introduce compound risks. At the same time, not all compound risks have a Systempunkt at their core.*

In a nutshell, *summarising risks points out where the major risk areas are*. This can be done at many levels of abstraction. When applied to the CIA triad, the holistic evaluation of risks demonstrates which parts of the triad are most affected by the security issues uncovered. If utilised for the assessment of operations, it can show which processes are more unsafe or have evident security flaws. Consolidating risks is likely to pinpoint high risk weak spots within the auditee ISMS organisation and structure. It can hint whether human, operational, policy or technical factors are the main contributors to the security risks faced by the entity. Comparing separate risks to the whole is a fundamental way of establishing their actual root sources. Is there a major strategic risk to which the tactical ones are evidently subordinate? On the basis of such comparison, some individual risks might be re-assessed, with their remedial priorities altered as a result.

Risks faced by large components

Our notions of the synthetic risk evaluation and analysis refer to assembling, disassembling and analysing the total summary of risks. The general scheme of how it could be done is introduced in Figure 32.

Figure 32: The process of synthetic risk evaluation

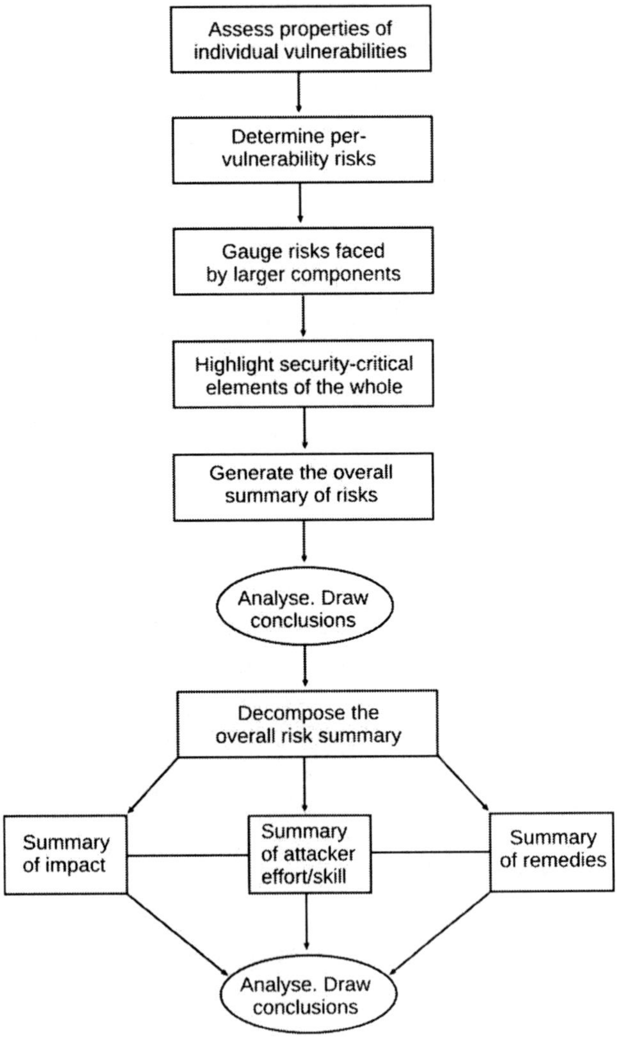

The first two stages depicted in Figure 32 culminate at assigning per-vulnerability risk levels for all applicable security issues. These stages were already covered in the previous section in sufficient detail, important modifiers included. Thus, we pick up the discourse from the third phase: '*gauge risks faced by larger components*'. This is the first stop at which risks introduced by individual vulnerabilities are summed up. An example of a typical 'larger component' in technical security assessments is a separate system. In software testing it can also mean a large part of a complex application, such as its kernel, back- or front-end. If a wide scope audit targets several networks at once, a separate net presents the next 'larger component' level as compared to its individual hosts. In human factor security evaluation, the 'larger component' can refer to a group of people united by common characteristics and aims. It can be a specific project team, a selected department's staff and so forth. When operational security is reviewed, the 'larger component' is typically a whole process, if assessing the premises security – a stand-alone building. In analysing security policies it would be a separate policy chapter. Depending on the size of the total, it could be feasible to split it into several components that co-exist in parallel, or nest one within the other, akin to Russian dolls.

We shall use a simple *external* technical assessment example, in which the large component is a modest size network. Firstly, look at the individual systems. How many vulnerabilities does a system have? What are their assigned levels of risk? Are they strongly influenced by any specific modifiers? Which vulnerabilities or their combinations are the most critical for the system? *Then approach the network as a composite entity*. The bar chart on Figure 33 shows the risks faced by a small network that consists of six nodes only. If the assessment was internal, it would also include any discovered network protocols-related risks.

Figure 33: A technical example of risks distribution

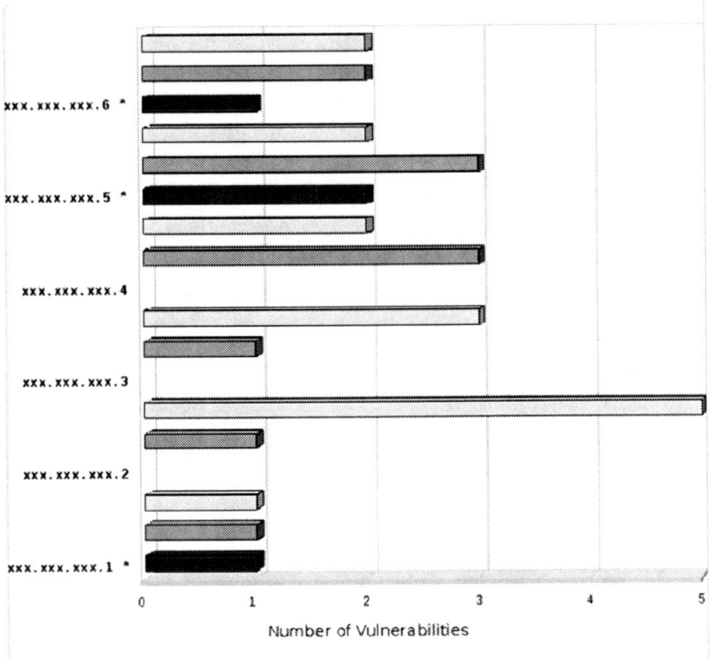

The colour of the bars represents the three levels of per-vulnerability risk from Low (light grey) to High (dark grey). Systems with network addresses ending on 2, 3 and 4 do not have any High risk security issues. The other half of the sample network evidently does. Thus, the hosts with addresses ending with 1, 5 and 6 are marked with a star as *security-critical*. To define the criticality, we suggest employing the following criteria:

- *The elements that have even a single High risk level vulnerability are security-critical.*
- *The elements with the number of Medium risk vulnerabilities exceeding the amount of their Low risk siblings can be security-critical depending on these flaws impact.*

System 4 of Figure 33 could satisfy the second criterion, as it has two Low and three Medium risk vulnerabilities. However, it is not labelled as security-critical on the chart. This indicates that none of the discovered Medium risk flaws have Severe impact whether on their own *or in combination.* Security problems embodied in the systems 1, 5 and 6 introduce higher risks and must be addressed first.

Compound risks, Systempunkts and attacker logic

At this stage of the synthetic risk evaluation we are likely to encounter the accursed compound risk/Systempunkt issue. *Addressing it will require a bypass of the boundaries of a single reviewed element, or even a re-evaluation of the scope and nature of the selected 'larger components'.* Revisit the Systempunkt example of Chapter 5. Earlier, we promised to supply non-network-centric illustrations of the same. The time has come to fulfil this promise. In the area of application security, a compound risk vulnerability can consist of:

1 Improper input validation, plus
2 Unsafe memory use, plus
3 Ineffective memory protection, plus
4 Violation of the least privilege principle.

Is it also a Systempunkt? Point 4 above hints at 'yes', as gaining privileged access to the system constitutes a definite 'collapse of its defences' and the Severe level of the vulnerability impact. On a larger scale of things, though, the correct answer will depend on the role of the penetrated application and system, and the sum of all repercussions of the breach. Thus, only a proper synthetic summary of risks, *knowing the whole risk state picture*, can provide the final answer.

Note, that in a real-life installation:

- Input validation can be done by a different application module (its front-end) or even a totally separate entity, such as the application layer firewall.
- Memory protection can also be performed by an extrinsic entity, e.g. the operating system or even in hardware.
- Violation of the least privilege principle can be an error of configuration, with the only fault of the application itself in being insufficiently fool-proof.

Even in such a case, the individual risks presented by all *distributed* constituents of the vulnerability are still inseparable from its summary risk level. It doesn't matter whether these constituents belong to the same or different entities or parts.

However, *separate components of a compound risk can have uneven individual contributions to its whole*. Thus, it is feasible to prioritise them when the remedy is considered. We shall use a common client-side targeting attack example to illustrate this vital point. This time the sample compound risk vulnerability comprises the following factors:

1 A cross-site scripting (XSS) issue on a corporate website that allows stealing user's log-in cookies if they click on a forged URL link.

2 The TRACE method enabled on the affected web server. It can assist the cross-site scripting attack.
3 E-mail addresses of employees can be harvested. Thus, the forged malicious link can be sent to all or selected members of staff.
4 Some users lack security awareness and will click on the insidious link if the e-mail that contains it is sufficiently enticing

Part 1 of the described compound risk flaw pertains to the Web application. Part 2 to the web server hosting it. Part 3 is an information leak that could either be allowed or violate the existing security policies. Part 4 is a human security issue.

In relation to this specific risk, the cross-site scripting flaw is the most critical. Eliminate it, and the problem is gone. This is a good illustration of how the compound risk can be reduced to a non-compound equivalent in practice. The use of the TRACE method is the least important. Providing that other relevant issues are solved, it can be safely retained as a Low risk level security weakness. The exposure of staff e-mail addresses is of great assistance to attackers. Nonetheless, in its absence a malicious link can still be sent via other available means like message boards, forums, social networks and instant messengers used by employees. Finally, the lack of security awareness exhibited by some users is nearly as important as the XSS, but does not lie at the very core of the sample compound risk. Increasing the awareness would reduce the risk without bringing about its complete avoidance, as removing the XSS issue will. However, under other circumstances and when reviewing a different attack, the security awareness problem can introduce far more serious risks than the specific technical cross-site scripting flaw!

Is this sample compound risk a Systempunkt? Again, the answer will depend on knowing more than the specifics of the complex vulnerability described. Who are the users whose accounts can be broken into and what are their confidentiality levels and rights? What would be the real consequences of the breach? What are the connections the exposed targets have? Is their exploitation able to create a domino effect propagating along these links? For instance, could the potential attackers utilise the breached accounts to disseminate the malicious URL within the organisation? Only the in-depth active security assessment is able to provide sufficient unbiased data on the basis of which any meaningful analysis of such compound risks can be performed.

The discussion of the compound risk example above highlights non-linearity of the strategic concepts when applied to the modern information security field.

- *Part of a Systempunkt in one attack can be a Schwerpunkt or Nebenpunkt of the other, and vice versa. The critical points and specific risks their exploitation creates can be independent, interlinked with a different connection strength, or even nested within each other.*

If you encounter such phenomenon when analysing the assessment results and summarising the risks, don't be surprised. When contemplating the remedies suggestion, take this complexity into account. Reducing a specific risk could diminish other risks. This is desired. Mitigating a specific risk may have no effect on any other risks. This is a typical view of risk reduction if the strategic considerations are totally ignored. Reducing a specific risk might increase other risks. This can be predicted and avoided.

The compound risks issue raises another interesting subject. Whether the atomic or complex elements of summarised risks are selected, their choice is usually based upon the objective auditee structures and processes. The auditors split the risks faced by applications, systems, networks, groups of people, separate departments, defined operational processes and so on. However, all examples of compound risks we have used are, in essence, reflections of the specific *processes of exploitation and structures, or scenarios of attack*. So, the compound risks emerge when these offensive processes and their elements do not match the individual or large components of their targets as seen from the defender's viewpoint. *This footprint mismatch is the real 'extrinsic' compound risks source. Among other things, the compound risks relate to exploiting differences and weaknesses of perception.*

Instead of adapting to the opponent as suggested since the times of Sun Tzu, the defenders operate in accordance with their own structure, categories and logic. Gauge the risks faced by the network A, process B, data set C, or team D. Treat them in accordance with this *objective, yet ultimately perceived and not the solely unique division*. However, the assailants can reach beyond such separation as it might have no actual relevance to the arrangements of a complex attack. They have their own offensive separation methods, as the given compound risk or Systempunkt examples demonstrate. How do we counter them?

If the entire all-encompassing view of both the risks and the corresponding security state is synthesised, we can divide it the way we want. It is possible to split it into the large and then the individual components the traditional way. This is probably how the whole was assembled in the first place. Alternatively, *it can be divided using the attacker approach and logic*. This would highlight the potential compound risks and allow the reduction of them to one or several key constituents that can be effectively mitigated. We would define it as the direct approach to the problem. Its indirect equivalent is treating the wide scope strategic risks, which is likely to reduce the compound risks by proxy. *This means countering breadth with an even larger breadth, fighting fire with a greater flame*. You can also compare it to the earlier passage on addressing the strategic risks in dealing with the 'black swan' problem.

Total risk summary utilisation and dissection

When the risks of *all large components, their constituents and interconnecting links* are thoroughly reviewed, a formal total summary of risks can be successfully produced. This is, in essence, a few word conclusion of the entire security assessment process. As Table 9 demonstrates, the criteria we advise to employ for this task are more granular than those utilised when designating individual security-critical elements.

Table 9: Defining the overall security state

Security state	Criteria
insecure	High risk level vulnerabilities are present.
insufficiently secure	The amount of Medium risk level vulnerabilities exceeds the number of Low risk flaws.
sufficiently secure	The amount of Low risk level vulnerabilities exceeds the number of Medium risk flaws.
secure	Only Low risk level vulnerabilities are discovered. They do not create a higher compound risk vulnerability if combined.

Draw a summary pie chart that presents the total percentage of High, Medium and Low level risks to supplement the general security state conclusion. At this point, it is helpful to stop and review the entire operation of coming to it. What are the key findings of the assessment? Are they interrelated? What do they pertain to in terms of processes, the CIA triad, vulnerability classes and types, infrastructure elements etc? List all critical findings and place any helpful explanatory commentaries and notes next to them. This would come in very handy when writing the assessment report.

The next step suggested in Figure 32, is to split the summary of risks according to the three chief contributing factors. This will produce the general summaries of all vulnerabilities impacts, attacker effort/skill estimates, and suitable remedies availabilities. Generate the corresponding pie charts to demonstrate total percentages of vulnerabilities split by their impact, attacker skill and remedy levels.

Finally, analyse the results. Which per-vulnerability risk levels and their constituents predominate? How do the breakdowns of the three parameters match the overall risks summary? What can be said about these parameters contribution to it? How do their distributions compare to each other? Which types and categories of impact are the uppermost? What about the suggested remedies? Are there any specific processes and areas with prevalent Severe impact, or User attacker skill, or Non-existent remedy level issues? How about their opposites? What could be the most likely explanations for answers to these and other relevant questions you can think of? Which information security elements would they apply to on the strategic, operational and tactical planes? In the next chapter, we will revisit such matters as the solid foundation for drawing the final conclusions to entire security assessments. For now, they shall remain as the engaging food for thought.

Apart from being the source of essential data for the audit report conclusion, executive summary and accompanying debriefs, the process of the synthetic evaluation of risks generates numerous graphical representations. At the very least, it will produce:

- The overall risk summary pie chart.
- Vulnerability impact level distribution pie chart.
- Attacker skill level distribution pie chart.
- Suitable remedy availability distribution pie chart.
- The component risk evaluation bar charts (similar to Figure 33).

Such schemes do not only help to analyse and make sense of the test results, but are also easily understood by the auditee management representatives. This is essential for the top-down endorsement of the audit, its follow-up reactions, and any future security assessments from the same auditor team. As stated by none other than Napoleon himself, '*the first quality for a commander in chief is a cool head which receives a just impression of things; he should not allow himself to be confused by either good or bad news; the impressions which he receives successively or simultaneously in the course of a day should classify themselves in his mind in such a way as to occupy the place which they merit; because reason and judgement are the result of the comparison of various impressions taken into just consideration*'.

Thus, if you want dedicated support from the 'commander in chief', it is best to offer the assessment results being already classified and prioritised on the basis of the respective summarised and individual risks. The language of risks is as universal as it is effective. Presenting the risks sum, distribution and main contributing factors concisely and accompanied by visual aids, goes a great way in getting your point across.

CHAPTER 7: PRESENTING THE OUTCOME AND FOLLOW-UP ACTS

'The comprehensiveness of adaptive movement is limitless.'

Mei Yaochen

As emphasised in the closing part of the previous chapter, properly presenting information security assessment results is essential for the overall success. Which tangible outcome does the company or organisation expect from the security audit performed? First of all, it is the assessment report. Besides, the accompanying presentations and debriefs are likely to be requested. In addition, assistance from the auditors can be called for during the assessment follow-up. After all, the ones who have offered the remedial advice are expected to be the experts in all the suggested remedies. There is no point in recommending a solution you are not well-familiar with yourself.

Remember, that even the most professional information security audits can be completely ruined by badly composed reports and an inability to present the materials. Who cares about the astonishing results or prudent and far-sighted recommendations if they are not understood correctly, by the right people, and in due time? A security assessment report that gathers dust with no action on its content ever done, is not always the auditee fault. Recall, that the audit itself can be viewed as the 'OO' part of the strategic risk treatment OODA loop. If the Observation and Orientation are not properly performed, the Decision and Action can go terribly wrong. The same applies to communicating the 'OO' findings to the decision makers. Damage the neurons that carry visual information to the brain, and the person can go blind despite having 100% eyesight.

On structure and content of the assessment report

'As a general rule everyone is more inclined to lend credence to the bad than the good.'

Carl von Clausewitz

An information security assessment report must match the competence, understanding, abilities and skills of all auditee professionals involved in the process of the assessment and its follow-up. In the majority of cases, the report will be reviewed by the CISO or equivalent, as well as the selected heads and appropriate members of all corresponding specialist teams. For instance, heads of risk management and compliance are expected to participate in studying and reacting to any information security audit outcome. However, there is always a chance that all relevant materials are going to be shown to senior management representatives. This is very likely to happen if the audit findings are considered as business-critical and require significant expenditure to mitigate the uncovered risks. These possibilities must be taken into account when assembling and composing various information security assessments reports.

The report audience and style

Since the competence areas of the aforementioned auditee specialists strongly differ, it is not possible to cater for everyone at the same time and place. Thus, there must be a clear division of the assessment report, at least into the management and focused specialist parts. Depending on the nature of the audit, the latter can be oriented at either technical or human resources professionals. If the security assessment is ISMS-centred, this division can be partially downplayed. Nonetheless, keep in mind that evaluating security policies, organisation and processes addresses strategic matters and is likely to be reviewed at the top. The professional expertise and background of a CISO strongly differs from, for instance, their CIO equivalents. Revisiting the discourse on the top-down approach and different levels of expertise in Chapter 2 of this book can provide insights which are highly applicable for the current subject.

Unlike the audit report, presentations and debriefs can, and should be arranged, to match the specific audience type. Giving a technical presentation to the techs, and management level debriefs to the appropriate managers, is a good practice based on common sense. Trying to preserve time by giving a mixed audience presentation would have exactly the opposite effect. One fraction of the listeners would be bored and confused during the 'technical' parts of the presentation, the other – in the course of its management counterparts. The cumulative question time would become a complete mess. Avoiding such mishaps is beneficial for both the auditee and the auditors.

Both security assessment reports and any auxiliary presentation materials must be clear, accurate and readable. All difficult or unusual terms must be explained, either within the text of the report or in a separate Glossary appendix. Usually, we do not utilise the Glossary as it would mean mixing technical and non-technical terminology in a single section. The style of the report, presentations and debriefs must aspire to reflect the assessment's objectivity based upon the thorough synthetic analysis of risks. Scaremongering is a no go, even when it might appear to be advantageous for the auditors in selling any additional services. Or even if the overall security state of the evaluated targets is determined as 'insecure'. Calmly explain what the major risks are and in which priority they should be dealt with. The aim of the assessment is to assist the auditee in gaining the upper hand in the 'FUD game', not inhibit their will or induce panic. As the epigraph to this section attests, people are inclined to lend more credence to the bad news anyway.

The style and structure of the audit reports must be streamlined while taking into account all peculiarities of the specific security assessment types. They should not be strongly distinct between the same assessment type reports submitted to different clients, or the same client in the course of time. Since '*information security assessment must be a part of a continuous process*', comparing the current and previous audit reports should not be clogged with unnecessary complications. This enables effective ongoing monitoring of the auditee security state. Typically, companies that provide security assessment services will have prefabricated templates for all common audit type reports. These templates must be regularly reviewed to incorporate the necessary modifications driven by relevant technological, regulatory and other developments. We suggest at least an annual review of the audit report templates. Also, a dedicated template, and not a different client's report, should be used to produce the document in progress. This simple measure prevents revealing any client details to a third party, either by accident or via metadata.

A proposed conceptual structure of an information security assessment report based upon our live documents is outlined in Figure 34.

Figure 34: Suggested security audit report structure

- Legal Disclaimer
- Report Summary
  - Executive Summary
  - Risk Review
  - Key Findings
  - Summary of Findings
- Report Interpretation
  - Assessment Background and Aims
  - Asssessment Scope
  - Assessment Methodologies
  - Definition of Terms
    - Vulnerability Types
    - Vulnerability Impact
    - Attacker Skill Level
    - The Remedy Criteria
    - The Levels of Risk
    - Specific Definitions and Terms
- Reconnaissance
  - Enumeration
  - Fingerprinting
  - Mapping
  - Abnormalities discovered
- Description of Vulnerabilities
  - Component or Vulnerability 1
  - Component or Vulnerability 2
  - Component or Vulnerability 3
  - ...
- Conclusions
- Appendices
  - Appendix A
  - Appendix B
  - ...

It is important to begin the report with the appropriate legal disclaimer reflecting the security assessment's nature. The disclaimer should strongly emphasise that the audit and its recommendations does not provide 100% insurance against future security incidents, and the auditor company cannot be held responsible if they take place. This might appear as the one-sided protection of the auditors against any negligence-related law suits. Nonetheless, such a statement also warns the auditee about the real state of affairs and prevents them from yielding to a false sense of security on the basis of the assessment results. Besides, the disclaimer should underline high confidentiality and non-disclosure of the report's content.

The report summary

The summary of the assessment report is probably the part everyone is going to pay the most attention to. It is safe to expect that any non-specialist management representatives will only read the report's summary and totally ignore the rest. So, it is this section of the entire document that will actually determine the top-down endorsement (or lack of thereof!) of the completed audit. Thus, it must be composed in a highly concise way using appropriate visual aids and language that will get all the described points across to the auditee management. Which is easier said than done, especially if the report is written by technically inclined specialists. To circumvent this problem, Figure 34 suggests splitting the summary into four distinct sections.

The executive summary proper should be brief, simple and to the point, while avoiding any technical terminology whatsoever. It should not exceed a single page unless in exceptional circumstances. Such situations might arise if the critical assessment findings are just too numerous to be outlined in one page, even in the most general and abridged terms. What is feasible to include within the executive summary? First of all, it must declare the overall security state level. Consult Table 9 for its possible definitions. Then, it should briefly explain which business areas, specific departments and operations, etc. are most affected by serious security issues. At this stage, utilising the CIA triad comes in handy. Which confidential data can be exposed to or modified by likely assailants? Which important services availability can be disrupted? What impact might it have on finance, ongoing business processes, compliance demands, or auditee image and reputation? The executive summary should never mention any specific vulnerabilities. It is there to highlight the general areas of critical risk.

The total risk review section should present all estimated information security risks in a clear, easily understandable, management-oriented manner. It should illustrate the distribution of vulnerability risk levels to justify the overall security state rating declared in the executive summary. Afterwards, the breakdowns of risks by their levels of impact, attacker skill and suitable remedy availability, as well as by the affected large or complex components, should be reviewed. This section of the report is where all the pie charts and diagrams created during the synthetic risk analysis, as described in Chapter 6, should go. Appropriate explanations and *strategic or operational level* conclusions derived from examining the summary of risks and its disassembly results should accompany every illustration.

The key findings section is the first part of the assessment report that addresses separate vulnerabilities, security weaknesses and gaps. Its aim is to list all security issues with a High level of risk and provide very short comments outlining their nature and impact. These commentaries should not go any further than 'an SQL injection flaw allows unauthorised access to the customer database' or 'a social engineering attack against selected accountancy department staff exposed personal employee data'. Note, that 'a security issue with a High level of risk' can be a compound risk problem comprising multiple individual flaws. In such a case only the whole issue, and not its specific components, should be covered in this part of the report.

The following summary of findings section lists all discovered security problems giving only the vulnerability name, risk level and reference number. The latter usually corresponds to the section number of the specific vulnerability outline in the Description of Vulnerabilities chapter of the report. It is best to present the summary of findings as a set of simple three column tables. It is also advantageous to arrange these tables according to separate tested components, such as systems, networks, processes or teams. Table 10 presents a simple instance of this approach.

Table 10: A fragment of a technical summary of findings

Summary of findings for host xxx.xxx.xxx.xx1:

Ref. N	Risk Level	Issue
6.1.1.	medium	HTTP – Cross Site Scripting vulnerability
6.1.2.	low	HTTP – HTTP TRACE method allowed
6.1.3.	low	HTTP/S – Disclosure of internal IP addresses, directories and files
6.1.4.	low	HTTPS – Weak cipher support
6.1.5.	low	HTTP/S – Test applications remain on the production server
6.1.6.	low	HTTP – Internet Printing Protocol (IPP) is enabled but not used

Summary of findings for host xxx.xxx.xxx.xx2:

Ref. N	Risk Level	Issue
6.2.1.	medium	ISAKMP - Aggressive mode with pre-shared key in use
6.2.2.	medium	ISAKMP – Weak cipher selection

However, if the components are too numerous (for example, systems in a large scope technical internal audit), sorting the summary tables by vulnerability type is more practical. Frankly speaking, the top management is unlikely to go through this final part of the report summary. On the other hand, it is comfortable to have a brief of all vulnerabilities in one place rather than skim through the entire Description of Vulnerabilities chapter. The readers of the report who are more technically inclined would appreciate it.

The report interpretation chapter

The report interpretation chapter aims to provide clear statements of the assessment scope and background. What exactly was tested? What were the main reasons for the audit? Is it a part of a continuous process building up upon the results of the previous tests? It should also specify the assessment methodologies and techniques used. The auditee must know what they are paying for. They need to estimate how well the approaches that were employed correspond to their specialist's expectations. This might assist the auditee in judging the quality of the assessments. But more importantly, it can also prevent a false sense of security from creeping in.

In technical security assessment reports, outlining the methods does not mean going into great detail down to the lists of used tools, configurations and commands. However, the report must state whether the audit is black, grey or white box, or if the intrusive or non-intrusive techniques were employed. It should note if multiple scanning tools were used in parallel and manual tests were performed. Any specific evaluation approaches towards assessing various safeguards must be outlined. Were the firewall access lists and filtering rules tested? How about egress filtering in the internal audits? Did the auditors assess centralised SPAM and malware filters, or intrusion detection and protection mechanisms?

For instance, a fragment from our current penetration testing reports elaborates that '*during the whole process of scanning we continuously verify that there are no interruptions in the assessed network functionality. The "noisiness" of the attack is gradually increased, thus testing the efficiency of the IDS/IPS, while also bringing the assessment closer to emulation of a determined Black Hat hacker behaviour. First, the services are tested for known vulnerabilities using slow-pace, cautious scanning. Only then any "noisy" fuzzing to search for new or unknown security flaws is performed.*'

Another relevant excerpt deals with the discovery of novel vulnerabilities, stating that '*if such flaws are found, or a "purely theoretical" vulnerability is detected, a proof of concept exploit code might be written, applied and provided in the report Appendices and/or in the electronic form. Such code will not be made available to the public domain, unless explicitly authorised by the client company or organisation*'.

It is also vital to declare what was not tested during the security audit, for a variety of situational reasons. To continue with the external penetration test report example, '*no attempts were made to access the targeted systems physically, or by means of wireless-based or social engineering attacks. No deep evaluation of resilience to various Denial of Service (DoS) attacks and poisoning of the external service caches has been performed during the tests in order to avoid serious interference with online business operations of the auditee. However, a few non-generic DoS issues have been discovered and reported*'. More often than not, the audit scope, objectives and hands-on methodologies are absolutely inseparable.

Finally, the report interpretation chapter must provide precise definitions for all specific categories and terms used within the entire document. For instance, in Figure 34 it covers all the levels and criteria of risk described in Chapter 6 of this book, since this risk evaluation approach is presumed. As for any other explanations that should be included, they will strongly depend on the nature of the assessment. For instance, in technical audit reports we casually include tables that define categories of IPID and TCP sequence numbers randomness, etc.

The bulk of the report

The reconnaissance chapter of the report should present all the recon data in a structured clear manner. Figure 34 represents it as split into Enumeration, Fingerprinting, Mapping and Discovered Abnormalities parts. In this division, the Enumeration corresponds to the overall listing of all uncovered targets and determination of their basic characteristics and types. The Fingerprinting goes further into detail, exploring a variety of separate target traits and their peculiarities. Mapping brings the recon information together in an attempt to generate the all-encompassing view of the entire 'attack surface'. Finally, the Discovered Abnormalities section should describe all deviations from the intended functions and standards spotted during the recon phase. Such oddities do not constitute vulnerabilities proper or, even, security weaknesses. However, they can negatively affect the auditee operations and should be taken into account.

Continuing the previous discussion thread, in penetration testing reports the Enumeration section should cover networks, systems and their characteristics, like the address ranges, domain names, packet paths, OS'es, system uptime and so on. The Fingerprinting part should describe separate services and, where applicable, network protocols. The Mapping should bring all this data together by presenting applicable infrastructure diagrams. Such schemes show how the assessed networks and systems are seen through the external or internal attacker's eyes. In black box application security testing, schemes demonstrating the overall application structure, logic and data flows can be provided instead, if possible.

Finally, the Abnormalities section is dedicated to the discovered misconfigurations that do not present a direct security threat. Nevertheless, as Dan Kaminsky pointed out years ago, 'network security and network stability are two sides of the same coin'. A system or network that does not operate properly is harder to defend. For instance, such behavioural oddities can generate plentiful false alarms that can decrease intrusion detection and monitoring efficiency. If the flood of false alarms is relentless, it can render these important security functions useless. At the end of the day, deviations in services, systems and networks operations contribute to the overall *self-induced friction*. The aim of any security assessment is to reduce it as much as one can.

The Vulnerability Description chapter lists and outlines all the discovered security flaws, weaknesses and gaps. As previously discussed, depending on the scope of the audit, this can be done in a per-component or per-vulnerability type order. A description of separate vulnerability we typically provide includes:

1 Vulnerability type
2 Vulnerability impact
3 Attacker skill level needed to exploit this flaw
4 Suitable remedy availability
5 Level of risk
6 Technical (or 'social') vulnerability description
7 Outline of the proposed remedial solution.

Note, that both points 6 and 7 should be sufficiently detailed to explain the vulnerability and its suggested remedies nature and hands-on utilisation. However, they should not be too elaborate and extensive, especially if it means a highly unequal distribution of attention and report space between different vulnerabilities that belong to the same level of risk. If a long detailed description of a specific security flaw and its elimination is clearly needed, it is better to move it into a dedicated appendix of the report. The vulnerability description should simply reference this appendix.

The conclusions chapter is akin to the report summary in bringing together the important discoveries of the audit. However, unlike the summary, the conclusions can be as 'technical' as necessary, so that all the uncovered security issues are properly addressed. Nonetheless, it frequently tends to deal with them on strategic and operational, rather than tactical planes. The subject of drawing appropriate conclusions is of such utmost importance that the next section of this chapter is entirely dedicated to these critical matters.

Finally, the appendices of the report might include:

- 'Crude' output of scanning and exploitation tools, or social engineering communications records where needed and considered as helpful for the auditee.
- Representative evidence of successful exploitation, such as screenshots, lists of cracked passwords, retrieved sensitive data etc (see Figure 29 and the corresponding discussion for more details).
- Extensive highly technical descriptions of specific security issues and their remedies.
- Exploit code.
- Other data deemed as important that does not quite fit the proposed assessment report format.

Some of the information listed above is highly confidential by its very nature. We wholeheartedly suggest that it should be submitted to a trusted auditee representative in person and in encrypted form. The auditor's security policy must also cover the retention of such data. It is best to delete it in a secure manner as soon as the assessment is over. However, if there is a need to preserve this information until the next planned assessment, or for any other reasons, it must be protected by strong encryption and stored on dedicated secure systems only.

On drawing conclusions

'The superior efficacy belongs not to the ***means*** *but to the* ***end****, and we are only comparing the effect of one realised aim with the other.'*

Carl von Clausewitz

The general conclusions to the security assessment performed belong to both the Report Summary (primarily, its Executive Summary and Risk Review sections) and the conclusions chapters. We shall start reviewing suitable and example approaches to drawing the assessment conclusions from the report summary part.

Explaining the overall security state

The first all-encompassing characteristic encountered in the report summary is the estimate of the overall security state. When discussing it, list the number of vulnerabilities that contributed to it and underline their general effects. A corresponding example excerpt from one of the assessment report's risk review is: '*The overall security state is judged as "insecure" since four High risk level vulnerabilities were identified. Three of these vulnerabilities allow remote access to highly confidential data. The fourth can be abused to launch attacks against third parties, thus creating potential legal and PR problems. There are also 11 Medium risk level flaws, which is close to the number of their Low risk counterparts (15). Such state of affairs is clearly unacceptable and requires urgent intervention*'.

More often than not, the 'Insecure' state means that the target is vulnerable to both determined and 'sweeping' automated attacks. The results of the breach are expected to correspond to the Severe impact level. The 'Insufficiently Secure' state indicates that there is more resilience to the low skill automatic attack approach, however the determined assailants are very likely to get what they want. The anticipated predominant impact of the attacks is Considerable or Severe. If the state is determined as 'Sufficiently Secure', the auditee company or organisation is still susceptible to a few Medium risk level issues which are likely to require significant skill and effort expenditure on the attacker's side. Take care to note the true extent of these issues impact. As previously discussed, retaining a hard to exploit but Severe impact flaw is closer to a gamble rather than a thoughtful risk treatment approach. 'Sufficiently Secure' is not 'Secure', these are different security risk categories!

Even if the overall state is evaluated as 'Secure', it is not a reason to sit back and slack. First of all, this is the current security state which can dramatically change tomorrow. Thus, an entity considered as 'Secure' on the basis of a performed audit, should concentrate on security processes and safeguards that relate to the change control procedures. Besides, the auditee professionals should clearly understand scope, depth and limitations of the assessment, as its final judgement is valid within these confines only. This is why the report interpretation chapter and its descriptions of methods and techniques used are so important.

Elaborating on breakdown of risks

The next stage is concluding the breakdown of the overall risks summary. Check which impact, attacker skill and suitable remedy availability levels are predominant (if any). Gauge them against each other, taking into account whether per-vulnerability risk estimates apply to the same or different security flaws. For instance, are Severe impact, User level and Non-existent suitable remedy vulnerabilities more common than Severe impact flaws which are easy to fix and hard to abuse? Or is it the other way? At this stage, a fine judgement of the specific circumstance is clearly needed. We strongly warn against 'assembly line stamping' of standard 'canned' conclusions based on the summarised risk criteria, without taking into account all the peculiarities of the given audit findings. Nonetheless, some general breakdown-based inferences can be applicable to a variety of situations.

More often than not, the prevalence of Severe impact vulnerabilities indicates an absence of proper defences-in-depth that could otherwise delimit the repercussions. This commonly signifies the existence of major strategic flaws pertaining to the infrastructure, application, process and overall ISMS design. Suitable examples may include situations in which:

- The breach of a vulnerable application provides high level access to the system. It could have been contained by sandboxing or virtualisation, kernel level countermeasures, and adherence to the least privilege principle.

- The exploitation of a system gives direct access to highly confidential data. It could have been contained by using strong encryption.
- The access to the DMZ server or corporate wireless LAN allows breach of the internal wired LAN. It could have been contained by secure network separation.
- Highly confidential data was accessed because it was stored too close to the network perimeter (e.g. on the publicly accessible servers). Alternatively, a social engineering attack has succeeded since far too many employees had access to the confidential information. It could have been prevented by policies and mechanisms effectively controlling dissemination of sensitive data.

A sample vulnerability impact distribution conclusions excerpt from one of the audit reports states that '*the presence of seven severe impact vulnerabilities clearly points at the general lack of proper defence-in-depth architecture and highly flawed elements of the ISMS design. Five of these vulnerabilities are due to weak authentication credentials and methods, or weak file and directory permissions. This demonstrates serious problems with access control and password policies and guidelines, and/or their practical implementation mechanisms. These problems are further underlined by the discovery that unprivileged user accounts and private, but not confidential or highly confidential data, can also be remotely accessed, as indicated by the existence of 11 related Considerable risk level flaws*'.

The prevalence of user skill level vulnerabilities typically points at low security awareness of the involved personnel, or low overall knowledge of applied information security. In relation to technical issues, it might signify the absence of a proper testing environment, with new insecure roll-outs being directly deployed into production and exposed to untrusted networks. In general, the skill level of defenders mirrors its estimated would-be attacker's counterpart. So, if the majority of vulnerability skill level estimates are 'Expert', the auditee professionals surely know their trade.

Human user skill level flaws commonly indicate a total lack of appropriate security awareness training. This is clearly a policy or operational fault. Technical user skill level vulnerabilities usually belong to three major categories:

- Easy-to-guess passwords (no proper password policies, guidelines or their enforcement).
- Password-unprotected services or unnecessary data disclosure due to weak or inappropriate permissions (no proper access control policies, guidelines or their enforcement, or weak data classification guidelines and controls).
- Plaintext transmission of sensitive information (no data encryption policies or their implementation).

A sample attacker skill distribution conclusions excerpt from a black box penetration test report elaborates that '*nearly equal distribution of this level estimates indicates highly uneven approach to security of all tested systems and services. Effective centralised security management solutions and related policies and procedures are clearly lacking. Most likely, different systems and applications are handled by several system administrators with large IT security skill gaps between them. If a single person is responsible for maintenance of the assessed network, then his or her knowledge of hands-on IT security is sufficient in some specific areas only. Alternatively, selected systems and services are viewed as less critical and thus ignored. However, the results of penetration tests demonstrate that if applied to this particular situation such an approach has already caused serious security issues, like the High risk level vulnerabilities described in this report*'. Further communications with the auditee have pinpointed which of the anticipated reasons were the actual causes of the nearly equal distribution of the attacker skill level estimates observed.

The predominance of the available suitable remedy flaws strongly indicates absence or serious gaps of vulnerability management policies, guidelines and procedures, or their working implementations. Evident slow or insufficient reactions of the responsible staff counterbalances all the benefits of a solution being immediately and widely available. Thus, when the summary of per-vulnerability risks is finally reviewed, the borderline risk level values of Table 8 should shift towards the increase. Appropriate technical examples might include situations in which:

- Some, but not all systems, run obsolete and vulnerable services (no centralised automated patching and upgrade system in place).
- Recommendations of previous security assessments are ignored (security audit mismanagement).
- The remedy is a configuration change and its distribution is highly uneven (weak centralised configuration management, or some systems are simply ignored).

Abundant easy-to-eliminate human security flaws go hand in hand with the corresponding user skill level estimates.

They demonstrate gross personnel mismanagement, lack of appropriate security training included. Quite often such mismanagement involves misplacement: people who have divided allegiances, are security unaware, incompetent, negligent or naturally naive must not have any access to critical data and systems.

A relevant excerpt from one of our technical security audit reports points out that '*the fact that the appropriate remedies are readily available for all the uncovered vulnerabilities except two, but are not actually applied, demonstrates the absence or total disregard of effective systems and software security maintenance and change control policies and procedures. If these were in place and properly followed, our consultants would have discovered only two vulnerabilities instead of 12. Alternatively, if the awareness of many gaps uncovered by this assessment already exists, the reaction of the tested IT infrastructure management to serious security issues is unacceptably slow*'.

It is not difficult to invert the aforementioned observations and examples, so that the opposite 'secure' conditions and situations can be concluded. However, we prefer to support the discourse from the 'negative' point of view. After all, '*advantages and disadvantages are interdependent – first know the disadvantages, then you know the advantages*' (Li Quan). It is finding the middle ground and inferring the results which pertain to the overall prevalence of Medium level risks that is the most difficult. This task is highly situational and usually demands taking into account large numbers of specific factors. Fortunately, more often than not, splitting the summary of risks into the integral components of impact, skill and remedy shows whether the situation tilts towards one of the extremes. This is the reason behind our use of four, and not three, general security state categories, as shown in Table 9.

Further insights can be gained from concluding the estimated risks faced by separate large components. To refresh the reader's memory, depending on the nature and scope of the audit these components could be:

- Company branches, business units or departments.
- Teams or other groups of employees.
- Different types of premises.
- Networks, systems or complex application modules.
- Complete processes and operations.
- Sets of policies, standards and guidelines.

At this stage, it is vital to look for evident risk patterns. How uneven is the distribution of evaluated risks between different assessed components? Which large or complex components present higher risk? Why is it so? What lies in common between them on strategic, operational and tactical levels? Who has the direct responsibility for their design, management and information security? Is it the same members of staff, or employees sharing common background and previous training? Are there any third parties involved? Are there also any apparent patterns of vulnerabilities distribution that clearly relate to their specific characteristics, classes and types? What are these patterns and how can they be explained? Answering these questions does not only provide important elements for concluding the review of risks, but can also assist at establishing the actual causes of uncovered security flaws, weaknesses and gaps. This is a subject we aspire to cover in the Conclusions chapter of the report.

Depending on the volume of the security assessment discoveries, the Conclusions chapter casually occupies one to three report pages. Its content is highly condensed and intense. The topics we might typically discuss in this chapter are:

- Scenarios of attacks that exploit the evaluated security flaws on their own, or in specific sequences and combinations.[3]
- Security weaknesses that do not qualify as fully blown vulnerabilities and cannot be included in the vulnerability description chapter.
- Examinations of the critical vulnerabilities causes, sources and roots.
- Descriptions of the strategic and operational level security issues that became apparent from the results of 'tactical' testing.
- More general and generic (as compared to their specific per-vulnerability counterparts) remedial recommendations.
- Risk treatment suggestions outlining what can be eliminated, reduced, retained or transferred.
- Risk treatments prioritisation.
- Suggestions regarding any future security testing in relation to the existing and planned auditee security programmes.

---

[3] If too numerous or extensive, the scenarios of attacks could form a separate chapter of the assessment report, placed in between the Description of Vulnerabilities and Conclusions chapters.

Analysing attack scenarios and trees

The attack scenarios form the essence of the qualitative risk assessment methodology and provide practical foundations for the estimated overall security state. Besides, evaluating and reviewing these scenarios is an effective way to address present compound risks and Systempunkt issues. Inevitably, it will include *dividing any existing compound risks and complex security flaws using the attacker separation approach and logic*. The limitations of the Description of Vulnerabilities report chapter dictate that it can only cover stand-alone problems without the analysis of any possible connections in-between. The following Conclusions chapter provides an excellent opportunity to outline how potential assailants can combine them to reach the desired aims. *The attack scenarios transform static descriptions of the uncovered vulnerabilities into dynamic, fluid, situational schemes*. Afterwards, the critical links in these schemes can be accurately identified. Such links correspond to gaps closing which can completely *ruin the flow of the attack, break the tactical exploitation cycle, or uproot the entire attack tree*. Elimination of these security flaws should be at the top of the suggested remedial priority list.

It is advantageous to categorise the suggested scenarios in accordance with the attacker effort and skill needed to execute them with success. To do so, contemplate on where, how, and how far the assailants can get, if only the user (or amateur) skill vulnerabilities are utilised. Then add the administrator (or conman) level vulnerabilities into the concoction. Finally, supplement it with expert (or spy-master) security flaws. How different are the attack scenarios corresponding to the three estimated skill levels? Do they resonate well with the Low, Medium and High levels of risk? Which skill category scenarios contribute the most to the determined overall security state? Needless to say, when it comes to the treatment of risks, priority should be given to preventing the attack scenarios which do not require a high level of opponent's dedication and expertise. However, there might be cases in which staving off high risk, severe impact and demanding skills scenarios first is preferential, as their easier-to-do counterparts are far less threatening. A related issue of deciding on the retention of risks, while gauging their impact versus attacker skill level, was already discussed in the previous chapter of this book.

Another feasible way of evaluating scenarios of attack is by looking at them from the specific threat, or estimated likely attacker's aims perspective. Taking into account all the discovered vulnerabilities, security weaknesses and gaps, is it possible to materialise the threat and achieve such goals? For instance, what needs to be done to obtain the trade secret, access personal data, or steal the customer database? How many steps would it take? What will these steps involve? Which security flaws will the assailants have to exploit and in which sequence will it have to be done? When these questions are answered, it becomes possible to estimate the level of attacker effort and skill required to reach the specific aim. Then, the conclusions outlining such incident's likelihood, as well as the specific risk reduction plans, can be deduced.

While analysing sophisticated attack scenarios that involve sequential exploitation of several security gaps, draw the corresponding attack trees or maps. You will find them incredibly helpful, and may even include such illustrations in the conclusions part of the audit report, or in a dedicated appendix. Security issues which are close to the attack tree roots or create its embranchments are likely to cancel the scenario or eliminate its vital parts if eradicated. If you prevent the initial breach that allows the entire attack scheme to proceed, the problem is solved. On the other hand, eliminating vulnerabilities that lead directly to the centres of gravity, while being well behind the attack surface, is a far sighted approach that lies at the core of defence-in-depth. *Thus, the most critical elements of the attack tree are likely to be encountered where it starts and ends, rather than in the middle.*

From a strategic viewpoint, the structure and flow of a complex attack have their own centres of gravity, represented by these vital points of the attack tree or map. It is even possible to categorise them as Schwerpunkte, Nebenpunkte and Systempunkts, as per Figure 21. Centres of gravity of the attack and exploitation process could also be reduced to a few key points and prioritised to assist the remediation. Then they can be effectively 'counterattacked' by closing gaps that allow these critical attack elements to exist. Correct priorities are crucial. They enable addressing the whole issue presented by the attack scenario as soon as possible, thus 'getting inside the assailant's OODA loop'. So, even the most crafty attack plots can be thwarted by utilising accurate scenario-based analysis of thorough security assessment results. This is the pinnacle of the defender's art, founded upon employing the attacker perspective and mindset. It goes hand in hand with the classic notion of winning the battle well before it starts.

When examining attack scenarios or going through the checklists in a more formal assessment, security flaws that do not constitute a vulnerability *per se* become apparent. For instance, the auditors may discover that there is no data leakage prevention or any egress traffic filtering at all. Or that the use of instant messengers, social and peer-to-peer networks by employees is excessive. Or, perhaps, highly confidential information is not strongly encrypted. All such problems clearly underline a lack of appropriate security controls. They emphasise the distinction between what allows the attack (vulnerabilities) and what does not stop it when it should (absent or inappropriate countermeasures and safeguards).

The assessment report of a dedicated internal white box audit will have separate sections that list and describe these issues. However, in black box assessments their discovery is secondary to vulnerabilities evaluation. Quite often, insufficiency of specific controls becomes apparent only when the testing results are analysed and conclusions are produced. 'The IPS should have blocked this attack.' 'The firewall should not have allowed such packets through.' 'The identity verification process must have stopped this social engineering attempt cold.' These statements are not independent, but present inseparable parts of the examined scenarios of attack. The earlier examples in this book also demonstrate that inadequacies of controls frequently constitute components of a Systempunkt. This provides sound reasons to outline important security weaknesses of the kind in the Conclusions chapter of the report and in relation to the relevant attack scenarios or complex flaws. This approach helps to conclude which insufficiencies of the auditee countermeasures and safeguards contribute the most to the ascertained overall security state.

Utilising vulnerability origin investigations

When pondering on the place of a specific security problem in the general scheme of things, it is possible to determine its original source, as well as the true extent of its impact.

The auditors should ask themselves the following questions:

- Which specific operations and processes the vulnerable element is a part of?
- Which flaws of these processes and operations could lead to this and similar security issues?
- Which security policies, standards and guidelines clearly relate to the uncovered problem?
- Which flaws of these documents, or their practical implementation and enforcement, could lead to this and similar security issues?
- Who are the people responsible for the design, management and security of the vulnerable element?
- What could they do in a wrong way and why would anyone commit such errors or misdeeds?
- Do any answers to the questions above fall into, or form, a specific pattern?

More often than many security professionals realise, even the most peculiar vulnerabilities have several contributing source factors that can belong to completely different realms (Figure 35).

Figure 35: General vulnerability source factors areas

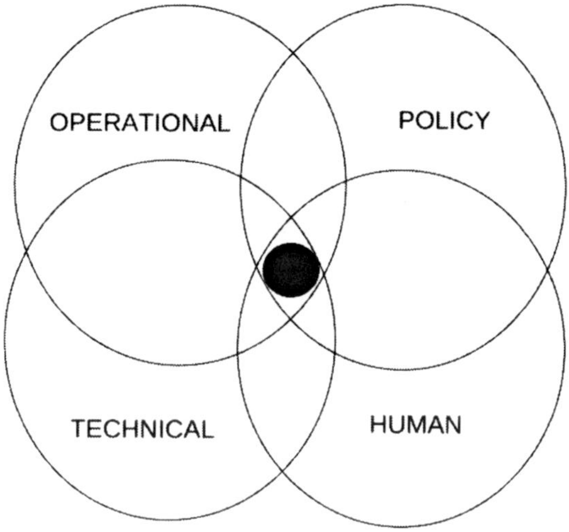

Numerous information security issues come to existence only if these factors are combined, as the intersection of the areas at the 'black security hole' in the centre of Figure 35 demonstrates. However, their contribution towards the flaw is typically uneven. Gauging this contribution correctly and determining which factors came first, can be a very difficult task. Is it human resources mismanagement, inappropriate policies, inaccurate guidelines, lack of knowledge, controls, attention or time? Is it a third party vendor's fault? Or, may be, a different and more secure solution should have been selected in the first place? User attacker skill vulnerabilities are commonly a result of sheer human incompetence or negligence. Nonetheless, it is not always clear who and at which level of corporate or organisational hierarchy, should bear the actual blame. In the majority of real-life situations it would be placed on subordinates by the management. However, if the true source of the problem has little to do with these subordinate's acts, it will persist, or similar security issues will appear. Finding a scapegoat does not make you more secure, and the attackers cannot care less.

Figure 36 is a version of Figure 35 redrawn in a traditional top-down hierarchical manner.

Figure 36: A top-down view of vulnerability origins

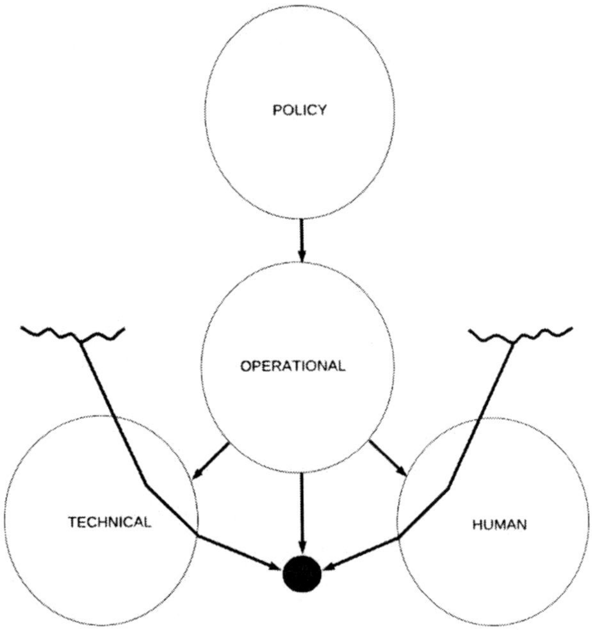

In accordance to this figure, strategic policy level faults negatively affect operations, processes and procedures. The problem is then propagated to technical and personnel levels, eventually producing vulnerability. When discussing the influence of top level policies on the actual combat,

Carl von Clausewitz noted that '*when people speak, as they often do, of the prejudicial influence of policy on the conduct of a war, they say in reality something very different to what they intend. It is not this influence but the policy itself which should be found fault with. If policy is right, that is, if it succeeds in hitting the object, then it can only act on the war in its sense, with advantage also; and if this influence of policy causes a divergence from the object, the cause is only to be looked for in a mistaken policy*'.

He has summarised this issue by stating '*it is only when policy promises itself a wrong effect from certain military means and measures, an effect opposed to their nature that it can exercise a prejudicial effect on war by the course it prescribes*'. Replacing 'military' by 'technology means' or 'human resources measures', and 'war' by 'information security' in the above quote, produces an accurate picture of common policy faults. In addition, the 'influence of policy' can be referring to its upholding processes and operations, thus generating a scheme very similar to Figure 36.

More often than not, investigating the initial source of a major security problem can pinpoint relevant operational level weaknesses. Consider how many security flaws are produced by poor processes of access and change control, background verification, patch, upgrade, configuration or vulnerability management, software development life cycle, etc. Such operational inadequacies can result from:

1 *Defective strategic security programmes, standards, policies, etc.*
2 *Negligence in implementing and maintaining the proper ones.*
3 *A combination of 1 and 2.*

The auditors should review all relevant documentation and processes to distinguish between these reasons. However, when searching for the vulnerability cause in a black box assessment it is frequently impossible to determine whether it is a wrong security policy, standard or programme, or a correct one which was not properly implemented and enforced. This should be reflected in the report conclusions, alerting the auditee team and letting them discover the truth themselves.

What if the origins of vulnerability cannot be established, even though the assessment has supplied reasonably accurate data to do so? In our observations, such situations usually apply to either technical or human security issues. Hence, two arrows that cross into these areas from the external 'great unknown' on Figure 36. If the skill level required to exploit the 'unknown source vulnerability' is very high, than it is a likely case of a dedicated ingenious attack 'creating a gap' in otherwise sufficient defences. What if it isn't? What if an easy-to-exploit, yet unknown or unclear origins vulnerability is discovered? There could be two feasible explanations for such an event. The first is the interference of pure chance. Even the most well-protected systems and security-conscious people are not invincible to accidental errors. In such occasions, the flaw completely falls out of pattern of an otherwise secure entity. Thus, it is reasonably straightforward to determine and attribute to friction.

The second possibility is sometimes observed in technical information security when an idiosyncratic, totally unexpected 0-day vulnerability is discovered. This is followed by quick release of an easy-to-use exploit (or a worm!) utilising such flaw before suitable countermeasures are available. It is likely that the very first '419' SPAM mails or other unaccustomed social engineering attempts had a similar impact. Such situations closely mirror medical epidemiology. When a totally novel virulent organism is encountered by its first human hosts with zero immunity to this threat, a lethal pandemic could occur. Black Death and smallpox attest that with gloomy perfection. In essence, these events clearly fall under the 'black swan' category.

We have already discussed dealing with chance and the obnoxious black birds, via employing rapid adaptability and effective containment based upon sound defence-in-depth. If the entity is properly protected, unexpected errors and novel means of attack can degrade its estimated overall security state to 'Insufficiently Secure'. However, they should not make it 'Insecure'. For instance, assailants might obtain highly confidential data utilising a 0-day exploit only to discover that it is strongly encrypted and cracking the key would take a million years or so. At the same time, the monitoring system generates alarms which trigger appropriate incident response and recovery actions. When the audit report conclusions related to this subject are produced, it is reasonable to elaborate that the vulnerability which allowed the breach exists due to error of chance, or cannot be effectively protected against at the moment. It is not a result of any systematic security fault, whether strategic, operational or tactical, policy, process, technology or human. Then, the conclusions should address the observed containment measures sufficiency (or lack of thereof).

Formulating the strategic conclusions

Drawing the deductions on strategic, high-level issues uncovered by security testing is probably the highest point of the Conclusions chapter and its key input to the Executive Summary of the report. This subject was already touched upon when investigations of vulnerability origins were outlined. Other major hands-on assessment elements that provide a strong contribution towards its strategic conclusions are:

- Generation and dissection of the summary of risks.
- Recognition and analysis of likely attack scenarios.
- Discernment of patterns formed by vulnerabilities, security weaknesses and gaps.
- Comparing the outcome of the current and previous security assessments.

If the security audit itself is directed at the evaluation of policies, standards, procedures, processes and so on, its whole conclusions are already dedicated to strategic (or, at least, operational) matters. Alternatively, different ISMS reviews can accompany technical or social engineering tests or, indeed, be triggered by them. In the latter case, they constitute a critical component of the follow-up action. *Where possible, the outcome of hands-on tests should be correlated with existing security documentation, processes and programmes.*

Scenarios of attacks, character and distribution of risks and their underlining security flaws, provide potent indicators of high-level areas plagued by strategic faults. As an example, a single access control vulnerability can be safely attributed to friction. A dozen of such flaws signifies that access control policies are absent, inappropriate, or completely neglected. If these gaps are evenly distributed, this is clearly the case. However, if they tend to concentrate within a single department, most likely the relevant policies are there, but the specific responsible personnel are unable to implement or enforce them.

Furthermore, compare the distribution of risks and corresponding types of security flaws between different systems (e.g. servers, workstations, network appliances) or employee positions and roles. Then do the same for the relevant operations and processes. Are there apparent gaps which are peculiar for any of the selected categories? What about the attack scenarios? Some elements and processes will be more engaged in their execution. Can it be due to weaknesses of relevant policies, guidelines, standards and programmes? Which particular areas of the above are more likely to be involved? Generate conclusions stating that a certain group of employees, class of systems, or a particular process are proven to be susceptible to a specific attack approach or vulnerability type. Supplement them with educated guesswork, explaining why it could be so.

The conclusions of the report could also elaborate on the high-level issues nature, rather than just the spheres affected. This is where our observations of various general strategic deficiencies can become helpful. They start as early as the Introduction, where the pitfalls of the prevalent cataclysmic approach to information security are outlined. Many of the strategic flaws can be deduced from the Chapter 1 fundamentals, or are outlined in its further discussions of aggressive defence and counteroffence. Finally, Chapter 2 is fully dedicated to such issues. Now it is a good time to revisit it. If you are a human resources or technical security specialist who found Chapter 2 to be of little relevance for your everyday work, perhaps this ongoing discourse will change your mind. We shall briefly review typical security strategy blunders to assist in forming relevant conclusions of the assessment report.

It cannot be overemphasised, that all information security plans, implementations and acts must correspond to the business aims, operations, models and procedures. Lack of such correlation can be manifested on lower levels by major usability versus security conflicts, important business infrastructure elements and processes being inadequately protected, impact of significant business changes on security being totally ignored, etc. Information security auditors should notice such an apparent discord and comment on it in the report's executive summary and conclusions.

Effective information security programmes must be present and carried out to full completion unless some dramatic shift of circumstances occurs. They should be continuous without any major interruptions, reinforced by a strong vision, and centred upon clear mission statements and goals as potent rallying points. Successive regular security assessments can determine whether this is the case. In fact, they are a form of monitoring the ongoing security programmes via evaluating their practical outcomes. An abrupt degradation of the overall auditee security state signals an important security programme failure. Analysing the specific factors that have contributed to such degradation can pinpoint which security programme has failed, and where. Besides, regular security audits can comment on the risks treatment tempo. Remember, that we need to get ahead of the opposition. Persistent, organisation-wide sluggish reaction to the uncovered security issues is a major strategic problem. Incomplete, or insufficient reaction, is a fault of security programmes that deal with risks and vulnerabilities management.

Failures of strategic security programmes and processes can be explained by bad planning and organisation, and resulting separate components desynch. The desynchronisation might originate from lack of, or ineffective, vertical and horizontal communications between departments, teams and separate employees. We have already covered this subject in Chapter 2: revisit Figure 7 and its corresponding discourse, then contemplate the sections dedicated to the top-down approach and its shortfalls. A thorough ISMS audit must detect and analyse such problems. Its conclusions should elaborate what is disorganised, desynchronised or amiss (Figure 7 should help). However, even the tactical level, hands-on assessments can indicate the presence of these strategic faults. Why does such a discrepancy between security risks faced by different large components exist? Is it related to the same or different processes? Were the results of the audit communicated to all members of staff that should be involved? How and by whom was the assessment handled? What about the follow-up reactions to the previous audit? If its specific technical recommendations were followed, but their policy and security management counterparts weren't, why is it so? An opposite situation is also possible. Search for the likely explanations on all levels: they must go into the report conclusions.

Lack of effective communication and organisation-wide propagation of the same security flaw with clear internal strategic origins, are potential signs of what we have dubbed 'the autocratic control and drill-machine approach'. Another good indicator is mitigating tactical, but not operational or strategic, vulnerabilities, weaknesses and gaps uncovered by the previous audit. The 'bottom' was not heard by the 'top' and bears all the responsibility and blame. This issue is difficult to reflect in the assessment conclusions and can be uncomfortable for many. Nevertheless, if it is detected, it must be described.

The next large set of strategic security faults can be grouped under the banner of unbalanced, or inordinate defences. The general term we have used to underline such situations is the 'Maginot Line mentality'. Of course, it is not feasible to state 'you demonstrate a typical Maginot Line mentality' in the assessment report conclusions. They are more likely to elaborate that 'the uneven defences coupled with insufficient defence-in-depth means are apparent'. Or, perhaps, that 'the listed information security elements are overemphasised at the expense of the following equally important areas, which creates exploitable security gaps'. Lack of defence-in-depth is a very common representation of the problem. However, the perimeter line defences can also suffer from it. This tends to happen because *the boundaries of the information security zone are not properly understood.*

There could be a variety of reasons behind the unbalanced state of defences, reflected through strategic, operational and tactical planes. It could be a belief in some sort of a panacea, whether technical, human or operational, that should instantly resolve the lion's share of information security headaches. The 'shiny box with flashing lights mindset' outlined in Chapter 2 of this book is an instance of it. 'The narrow compliance-centric approach' described in the same chapter can also be the source of the issue. If the areas or methodologies not covered by specific regulatory or compliance requirements are ignored, in order to dedicate all effort to satisfying these demands, they will remain, or become vulnerable. To summarise, practically all situations in which we have encountered the unbalanced defences, involved gross misunderstanding of information security fundamentals. This makes this issue strategic by its very nature. Evidently, the real lines of defence of any level and type cannot represent a homogeneous monolith. However, their unevenness must be based upon calculated analysis and treatment of risks, not misconceptions and lack of knowledge!

Finally, organisation-wide deficiency or poor quality of appropriate security documentation also constitutes a strategic flaw that must be noted in the assessment report conclusions. Not documenting information security intent, directives, standards, processes, procedures, methodologies and means, signifies crass deficit of consistency and is a glaring form of negligence. At the end of the day, security documentation of any kind is an important formal way of communication. As emphasised several times in this book, lack of effective communication could lead to the formation or retention of gaps, and is a security weakness *per se*.

Determining the character of strategic faults is a more complex business than pinpointing that, for instance, the change control process is unsafe or proper in-house secure software development guidelines should be introduced. In the majority of cases, a thorough internal security audit which includes detailed ISMS review is required. However, the above discussion highlights that at times the presence and nature of such problems can be effectively deduced by analysing results of specific technical or human security tests. The earlier schemes in Figures 8 and 9 provide general illustrations of such assessments contribution towards accomplishing this intricate task.

On audit recommendations and follow-up reaction

'The essence of the problem is to select a promising course of action with an acceptable degree of risk and to do it more quickly than our foe.'

MCDP 1 *Warfighting*

The suggestions on treating all uncovered risks can appear in several parts of the assessment report. Advice on specific remediation of separate security flaws must constitute a part of the vulnerability description. More general and strategic recommendations, as well as any suggestions on dealing with complex vulnerabilities and compound risks, should go into the conclusions. Treatment of security weaknesses and gaps that do not make a fully-blown vulnerability on their own, could also be described there, especially if they are related to compound risks or play a significant role in any of the attack scenarios. Just like the scenarios part, if the general remedial advice is too extensive, it might form a chapter on its own that finishes the report. Alternatively, lengthy descriptions of mitigating specific security issues can be included in a separate dedicated appendix.

In technical and social engineering assessment reports, all per-vulnerability remedies are 'tactical' and typically do not correlate with each other. Their descriptions must be brief, but very precise. If a configuration change is needed, a suggested configuration line should be supplied. If it is a question of patching or update, a secure version of the application or patch must be stated. In social engineering reports, what should be corrected first to prevent the specific attack against the given target has to be outlined. Recommendations like 'provide security awareness training for the finance department personnel' are far too general and should go into the conclusions. Wider scope technical suggestions, such as 'consider installing an application layer firewall' should be treated in a similar manner, as they address multiple vulnerabilities at once.

Delivering a risk reduction plan

Whether the assessment is directed at ISMS, people or technology, its strategic recommendations should include a basic risk reduction plan. This is the approach advocated by the OCTAVE methodology. It constitutes an integral part of the OCTAVE risk evaluation Phase 3. This plan must be priority-centred. Time is essential: it is better to eliminate the most critical vulnerabilities now than all uncovered security flaws in a few weeks. To prioritise the remedies for risks belonging to the same level, review these risks constituents. While all high risk problems must be dealt with ASAP, those which are easier to abuse and fix should have higher priority than their harder-to-exploit-or-eradicate counterparts. If doubts remain, revisit the descriptions of various modifiers in the per-vulnerability risk evaluation section of the previous chapter. For a specific situation, one or few of these modifiers can prove helpful.

Ideally, a risk reduction plan should aspire to eliminate the actual sources of risks and address multiple issues at once. This commonly means correcting strategic, or at least operational, shortfalls. However, dealing with such high-level issues can take a rather extensive period of time while being both effort and resource-consuming. The detailed recommendations on how to do it can make the plan unnecessarily complex and even create confusion. Thus, subscribing to '*a good plan violently executed now is better than a perfect plan executed next week*' MCDP 1

Warfighting motto is a very sensible idea. So, what makes a good risk mitigation plan to include within a security assessment report?

Firstly, it should be concise. Then, it should have clear priority and risk treatment sequence marking. Consider the following theoretical example of such a plan:

1. Eliminate high risk vulnerabilities A and B.
2. Eliminate medium risk vulnerabilities C and D.
3. Eliminate low risk vulnerability E, since it can be used to enhance the exploitation of C and D.
4. Low risk vulnerabilities F and G can be retained until more critical flaws are eradicated.
5. The set of security policies N is strongly related to vulnerabilities A, B, D and F. It is either flawed, or not properly enforced. Review N, its supporting documentation and the implementation processes.
6. Fully upgrading or replacing the large component X is expected to eliminate vulnerabilities A, B, C, D and F, as well as prevent any similar security issues in the future. Deploying safeguards Y and Z would have the same effects.
7. We suggest performing the next security audit when all security problems described in this report are corrected.

The hypothetical vulnerability E is a part of a compound risk. It is either a component of a Systempunkt together with C and D, or constitutes a Nebenpunkt in relation to them. Thus, it has a higher priority than F and G, in spite of formally belonging to the same per-vulnerability risk level. Point 5 of the sample plan is strategic in nature and can address multiple vulnerabilities at once. Point 6 could be a consequence of the previous point spanning into operational and tactical planes. By all means, it will require at least amending the relevant guidelines upon the implementation.

Following the suggestions of 5 and 6 can do more than simultaneous *extirpation* of several serious flaws. It can prevent similar problems from happening hereafter. This is highly desirable. However, reviewing a set of security policies with all relevant downstream guidelines, manuals, procedures and processes is time-consuming. Correcting all the uncovered errors, especially those of practical implementation, is likely to take even more time. It is also evident that the solutions outlined by point 6 are not instantaneous and easy to deploy. Otherwise, taking into account the advantages they provide, these solutions would have had a higher preference than the specific 'tactical' recommendations of points 1-4. In the example situation, the suggestions of point 6 would require additional planning, budget allocation, a pilot study, applicable personnel training, etc. In the meantime, the tactical remedies for all critical vulnerabilities must be applied ASAP according to the priorities set forth by the plan.

In the words of Clausewitz, '*if we quit the weak impressions of abstract ideas and descend to the region of practical life, then it is evident that a bold, courageous, resolute enemy will not let us have time for wide-reaching skilful combinations, and it is just against such a one we should require skill the most. By this it appears to us that the advantage of simple and direct results over those that are complicated is conclusively shown.*' According to John Boyd, strategic OODA loops spin slower than their tactical counterparts. We need to get inside the opponent's OODAs in order to win. In fact, many attackers do not have any strategies whatsoever. Possessing something they don't, gives the defenders a strong advantage in the long run.

Nevertheless, it is absolutely necessary to defeat the immediate adversaries on the tactical plane first.

An important element of the sample plan point 6 is suggesting two different solutions, thus giving the auditee some choice and manoeuvring space. Whenever the valid comparable alternatives exist, they should be suggested side by side. The differences between them should be briefly outlined, which could be done in the appropriate report appendix, or even during a post-audit presentation or debrief. This is one of the reasons why vendor-independent auditors ought to be preferred. Even if one remedy provides more advantages, or addresses the problem better from the auditor's viewpoint, the auditee selection can be influenced by a plethora of factors. These can include:

- The budget considerations.
- Company politics and vendor preferences.
- Internally available skills.
- Estimated implementation time and effort.
- Regulatory and compliance issues.
- Compatibility with other elements, including those of partner companies or organisations.
- Third party (e.g. service providers) relationships.

The auditors should explain why they think the suggested solution A is preferable, as compared to B and C, but the final word belongs to the responsible auditee management. As a technical instance of such a situation, eradicating and preventing security flaws of a complex critical internally developed Web application, is better than deploying an application layer firewall/IPS. However, it could require a major overhaul of the existing software development cycle, extensive additional training, and even hiring a dedicated full-time software security specialist. This is a long process, which may not have sufficient funds allocated to it until the next accounting year begins. In the meantime, a properly configured and maintained application layer firewall might well do the job, while meeting the financial circumstance. It is also relatively quick to acquire and deploy.

The final, seventh point of the example plan, advises to perform a similar security audit after the reported flaws are eliminated. This highlights the role of information security assessments as a form of quality control. Every security audit should carry a seed of the next assessment within. The previous section of this chapter argues that apart from being an effective tool of security monitoring, regular auditing enables discovery of important strategic security issues which cannot be deduced otherwise. Nonetheless, security assessments might fall out of the pre-planned schedule. Usually, this happens when demanded by change control procedures because major changes took place. It can also occur if an additional assessment constitutes a part of the follow-up reaction and its risk reduction plan. It could be suggested to verify that all discovered critical flaws are fully rectified without additional risks being introduced. Such recommendation typically applies to situations in which the overall security state is determined as 'Insecure' and the problems are hard to eliminate.

Quite frequently, we suggest that the black box assessment should be followed with a logical grey box sequel. Or, that the successful external audit should be supplemented by future internal tests. This relates to evaluating defences-in-depth and discovering the sources of security issues which are not clear from the current assessment's outcome. In a similar manner, the auditors might recommend that the specific technical, premises or human tests should come next after the ISMS-centric reviews. Or vice versa. Whether to follow such advice or not, is of course, up to the responsible auditee management.

Post-audit assistance and follow-up hurdles

Aside from the future scheduled or auxiliary assessments, after the report is submitted the auditors might participate in a variety of activities directly related to the accomplished tests or information security reviews. The most obvious ones are briefings and presentations, typically dedicated to:

- Explaining to the auditee representatives all matters they find unclear in the report.
- Giving a more technical or management-oriented overview of findings.
- Discussing the recommended remedies and the risk reduction plan.

The latter might lead to a request for assistance from the assessors, who are often more experienced at the suggested solutions than the auditee team. Or, at times, they can recommend a suitable third party that is a true expert on the matter. Any follow-up remediation work by the auditors is usually done for an additional charge, although it might be previously agreed as part of the expected service covered in the contract.

In our experience, the subject frequently brought up during such presentations and debriefs is deciding which risk treatments should be applied to the specific discovered risks. Which risks can be completely eradicated or partially reduced giving the available resources, time and expertise? What about those that can be retained, and is it really safe? If any risks are transferred, how could it be done and to whom? To summarise, the auditee team might not be sure regarding the precise course of the follow-up reaction and may need some help in making their decisions. This happens even when the risk reduction plan is to the point and general suggestions on how to deal with various risks are provided within the report conclusions.

For a cautious mind, it is natural to verify all critical information one more time before any important decisions are made. When the volume of such information is high and its content is rather complex, it is easy to get stuck at the second 'O' of the OODA loop. Besides, the auditee might have a different view of the situation, including the priority of some risks and their corresponding remedies, whether tactical or strategic. Before such differences between both sides are effectively resolved, the follow-up acts are unlikely to receive their go ahead. The auditors should aspire to understand financial, political and other factors that affect the other side. They should be ready to compromise, unless it would lead to retention, or increase the likelihood of emergence of serious vulnerabilities and high-level risks. The applicable wisdom from MCDP 1 *Warfighting* is '*as a basis for action, any decision is generally better than no decision*'.

There are several issues both the auditors and the auditee have to be careful with when solutions for the uncovered problems are considered and prioritised. One such dilemma is balancing the competing risks. In this book we are naturally concerned with information security risks and their reduction. However, a challenge might arise when acts directed at dealing with this important matter create other, security unrelated risks at the same time. Then the risks collide, and the auditee is left at a crossroads, having to weigh the competing risks against each other, prior to deciding on the remedial and other security-enhancing measures and means.

The *resource-related risks* (budget, but also working hours, level of effort and resources of systems and networks) are the most commonly cited instance of risks that have to be gauged against their security counterparts. The subject was contemplated thousands of years ago, when ancient Chinese strategist Mei Yaochen wrote that '*the more defences you induce your enemy to adopt, the more impoverished your enemy will be*'. On the technical side, there were times when introducing certain security measures, such as strong encryption, could put an unacceptable strain on servers, workstations and network appliances. Nowadays, this issue still persists in relation to embedded devices and RFIDs security. Besides, even the powerful servers can experience shortfalls of internally generated entropy. The entropy here refers to random numbers collected by an operating system or a specific application for use in cryptography. If it is depleted, the process of encrypting can become painfully slow and lead to serious service availability issues. To rectify this problem, the affected systems have to be upgraded, or external hardware sources of randomness acquired. If we are talking about a large-scale installation, this could be quite costly. Is there a budget for it? This is a good example of technical details that are unlikely to be uncovered in the process of assessment, but should be taken into consideration when the suggested security solutions are reviewed.

Systems, services and applications usability can be viewed as a type of productivity-related resource. If the suggested countermeasures or safeguards reduce usability below a certain level acceptable for the auditee employees, they become self-defeating. Thus, it is feasible to talk about competing *usability risks*. Note, that such risks are relevant for operations and processes, not just the technology. If improving the security of a process makes it too complicated, with far too many complex steps for its users to go through, its usability risks can easily outweigh their security counterparts. Besides, sophisticated processes are more error-prone. The similar principles pertain to important security documentation, especially manuals and guidelines. As the end result, the auditee friction goes up, which is completely the opposite of what a security assessment and its follow-up reaction should aspire to achieve. Again, the auditors can only guess which usability requirements are reasonable for the auditee employees, until this subject is brought up by post-assessment discussions.

Another competing risk which has to be frequently considered when follow-up actions are reviewed is the *risk of delay*. Here it refers to the downtime of systems, services, networks or processes, due to the treatment of security risks. It can cause productivity losses, employee and customer dissatisfaction, and other unpleasant effects. Essentially, *availability becomes the enemy of security instead of being its integral part*. The risk of delay is highly likely to arise if the evaluated vulnerabilities remedies are categorised as 'Non-existent' or 'Temporary', or are difficult to implement. It can be reduced by thorough pilot studies employing appropriate testing environments. *The more refined the processes and procedures of change control are, the lower is the risk of delay*. Take note that implementing strategic security improvements in practice can introduce significant delay risks. However, since doing it is typically a lengthy gradual operation, good foresight and advanced planning can help a lot. For instance, important processes or parts of infrastructure can undergo major overhauls at the periods when it will put minimal strain on business, such as during the holiday seasons.

The last subject that needs to be considered in this section is the balance between remedies, countermeasures and safeguards of different types. As previously emphasised, effective solutions for security problems can lie within the different areas. This is especially true when the roots of security flaws are eradicated. Resolving a technical issue can belong to the sphere of personnel management and involve training, disciplining, reassigning or hiring the responsible employees. Human security shortfalls can be addressed via technology, such as deploying more efficient authentication and monitoring systems, or improving existing channels of communication. Information security of various processes commonly includes both human and technological elements and can correct, or be corrected, by them. When both per-vulnerability and more general or strategic remedies are taken into account, risk treatment recommendations provided within the majority of audit reports will affect several areas at the same time. The sample risk treatment plan we have reviewed can apply to both technical and social engineering vulnerabilities alike. It also covers security policies and their downstream documentation. No doubt, all corresponding processes will also be influenced.

It is vital that all areas that pertain to reduction of the discovered risks receive due attention and effort. This is why it is so important that all relevant specialists of the auditee participate, if not in the process of assessment, but at least in its follow-up acts. For example, if a social engineering-centric audit report suggests using specific technologies to rectify the evaluated problems, the corresponding technical specialists must be invited to review and contemplate its summary, recommendations and results. In a similar manner, if a technical assessment indicates a clear necessity of personnel management-related measures, participation of the Head of Human Resources or other appropriate HR department representatives is a must. Ignoring any risk treatment areas or concentrating on a single one at the expense of the others, is an instance of the strategic unbalanced, or uneven defences fault, addressed in this chapter's previous section.

Overreliance on purely technical means is a very common error. On the one hand, 'those who cannot deploy their machines effectively are in trouble' (Du Mu). On the other hand, MCDP 1 *Warfighting* has a perfect summary of this approach's shortfall:

- *There are two dangers with respect to equipment: the overreliance on technology and the failure to make the most of technological capabilities. Better equipment is not the cure for all ills; doctrinal and tactical solutions to combat deficiencies must also be sought. Any advantages gained by technological advancement are only temporary for someone will always find a countermeasure, tactical or itself technological, which will lessen the impact of the technology. Additionally, we must not become so dependent on equipment that we can no longer function effectively when the equipment becomes inoperable.*

When selecting the technical remedies for any uncovered security flaws, the auditors should contemplate using the capabilities of the existing systems and applications first, and consider deploying any additional safeguards second. Where appropriate, a thought to what will happen if the suggested safeguard 'becomes inoperable' is ought to be given. *Thus, the recommended security solutions should contain an element of redundancy.* This principle might apply to non-technical recommendations just as well. The fact that the suggested technology-centric measures cannot substitute their concurrent non-technical counterparts (or vice versa!) could be highlighted in the report conclusions.

Finally, whether the advised risk treatment means are technical, human, operational or strategic, engage the auditee to find out which actions *that lead to elimination of high risk vulnerabilities* can be done right away. As the old boxing proverb states, 'the fastest with the mostest is the bestest'. By identifying and immediately utilising the elements of remedial actions and solutions that are effective at preventing serious attacks, yet require little time to accomplish, the defenders can outrun their adversaries, despite having a complex and large structure to protect. '*Some win through speed, even if they are clumsy*' (Cao Cao). This constitutes a key method of 'getting inside the opponent's OODA loop'.

CHAPTER 8: REVIEWING SECURITY ASSESSMENT FAILURES AND AUDITOR MANAGEMENT STRATEGIES

'The essence of strategy is not to carry out a brilliant plan that proceeds in steps; it is to put yourself in situations where you have more options than the enemy does.'

Robert Greene

Even if you studied and comprehended everything said in this and other relevant sources on information security auditing, everything can still go blatantly wrong. There are always some inevitable influences of chance, human error, technical fault and environmental pressures. Because of the latter, quite often both the auditee and the auditors have to make important decisions on the basis of insufficient information and in a very limited timeframe. This might lead to a variety of shortcomings on both sides, which can easily amplify their net negative effects when synchronised. As a result, a security audit or, even worse, successive series of security assessments could become a complete failure. To understand and know what needs to be done is one thing. To implement it properly is an entirely different matter. Especially, if it involves numerous people, complex processes, sophisticated technologies and unfavourable circumstances.

An information security assessment is unsuccessful when:

1. *It does not address critical security issues of the auditee.*
2. *It fails to produce proper evaluation of individual risks and the overall information security state.*

3 *The follow-up reaction is insufficient, incorrect or simply absent.*

In our observations, point 1 is more often the auditee fault. This is the reason behind dedicating an entire chapter to pre-assessment planning and preparations, including the initial gap analysis. These are not straightforward, easy to perform tasks. The auditee team should not be ashamed to ask their auditors, or any other third party, to assist with the preliminary gap analysis if in doubt. Spending additional money saves on the audit itself. It ensures that the right things will be done. Nevertheless, in any black box assignments that do not have a pre-defined set of targets (alas, they may have a desirable trophy), the responsibility of identifying and prioritising security issues is transferred to the auditors in full. Thus, it is a good option to consider if for some reason performing a decent pre-assessment gap analysis presents certain difficulties.

Point 2 is usually blamed on the auditors, since this is what they are expected to deliver. In the majority of cases such reproach is entirely justified, unless there was a clear lack of co-operation, or even obstruction at the auditee side. However, this problem could stem from inaccurate pre-assessment planning, that could pick the right targets but err when it comes to preferences of relevant methodologies. A typical example is subscribing for basic vulnerability scanning when in-depth penetration testing is required. Or, if a black box approach is embarked upon where its grey, or even white box equivalents are far more appropriate. Also, it is worth revisiting the 'audit the auditors' section of Chapter 4. Perhaps, if the auditors could not deliver a quality service, a different specialist team should have been scoped out in the first place.

In contrast, point 3 of the above is commonly viewed as the result of auditee carelessness, if not plain negligence and ignorance. However, if the auditors did not:

- Clearly communicate testing approaches and results
- Accurately prioritise risks
- Suggest realistic effective remedies
- Produce a workable risk reduction plan ...

it is senseless to accuse the auditee in not acting upon the assessment discoveries with precision and vigour.

To conclude, depending on a specific situation the actual responsibility for security assessment failures could be on any of the sides, or shared between both. The first four chapters of this book provided extensive coverage of the auditee perspective and some of the strategic fallacies they can fall prey to. In this chapter the issues faced by the auditors will be accented to restore the balance.

On information security assessment follies

'The influence of theoretical principles upon real-life is produced more through criticism than through doctrine, for as criticism is an application of abstract truth to real events.'

Carl von Clausewitz

A previous discourse has illustrated that dedicated attackers are able to create gaps by exploiting depth, breadth, or utilising a skilful combination of both approaches. Flawed information security strategies of the defenders could also produce gaps via insufficiencies related to depth (for instance, lack of suitable echeloned protection) and breadth (desynchronisation of security processes, countermeasures and safeguards). In both cases, these shortfalls disrupt the balance of defences producing their unjustified unevenness. A flawless security strategy (if such thing is actually possible in practice!) compels the opponents to look for weaknesses of implementation. That is, if the adversaries cannot counter the strategies, they are forced to attack the tactics. The auditors can encounter, and should be prepared for, a variety of such situations while discerning information security issues on all applicable levels.

However, the organisation and performance of security assessments by the auditors is, indeed, subjected to very similar problems. It is fascinating to observe that the strategic follies of the auditors often mirror those of the auditee companies or organisations! To remove any doubts, this discussion is not about information security issues faced by the auditors themselves. It is more akin to the reflections on 'weak points' of the attack structure and processes in the previous chapter's discourse of attack scenarios and trees. Security assessors have their share of strategic, operational and tactical failures that can turn any affected audit into a waste of resources, effort and time. We shall review them in a top-down order.

The fundamentals infringed

It is hard to provide a totally unbiased view of what the security audit shortcomings could be. Especially, after outlining how, according to our estimations and experience, the assessments should be done. The first method that immediately springs into mind when looking at the issue at the higher levels is to revisit the basic principles from Chapter 1 and see what can happen if they are violated. Where would it lead? Would it correspond to the actual failures we have observed in the past, including, perhaps, some of our own faults? Would you recognise any well-familiar problems in the following list of commentaries on the Chapter 1 fundamentals non-observance?

1 Breaking the first fundamental principle means not taking into account the strategic circumstance of the assessment.
2 Its second counterpart also addresses important lower level factors and conditions that cannot be ignored.
3 Violation of the third principle is reflected by failures to trigger appropriate follow-up reactions. Which, as previously discussed, could well be the auditor's fault.
4 The fourth 'incompleteness principle' brings up several critical subjects. One of them, the auditor's perfectionist attitude, was already discussed when the principle was outlined. It can be mirrored by the 'false perfectionism': thinking and announcing that the accomplished assessment is impeccable and nothing else could be done. This is likely to instil a false sense of security in the auditee and is a blatant misunderstanding of the assessment's limitations and scope. Note, that the imperfection of a security assessment is reflected in the suggested legal disclaimer that should open the audit report.
5 Breaking the fifth 'continuity principle' destroys the assessment's value as a mighty security monitoring tool and eliminates possibilities to deduce several important strategic security issues, as illustrated in the previous chapter's discourse on producing the audit conclusions.
6 Imbalance between the assessment tempo and depth signifies mismanagement and a clear lack of planning on the auditor's side.

7 A narrow mechanistic perception of the audit scope and aims ensures that the sources and roots of many uncovered security issues will not be discerned.
8 Any security problem is somehow related to ISMS shortfalls. If these relations are not contemplated, the ISMS will remain deficient.
9 In a similar manner, if the actual sources of security flaws are not discovered and addressed, the audit is not fully accomplished, and its suggested remedies and other risk reduction measures are incomplete.
10 If the underlining strategic shortcomings are not discerned and rectified, any proposed tactical solutions won't be more than a temporary patch.
11 Without the top level initiative, a security audit would be a purely mechanical exercise at its best. Any strategic, or even operational level advice, will not be implemented, or simply heard.
12 Without the corresponding initiative at the lower planes, the process of assessment will not be adequately supported, and its suggested remedies – properly implemented.
13 A failure of communicating the audit outcome to all auditee managers and specialists involved, means that important areas addressed by the assessment will be misunderstood or ignored.
14 If the audit has produced sophisticated, confusing and difficult to accomplish recommendations and plans, it could easily turn into a useless exercise. Citing Clausewitz, '*far from making it our aim to gain upon the enemy by complicated plans, we must rather seek always to be beforehand with him just in the opposite direction*'. The assessment should shed light on the auditee security state, not obscure it behind the hailstorm of ambivalent

descriptions and vague terminology. Unless absolutely necessary to rectify critical security flaws, any recommended risk reduction means should not make already complex processes and structures even more complicated.

15 A security audit properly executed, reported and explained has immense educational value for the auditee professionals. This aspect of information security assessments is frequently underestimated.

16 The fact that the descriptions of the audit outcome have to be clear does not mean that its results are black-and-white. Failures of risk analysis that stem from unaccounted factors and underestimated complexity of the entire situation, can easily lead to wrong conclusions and erroneous recommendations. The latter are particularly detrimental when it comes to remedial priorities and the risk reduction plan.

17 While it is 'better late, than never', still the earlier, the better. If information security assessments are one of the very few effective ways to get ahead of the opposition and even the negative chance, not utilising them as soon as favourable opportunities arise, can lead to troubles in the long run.

18 If security assessment conclusions and advice are clouded by any business or personal agendas of the auditors, they may not reflect the actual auditee security state and offer the most appropriate and effective remedies and solutions.

19 If the assessors are somehow bound to the auditee structures, systems, processes etc, it would be hard for them to 'think out of the box'. Such auditors are unlikely to discern security problems and solutions that the

auditee themselves cannot see. Which, in essence, defeats the whole purpose of the assessment.

20 Breach of the security audit confidentiality is a grand disaster.

How many of the listed points clearly assign the major blame to the auditee side? Point 5 is likely to do it, since the auditors are expected to be genuinely interested in providing regular services, if only for purely financial gain. Similar reasonings can apply to point 17. Although, an assessment not done in due time effectively responding to the auditee request, can be a fault of the auditor's management of timetables and multiple clients relations. Points 11 and 12 are also more of an auditee problem, even though they might equally apply to managing the auditor team. Besides, security assessors should aspire to generate interest and initiative in the auditee to support their effort. This leaves us with 16 points out of 20 where the responsibility for failure is, to a large extent, on the auditor's side.

To provide a concise summary of the aforementioned and related issues, the major high-level slips of security auditors frequently fall under the following categories:

- *Lack of strategic vision.*

On the one hand, it applies to not being able to discern all factors and circumstances that apply to particular security assessments, their actual requirements, scopes, targets, expectations and aims. Besides, the auditor company or team must have a continuous strategic programme of service improvement, of which all assessments are integral parts.

- *Desynchronisation.*

An assessment can be out of synch with what the auditee actually needs or can afford. The desynchronisation can relate to the targeted areas, depth, breadth, suitable risk reduction means, tempo and any specific (e.g. regulatory and compliance) needs and demands. There is also a potential problem of various audit processes being desynchronised within the assessor company or team.

- *Poor communication.*

The problems of communication can negatively affect all interactions between the auditors and the auditee, from the pre-assessment planning to post-report submission debriefs. It could also be an internal problem of the auditors, especially if the assessment involves specialists with different backgrounds, knowledge and skills.

- *Excessively formal approach.*

When the approach to security auditing is too formal, it can easily become perfunctory. By reducing initiative and suppressing creativity, it can transform any presumably active security assessment into a purely passive set of tasks. However, even the passive information security audits can also suffer from excessive formality. One has to be quite creative to generate quality checklists, or analyse results and produce high-level conclusions and recommendations for yet the most standard and streamlined tests. Points 7, 8, 9, 10 and even 16 of the fundamental shortcomings listed above, can be caused by the auditors being far too formal. In addition, unless the agreed conditions of the engagement strictly define all targets or even the testing methodologies to a minute detail, the auditors should not treat the auditee suggestions as bona fide formalists. Recall the earlier

Chapter 5 examinations of how different the critical points can be if viewed from the perspectives of the assessors and the assessed.

- *Bias, personal agendas and injurious politics.*

These factors can lead to non-observance of practically any fundamental information security assessment principles we have reviewed. Violation of the very last principle due to such reasons is particularly unsettling. They should never interfere with the assessment objectivity, veracity and effectiveness. If they do, earlier or later it will be discovered, disclosed and ruin the auditor's reputation. Disciplinary, legal, customer relations and other negative repercussions are highly likely to follow.

More often than not, these and other (e.g. skill and organisation-related) problems are caused by incompetent assembling and management of the auditor team. This subject will receive its share of coverage in the next section. But before that various tactical and implementation security assessment shortcomings have to be contemplated in brief.

Bad tactics and poor tests

From a vertical perspective, tactical assessment errors often originate from the strategic faults, like the ones we have just outlined. A horizontal view can be founded upon the corresponding lower levels OODA loops being incomplete or improperly executed. Often, this suggests badly designed and orchestrated testing processes. The lowest plane at which security audit blunders take place relates to a lack of specialist knowledge and skills. Of course, this problem does not materialise from thin air and signifies either insufficient or inappropriate training, misassignment, or poor personnel hiring practices.

In a tactical security assessment OODA the first 'O' stands for recon. The consequences of improper reconnaissance are quite obvious: missing the important targets and going after the wrong ones, or selecting inappropriate testing methodologies. Frequently, poor recon underlines a lack of an effective lateral approach. Metaphorically speaking, the auditors can spend days banging at the armoured front door while a window around the corner is wide open. In human security testing, there could be an obvious person who has what the social engineers want. However, that person is well aware of this fact, and is highly security conscious, vigilant and careful. At the same time, more vulnerable colleagues might have access to the very same trophy, even though it is not so apparent at first sight.

Selecting a wrong target by mistake can sometimes have highly negative legal consequences. Think what can happen if during the test a breach of data or system which was not authorised by the auditee and does not even belong to them occurs. Or a totally wrong person is approached by a social engineer. We have recently heard of such blunders in relation to wireless security assessments, in particular their client-side evaluation parts. The auditors can hook up a wireless-enabled laptop to a rogue access point, breach its security, and then discover that this computer actually belongs to an employee of a different company or a business visitor. When wireless security tests are performed for an auditee that shares a large office building with other organisations, errors of this nature are highly likely and should be watched for.

Another common situation that clearly relates to this obnoxious issue is evaluating security of hosted services with resources shared between numerous client entities. The growing popularity of virtualisation, clouds and SaaS dictates that any assessments of such installations must be done with the utmost care. In these environments, it is very easy to target and affect another company's data, service, or entire virtual system by mistake. Besides, the last thing any security auditors would want is to accidentally bring down a critical application or element of infrastructure used by thousands of organisations, out of which only a single one is the actual auditee. *We strongly suggest employing the grey box approach when hosted multi-user set-ups security is scrutinised.* At least, this should alleviate recon-related hardships.

Just like with any stage of a process OODA loop, it is possible to get mired at the reconnaissance phase. In fact, this is a very common misadventure. Always allow sufficient time for the tests while splitting it between different assessment milestones and preserving the needed balance between them. Reconnaissance can take plenty of time, however, it is rather predictable and can be thoroughly planned in advance. For instance, hands-on experience allows the auditors to estimate how long different portscans will take, or how quickly a sweeping social engineering mailshot is usually responded too. The same applies to physical and premises security checks, for as long as the approximate scope and scale of the assessment are known. The only exception that makes such planning rather difficult is fully black box assignments, with their range of targets not being initially known.

The next 'O' of our tactical OODA loop is orientation, based upon the reconnaissance results. At this critical testing process stage the appropriate targets, techniques and tools are opted *and prioritised.* Unless we are talking about the specific case of mutation fuzzing, throwing everything but a kitchen sink at the targets is a very ineffective approach. It is also highly noisy and intrusive, which can cause a variety of troubles, such as crashing the evaluated systems and their monitoring safeguards. Unfortunately, many technical security assessors do just that by pressing the big 'select all' button of all-purpose vulnerability scanning tools, without any regard to the target's nature estimated during the recon phase. On the other hand, good orientation allows one to decide which tests would be the most suitable in a given situation, and which are clearly out of place and should be discarded. Then the priorities of carefully selected tests and their targets can be decided. This saves the auditors time and reduces unnecessary testing intrusiveness-related risks.

Proper orientation applies to assembling and analysing the whole picture, as well as examining its minute details. Inability to do the former means that the correlations between different elements of a complex evaluated target are not deduced. Further down the testing path, the same problem would inevitably apply to connecting together the uncovered vulnerabilities, security weaknesses and gaps. Thus, any Systempunkt flaws will go amiss, proper attack scenarios creation will become impossible, and both the analysis of risks and the assessment conclusions will heavily suffer.

In respect to considering the details, a good observation phase is expected to produce a massive amount of data. It is the orientation that assigns its separate bits with the implied levels of importance. If such assumptions are wrong, some weighty components of the evaluated target can be treated as insignificant and not worthy of any further checks. Personal convictions of the auditors can heavily interfere with orientation and result in detrimental misjudgements. For instance, it is possible to treat certain types of applications, systems, appliances, employee roles, etc. as genuinely uninteresting, while in reality they might hold the keys to a successful breach, or become the sources of rather unpleasant passive security incidents. Hopefully, the previous discourse on the critical points and the strategic exploitation cycle can assist in streamlining orientation and avoiding common pitfalls that plague this stage of security assessments OODA loops.

The soundness and accuracy of decisions could be equally botched by specific preferences and dependencies of the auditors. In the beginning of Chapter 5 we highlighted that overreliance on a single general purpose vulnerability discovery tool is a folly. In a similar manner, it can apply to overreliance on a selected method, technique or even a skill set. This type of problem can be summarised under the banner of '*failures of adaptation*'. The so-called 'law of the instrument', or Maslow's hammer, states that 'if all you have is a hammer, everything looks like a nail'. We can reformulate it as 'if all you can use very well is a hammer, everything looks like a nail'. In fact, the first part can even be rephrased into 'if all you truly enjoy using ...'. This shifts the accent from the instrument to specific skills or personal preferences. Unfortunately, the surrounding reality has a limited number of nails, some of which could turn out to be screws under more close scrutiny. To aggravate the issue, it also contains highly precious objects artfully made of fine glass which are not particularly hammer-friendly.

Common sense dictates that differing situations demand dissimilar approaches. Thus, methodologies and techniques have to be adapted to the audit circumstances and the evaluated target's nature. Where necessary, new skills must be learned and testing instruments suitably modified. Even the purely passive security assessments presume accurate selection and timely update of all appropriate checklists and corresponding automated toolsets. Nonetheless, we have observed plentiful violations of these basic tenets. For instance, on numerous occasions exactly the same procedures, methods and tools are applied to external and internal, black and grey box security tests. What are the reasons behind it? 'We have acquired a great gimmick, so we have to use it.' 'We have honed this skill to perfection, so it must be applied.' 'It worked so well before, so why shouldn't it work now.' However, everything has its time and place that can be accurately determined by utilising proper 'OO' of the OODA loop.

Apart from various applications of the 'Maslow's hammer', there could be other misjudgements that can negatively affect the auditor's decisions. For example, unjustified preference might be given to approaches considered as orthodox, or unorthodox. As highlighted in the final section of Chapter 5, at times, simplistic and straightforward assessment techniques can be utterly neglected. Everyone knows that 'thou shalt not click on a suspicious URL link', right? Or, how secure passwords should be chosen – that's what the existing good password guideline is for. Of course, all users must have read this refined document and follow it to the point. Sometimes, a security problem lies on the very surface but ends up unnoticed. A far less critical issue is if the complex evaluation methodologies or instruments are avoided because they are viewed as too sophisticated for the likely attackers to use. However, are you sure that all potential adversaries share the same view?

Finally, if the 'OOD' part of the loop is flawless, the act should be seamless and smooth. In practice, it is not always so. When we discard the inevitable interference of human error and technical fault (or anything else clearly falling under the general category of 'chance'), what remains is either lack of hands-on experience or plain negligence. The former will go away with training and time. The latter shall require some form of reprimanding or other disciplinary action. However, if such dereliction persists, it is also the auditor team management fault.

On assembling and managing the auditor team

'The subordinate agrees to make his actions serve his superior's intent in terms of what is to be accomplished, while the superior agrees to give his subordinate wide freedom to exercise his imagination and initiative in terms of how intent is to be realised.'

Colonel John Boyd

The available sources that cover managing an information security auditing team are very limited and restricted to periodic or online publications. Perhaps, it is not considered to be an issue since such teams are usually somewhat limited in size. Or, when it comes to penetration testing or social engineering, it is expected that the group of testers consists of dedicated specialists driven, to a large extent, by sheer enthusiasm that provides cohesion and intent. At the same time, what we define as passive security assessments is often viewed as a mere mechanical routine. So, managing a team of such auditors is treated as 'business as usual' and does not sufficiently differ from running a typical group of office clerks. Spare, perhaps, for more in-depth background checks, since handling confidential client data is inevitable. This might, or might not be, the actual case. In our humble opinion, at least some elements of the auditor team creation and management should be reviewed and highlighted.

On the assessment team ordonnance

The composition of the auditor team is strongly determined by its mission and most likely assignments. The services offered can be highly specialised, e.g. source code security auditing, selected compliance or physical security checks. In a very specific, narrow field of knowledge this could even be a one-man job. However, more often than not, information security companies aspire towards the Jack-of-all-trades operating model, so that a wide variety of client requests can be answered. The same applies to internal security auditor teams of large corporations, although these have a tendency to lean towards attracting experts in solutions from selected vendors commonly used by the enterprise. If the major overhaul of the IT infrastructure occurs, such technical specialists can be re-trained or replaced.

A well-rounded Jack-of-all-trades security auditing team should at least have:

- *An application security specialist.*

In the current technical environments and market conditions this is an absolute requirement. Skilful application security consultants are typically security-oriented programmers capable of performing some reverse engineering work and writing (or modifying) the needed testing utilities.

- *A network security engineer.*

While this role is beneficial when running external technical assessments, for instance, in doing recon and evaluating security of remote access means, keep in mind that for their internal counterparts a good knowledge of network-centric security is a must. If there is no dedicated wireless security consultant in the team, a network security engineer must be able to handle these assignments as well. Another important area of testing that should be covered by these specialists is VOIP security assessments.

- *An expert in common technical safeguards, such as firewalls, IPS/IDS, monitoring and authentication systems, and VPNs.*

In a very small team this role might be appropriately shared between the network security engineer and the application security specialist. Alas, it pays to have a dedicated full-time professional, since the modern safeguards are both highly abundant and increasingly sophisticated. Notice, that apart from examining the safeguards, this specialist can play an important role when the advice on remedies and solutions for the uncovered security weaknesses, gaps and flaws is considered.

- *A social engineer.*

Basic social engineering tests over the Internet or telephone can be performed by other information security consultants. However, if human security evaluation assignments are complex and involve personal contact, it is advantageous to have several social engineers available. Perhaps, they could be hired from a known and trusted pool on a contract basis. The obvious problem with any visual or voice contact with the regular testing targets is that the auditee employees are likely to remember the social engineer and will not fall for her tricks again.

- *An ISMS specialist also versed in the areas of risk assessment, regulations, compliance and applicable laws.*

Apart from executing security management-centric audits like documentation and processes reviews, or assisting with any audit-related compliance issues, these professionals can be of great value when estimating risks and producing conclusions of lower level assessment reports. In addition, they make perfect negotiators with the auditee managers of all sorts, being able to speak their language and address their doubts and worries.

Thus, at the very minimum and if some of the listed critical roles are combined, a decent security auditing team must contain three-four full-time professionals highly skilled in the aforementioned areas. An individual person cannot absorb different spheres of competence without sacrificing their level of comprehension, proficiency and depth. If the auditor team is quite large and has narrowly focused experts (such as full-time security compliance consultants, malware specialists, wireless security engineers or dedicated vulnerability researchers) on board, shortfalls of effective communication between its members can become a rather demanding issue. Another obstacle that could easily arise is synchronising the testing procedures, processes, and their end results. A designated role of the audit team manager becomes a requirement for proper fulfilment of its purpose.

The discussion above is centred on the specialist competence and skill sets only. Nonetheless, there are more factors pertaining to the audit team structure and function that have to be taken into account. They relate to the auditor's natural cerebral capabilities and mindsets. Many years ago and in a place far away, one of the authors of this book played a popular team-based televised quiz game called the 'Brain Ring'. The official rules of the Brain Ring were as follows:

- The questions must be composed in a way that their answers could be guessed. Thus, it was not a direct knowledge exercise.
- It was played one team against another team, or two. A separate team consisted of six people.
- After a start signal, whoever's team pressed the button first and provided the correct answer, won a point.
- Otherwise, the right answer must be provided within a minute.
- If no one gave the correct answer, the next question followed.
- The team that scored a pre-defined amount of points first won.

So, the game required teams to deduce the right answer in the shortest time possible. It became apparent, that in order to gain the upper hand, the team must be structured and operating in a certain way (Figure 37).

Figure 37: The Brain Ring team organisation

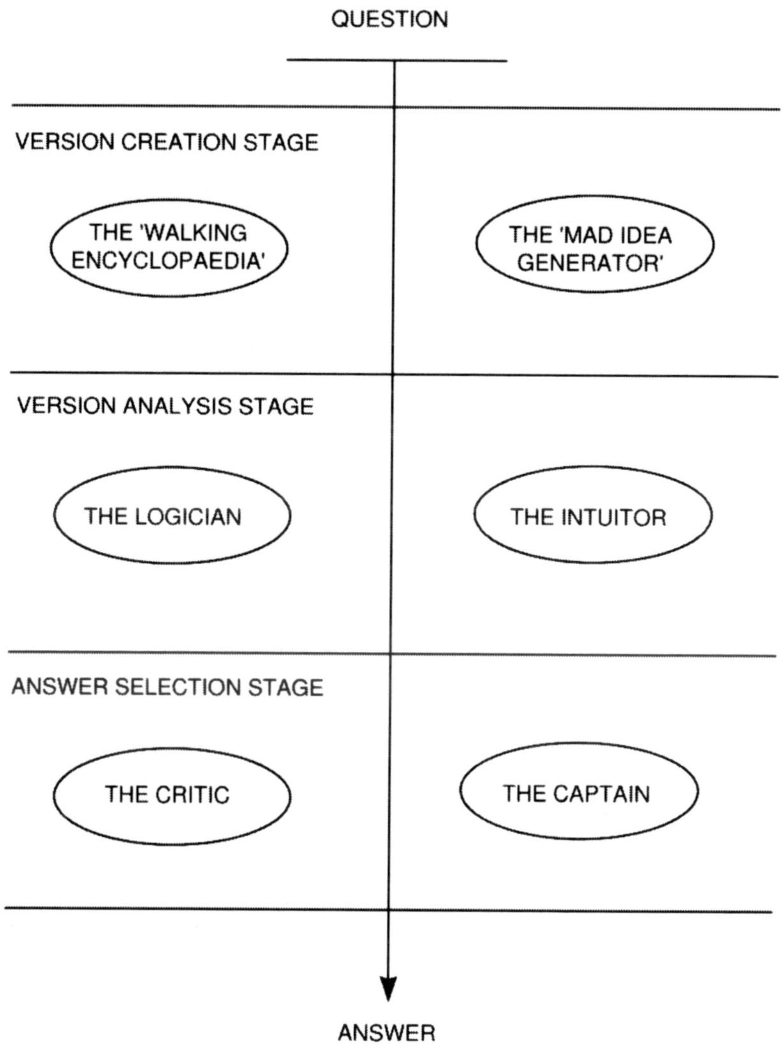

The answer generation process is split into three phases. At the first stage different versions of the answer are produced. If the relevant direct knowledge is available, the 'walking encyclopaedia' player supplies the most likely answer. However, if this is not the case, this player can still give some information potentially related to the question subject. The main attribute of the 'walking encyclopaedia' is, thus, an extensive and powerful memory. In contrast, the 'mad idea generator' is the player with the highest level of creativity and lateral, or unorthodox, thinking. It is the 'what if' person, the 'living fuzzer'. If no obvious version of a likely correct answer is in the air, the 'mad idea generator' can supply a wide variety of useful insights on what this answer might be. Obviously, such insights need further scrutiny. In fact, the 'walking encyclopaedia' is not flawless and could also err.

So, the next version analysis stage kicks in. The players with the strongest logical reasoning and intuition in the team apply their capabilities to the outcome of the first phase. Besides, they can also deduce or viscerally discern the answer themselves, especially if this outcome is highly inconclusive. At the end of the second answer generation stage, a few relatively refined versions can be produced. Then they are attacked by the critic – the most sceptical, incredulous and sober-minded member of the team. The critic finds flaws in the proposed answer variants and discards those which are clearly at fault. The final word belongs to the captain. This player decides:

- Which precise version of the answer will be given.
- How it will be formulated (badly worded answers can be rejected by the jury).

- Who will answer (this is important to satisfy the previous points).

The captain is usually the player who presses the button. He or she also oversees that the answer generation process runs smoothly and all members of the team have their say. It is the team manager, strategist and psychologist all in one breath. Typically, it was the captain that assembled the team in the first place.

To complete this 'Brain Ring interlude', notice that:

- The answer generation process we have described takes seconds to accomplish (or a minute at its best if the other team is indecisive or wrong).
- It forms a perfect OODA loop, with pressing the button and giving the answer for 'Act'. The aim of the game is to get inside the other team's OODA.
- The left and right sides of Figure 37 roughly correspond to what psychologists generally view as left and right human brain functions.

There is a lot that could be learned from it. Take Figure 37 and replace 'question' by 'the problem', and 'answer' by 'the remedy' or 'the solution'.

A very similar process with its stages and roles can be applied to many important information security assessment tasks, especially if handled by a group of professionals with similar areas and levels of expertise and skills. For example, it could be utilised when deciding upon the audit tactics, gauging risks, producing the assessment conclusions, contemplating the suggested remedies and generating the risk reduction plan. The described process is reusable, adaptable and flexible. As far as the auditor team goes, it might consist of three professionals only, or two dozen of them. Just like with the specialist skill sets, in a very small team an individual member can share several of the listed player roles. Its large counterpart might have a collective 'logician', 'intuitor', 'mad idea generator' (hence, the practice of group brainstorming) or 'critic'. There could be several 'walking encyclopaedias' in respect to different spheres of competence. However, to preserve *the unity of command* there should be only one 'captain'.

In his 'Avoiding the snares of groupthink: the command and control strategy' chapter of *The 33 Strategies of War*, Robert Greene provides sound advice on building and managing effective teams attuned to rapid and adaptable complex tasks. By the term of 'groupthink' he has referred to '*the irrationality of collective decision making'*, stating that *'the need to find a compromise among all the different egos kills creativity. The group has a mind of its own, and that mind is cautious, slow to decide, unimaginative, and sometimes downright irrational*'. We are aware of other definitions and descriptions of 'groupthink' in various management-related publications, but for the purpose of this discourse they are of no concern.

Since every bird likes its own nest, when specialists with very different areas of in-depth expertise and skills are intermixed into a single group, the problem is aggravated by the necessity to compromise between the professional views. Everyone would like to assign the highest priority and importance to their particular methods, targets and findings. Application security specialists will insist that the software flaws they have discovered should be addressed first in the report summary, conclusions, and the suggested risk reduction plan. Network security or social engineers might disagree. At the same time, an ISMS specialist could say 'all your discoveries are interesting and fine, however, this is what the auditee really need in order to be compliant to <insert the standard or regulation here>, and the compliance audit is looming'.

To give all members of the team their say, synchronise their approaches, operations and findings, produce well-founded prioritisation of risks, accurate assessment conclusions and apt risk reduction advice, a sole experienced and qualified 'final word authority' is necessary. Without such unity of command, chaos will inevitably reign. In the technical parlance, a situation of this kind is sometimes ironically referred to as 'design by committee'. This term implies poor results of insufficiently unified vision and divided leadership in 'let's get together and do the job that will please us all' projects. Remove the central OODA loop from the scheme depicted in Figure 7 and contemplate the likely repercussions. The auditors have their strategic processes too, even though they might not strictly conform to PDCA. As suggested by Robert Greene in relation to this highly critical issue, '*rely on the team you have assembled, but do not be its prisoner or give it undue influence*'.

Another advice he has provided is '*never choose a man merely by his glittering resume. Look beyond his skills to his psychological make up*'. This statement can have various interpretations. For instance, it might relate to verifying personal background and any related undesirable traits, like being particularly arrogant and conflict-prone, or unable to sustain serious commitments. Nonetheless, it might also be viewed in the light of the elaborated team-based answer or solution-seeking process. Apart from the required focused specialist skills, do you think that the auditor team needs the 'walking encyclopaedia', or the 'mad idea generator' types? Would it be more advantageous to get a 'logician', or someone who can sense the situation well, due to having a rich previous experience? Or, maybe the 'critic' is rather indispensable to assure the accuracy of security testing results and their interpretations? Do you require an independent creative thinker to participate in active security assessments, or someone more meticulous and persistent to handle their large-scale passive counterpart's routine?

Note, that these matters equally apply to both hiring people and assigning the already available professionals to perform the specific tasks. In the latter case, keep in mind that depending on the character of engagement, the discerned process roles can alternate. A 'walking encyclopaedia' in a particular area of expertise could make a great 'logician' in a somewhat different field. The 'logician' in one sphere of competence might make a perfect 'mad idea generator' in the other. Where necessary, the 'captain' may pull up the sleeves and do the job of a 'critic', or 'intuitor', or else. Taking notice of such 'situational artefacts' and utilising them when similar circumstances arise the next time, can tremendously expand the capabilities of the auditor team.

Of serpents and eagles

What about the more specific inclinations and traits of the relevant professionals and any influence these might exert on running an effective information security assessor team? Much was said about the so-called 'hacker mindset'. To summarise, it is usually described as the combination of unorthodox 'lateral' thinking with the 'disassemble and/or reassemble everything' attitude. Previously, we have highlighted that this approach can be applicable to a wide selection of information security auditing engagements. It is entirely possible to be quite 'hackish' at analysing the ISMS. Conversely, hands-on technical or social engineering testing, commonly viewed as 'the hacker playground', can be reduced to repetitive and methodical template chores. Notwithstanding, generating, correcting and modifying these templates could be quite a challenging and creative task. Thus, a 'hacker mindset' is generally desirable for an information security auditor and should be encouraged and looked for. However, when coupled with highly focused specialisation, it could have interesting side effects on the human mind.

For instance, such a combination frequently leads to what can be labelled as 'tunnelled lateral thinking'. This mindset is capable of generating rather ingenious ideas, but within the particular area limits and not without some contamination by the Maslow's hammer law. Because of the former, the latter influences and constrains are not realised, or even actively denied. Consequently, shrewd and hard-headed tacticians who are not very responsive to outside advice from anyone not matching their advanced degree of specialist expertise, are produced. These professionals surely know their job and do it well. At the same time, they do not like to be bothered by instructions and tend to treat strategic level inferences and intents as big and impractical words. This does not help in directing a highly skilled security assessor team where this way of thinking is clearly predominant. Which is often the case.

A popular notion regularly applied to handling a team of software developers, compares it to herding cats. If we attempted to write an article about managing a group of hardcore information security testing experts, we would probably entitle it 'How to herd serpents'.

A venomous snake is a highly evolved organism well-adjusted to its habitat. For an outside beholder its strike is swift and effective, but comprises somewhat limited options of movement. Unless the observer is an expert toxinologist, the complexity of the snake venom composition is completely eluded and not given deep thought. In reality, typical snake venom contains dozens of select components that specifically target any creature the snake can encounter in its natural milieu. All of them are also optimised to produce the exact desired effects, such as paralysing the prey in a given period of time. This can be compared to a dexterous and advanced attack toolkit, or a scrupulous collection of working exploits attuned to the likely target systems range. Combine it with the economy of action and formidable speed, and you shall penetrate the mystery of the snake.

However, to list the relevant allegoric issues:

- Generally, snakes do not hunt in packs (but zoologists say that some sea serpents do, so it is not impossible).
- Snakes have no outer ear and do not hear sounds travelling through the air well (however, they are not deaf – they have their very own way of hearing).
- They have a rather peculiar vision, often attuned to things up close while ignoring those 'irrelevant' far away objects.

Thus, anyone who would want to collaborate with the metaphorical serpents would have to develop distinct communication ways that appreciate their specificity.

In contrast, the power and sweep of the eagle eye, amalgamated with the ability to reach high attitudes, has earned it a well-deserved place in the very beginning of this book's Introduction. We used it to illustrate the strategic connotations of the 'bird's eye view' idiom. At the same time, an eagle has a wide variety of striking options combining its beak, claws and wings. It is also just as swift as any snake could be. What it lacks is highly specialised venom that our serpents possess. Besides, when objects are covered by thick darkness the eagle's sight strongly deteriorates. Snakes have their own 'technical' method of detecting important objects in the dark – they sense their temperature. A far-sighted and soaring, but not highly focused on the minute technical details strategist within the team of more field-specific experts, is akin to an eagle amongst the serpents. Whether they realise it or not, they surely need one. The eagle's scope of vision and perspective enable a correlation between distant objects or events, and ensure the enduring, rather than temporary success.

In fact, an information security auditor team should have two types of strategists on board. One of them must be directed at the team itself, defining and maintaining its long-term, large scale development goals, intent, programmes and plans. This is typically the role of the dedicated team manager. The other kind should be focused on the strategic aspects of different information security assessments *per se*. These, as was elaborated earlier and in great detail, include assembling and disassembling the summary of risks, producing high-level conclusions and risk reduction advice, etc. This could be the ISMS expert within the group, even though depending on its composition and aims, other viable alternatives are possible. If there is a need to formalise these important roles, the first can be called the internal (centred on the auditors), and the second – the external (focused on the auditee) strategist. Again, in a small team that handles a limited number of clients both roles can sometimes be fulfilled by the same person.

However, could the same individual perfectly combine both tactical and strategic functions without losing the offered security assessment service's quality and depth? In theory, this is possible. The phenomenon of the winged serpent is widely reported in dragon-centric mythology but is, apparently, exceptionally rare to be seen. So, how can we reach the productive union between the eagle and the snake? The 'boydian approach' towards flexible and adaptive command and control, or '*leadership-monitoring-appreciation-error correction flow*', is as directly relevant for the auditors as it can be. To quote Colonel John Boyd himself:

- *Decentralise, in a tactical sense, to encourage lower-level commanders to shape, direct, and take the sudden/sharp actions necessary to quickly exploit opportunities as they present themselves. Centralise, in a strategic sense, to establish aims, match ambitions with means/talent, sketch flexible plans, allocate resources, and shape focus of overall effort.*

Now you can simply substitute the '*low-level commanders*' by the '*narrowly focused specialists*', to get an accurate, eagle-sighted recommendation.

Science and art of information security evaluation

'Science must become art.'

Carl von Clausewitz

In medieval times, being able to follow the approved cannon to the last detail was considered a hallmark of a master artist or craftsman. It was aspired to as the pinnacle of advancement. Later, when the Renaissance arrived, some deviation from the prescribed standards finally became acceptable. As time passed by, this slack was widening more and more, providing the necessary space for innovation and the unorthodox. The norms were broken, stereotypes discarded, and new principles created from the ashes of the old. Eventually, this process brought us the Enlightenment, then the Industrial Revolution, and then modern science and engineering as we know it. At the same time, valid discoveries of the past were not dismissed and remain in good use, not to mention that we still marvel at the artworks of maestros of old. At least in Europe, this entire transformation of scholastics and craft into science, art and contemporary engineering took about a millennium. Notice that the arts were leading, and sciences following.

40 years ago, the majority of critical information was still disseminated by personal contact, on paper, over the phone or via unencrypted radio transmissions. The first message over the ARPANET was sent at 10.30 pm on 29 October 1969. It was supposed to be 'login', however the system crashed and it turned into 'lo'. So, the very first remote log-in over a packet switching network encountered a severe availability problem that could also be viewed as a passive security incident of a kind.

Only 10 years ago, the greater part of hackers, even the most malicious ones, were computer enthusiasts who wanted to prove a point. A phrase commonly ascribed to Kevin Mitnick is 'because I can'. Nowadays, it is either cybercriminals, casually linked to organised crime with money laundering channels, or sly insiders advancing their personal agendas via illicit means. To effectively counter these rapidly developing threats, information security must fully evolve into proper science and art as we speak. This cannot wait for centuries to happen. Information security auditing, which is more of an art right now, could take the lead.

Unfortunately, the rigid approaches to information security assessments that can be clearly described as 'craft and scholastics' are still abundant and they do have numerous acolytes. Security auditors that strictly follow the exact prescriptions whether coming from standards, textbooks or various forms of professional training, strongly resemble the medieval craftsmen. Their colleagues, who fiddle with these prescriptions applying limited creativity and imagination, are similar to their counterparts from the Renaissance times. This would not address modern day information security threats and risks, especially when it comes to deliberate, planned and timely attacks that tend to come as a total surprise.

When discussing the art of (military) intrusion, the MCDP 1 *Warfighting* elaborates that:

- *There are three basic ways to go about achieving surprise. The first is through deception—to convince the enemy we are going to do something other than what we are really going to do in order to induce him to act in a manner prejudicial to his own interests. The intent is to give the enemy a clear picture of the situation, but the wrong picture. The second way is through ambiguity—to act in such a way that the enemy does not know what to expect. Because he does not know what to expect, he must prepare for numerous possibilities and cannot prepare adequately for any one. The third is through stealth— to deny the enemy any knowledge of impending action. The enemy is not deceived or confused as to our intentions but is completely ignorant of them.*

A proper information security assessment should be able to counter all three key elements of surprise. The adversaries' options are very much limited by their target's weaknesses. *Deception* can be confronted with thorough reconnaissance and evaluation of security gaps. This produces the right information security state picture that no opponents are able to distort. *Ambiguity* can be defeated by decent analysis and prioritisation of risks. Thus, their reduction will be fully adequate. *Stealth* can be refuted with select measures based upon the detailed scenarios of attacks. These scenarios should exhaust all valid choices the potential assailants might have. However, there is no universal panacea recipe that can successfully stand against all three.

Instead, the auditors need to adapt a flexible, evolving system or framework of knowledge based upon extensive observations and security research. This is the science half. By having a go at formulating fundamental information security auditing principles and systematising strategic, operational and tactical assessment approaches, we have tried our best to advance it as far as we could. It might be a complete failure, and it is up to the readers to judge – on the grounds of their own practice, either as auditors or the audited. This living experience, in fact, constitutes the art side of the subject. The only way to express the art of information security auditing is via effective action and its wholesome results. Incidentally, this is exactly how Carl von Clausewitz distinguished between science and art:

- *Science when mere knowing; Art, when doing is the object. The choice between these terms seems to be still undecided, and no one seems to know rightly on what grounds it should be decided, and yet the thing is simple. We have already said elsewhere that knowing is something different from doing. The two are so different that they should not easily be mistaken the one for the other.*

The further astute, apt and detailed definitions of both, on the strength of their actual applicability and functionality, are provided within the MCDP 1 *Warfighting*:

- *Various aspects of war fall principally in the realm of science, which is the methodical application of the empirical laws of nature. However, science does not describe the whole phenomenon. An even greater part of the conduct of war falls under the realm of art, which is the employment of creative or intuitive skills. Art includes the creative, situational application of scientific knowledge through judgement and experience, and so the art of war subsumes the science of war. The art of war requires the intuitive ability to grasp the essence of a unique military situation and the creative ability to devise a practical solution. It involves conceiving strategies and tactics and developing plans of action to suit a given situation.*

This excerpt provides a perfect substrate for the very final 'substitution exercise' to conclude this tome, as we could not agree more.

BIBLIOGRAPHY

Information and IT security sources

A Practical Guide to Managing Information Security, Purser S, Artech House (2004). ISBN 1-58053-702-2.

Beyond Fear: Thinking Sensibly About Security in an Uncertain World, Schneier B, Springer (2003). ISBN 978-0387026206.

CISSP All-in-One Exam Guide, Fourth Edition, Harris S, McGraw-Hill Osborne Media (2007). ISBN 978-0071497879.

Effective Information Security Strategy, Torner J, Presentation, California State, San Bernardino (2004).

Establishing a System of Policies and Procedures, Page S, Process Improvement Publisher (1998). ISBN 978-1929065004.

Hacking Exposed Cisco Networks: Cisco Security Secrets and Solutions, Vladimirov A, Gavrilenko K and Mikhailovsky A, McGraw-Hill Osborne Media (2005). ISBN 978-0072259179.

Handbook of Research on Information Security and Assurance, Gupta D, Jatinder N and Sharma, S K, Information Science Reference (2009). ISBN 978-1-59904-855-0.

Information Assurance: Managing Organizational IT Security Risks, Boyce J and Jennings D, Butterworth-Heinemann (2002). ISBN 978-0750673273.

Information Security Management Handbook, Sixth Edition, Volume 1, Tipton H F and Krause M, Auerbach (2007). ISBN 978-0-8493-7495-1.

Information Security Management Handbook, Sixth Edition, Volume 2, Tipton H F and Krause M, Auerbach (2008). ISBN 978-1420067088.

Information Security Management Handbook, Sixth Edition, Volume 3, Tipton H F and Krause M, Auerbach (2009). ISBN 978-1420090925.

Information Security Policies and Procedures, Second Edition, Peltier T R, Auerbach (2004). ISBN 0-8493-1958-7.

Information Security Policies, Procedures, and Standards: Guidelines for Effective Information Security Management, Peltier T R, Auerbach (2001). ISBN 978-0849311376.

Information Security Risk Analysis, Second Edition, Peltier T R, Auerbach (2005). ISBN 978-0849333460.

Insider Threat: Protecting the Enterprise from Sabotage, Spying, and Theft, Cole E and Ring S, Syngress Publishing (2006). ISBN 1-59749-048-2.

IT Governance: A Manager's Guide to Data Security and ISO27001/ISO27002, Calder A and Watkins S, Kogan Page (2008). ISBN 978-0749452711.

Managing a Network Vulnerability Assessment, Peltier T R, Auerbach (2003). ISBN 978-0849312700.

Network Security Technologies and Solutions (CCIE Professional Development Series), Bhaiji Y, Cisco Press (2008). ISBN 978-1587052460.

No Tech Hacking: A Guide to Social Engineering, Dumpster Diving, and Shoulder Surfing, Long J, Syngress Publishing (2008). ISBN 978-1-59749-215-7.

Open Source Security Testing Methodology Manual (OSSTMM 3), Herzog P, ISECOM (2009).

Open Web Application Security Project (OWASP) Testing Guide Version 3, Meucci M, (Project Leader) et al. OWASP Foundation (2009).

Penetration Testing and Network Defence, Whitaker A and Newman D, Cisco Press (2005). ISBN 978-1587052088.

Schneier on Security, Schneier B, Wiley Publishing (2008). ISBN 978-0470395356.

Secrets and Lies: Digital Security in a Networked World, Schneier B, Wiley Publishing (2004). ISBN 978-0471453802.

Security Planning & Disaster Recovery, Maiwald E and Sieglein W, McGraw-Hill/Osborne (2002). ISBN 0-07-222463-0.

Service Design, ITILv3, The Stationery Office (2007). ISBN 9780113310470.

Service Operation, ITILv3, The Stationery Office (2007). ISBN 9780113310463.

Service Strategy, ITILv3, The Stationery Office (2007). ISBN 9780113310456.

Social and Human Elements of Information Security: Emerging Trends and Countermeasures, Gupta M and Sharman R, Information Science Reference (2009). ISBN 978-1-60566-036-3.

Tactical Exploitation or 'The Other Way to Pen-Test' or 'Random Pwning Fun Bag', Moore D and Valsmith H (2007).

The Art of Deception, Mitnick K D and Simon W L, Wiley Publishing (2002). ISBN 978-0764542800.

The Handbook of Information Security, Volume 1, Bidgoli H (editor), Wiley Publishing (2006). ISBN 978-0-471-64830-7.

The Handbook of Information Security, Volume 2, Bidgoli, H (editor), Wiley Publishing (2006). ISBN 978-0-471-64831-4.

The Handbook of Information Security, Volume 3, Bidgoli, H (editor), Wiley Publishing (2006). ISBN 978-0-471-64832-1.

The Official Introduction to the ITIL Service Lifecycle, ITILv3, The Stationery Office (2007). ISBN 9780113310616.

Wi-Foo: The Secrets of Wireless Hacking, Vladimirov A, Gavrilenko K and Mikhailovsky A, Addison-Wesley Professional (2004). ISBN 978-0321202178.

Writing Information Security Policies, Barman S, Sams Publishing (2001). ISBN 978-1578702640.

Zen and the Art of Information Security, Winkler I, Syngress Publishing (2007). ISBN 978-1-59749-168-6.

General/military strategy and related sources

A Discourse on Winning and Losing, Boyd J, Presentation (1992).

Chaos Theory for the Practical Military Mind, Durham S E, A research paper presented to the Research Department, Air Command and Staff College (1997).

Clausewitz, Nonlinearity and the Unpredictability of War, Beyerchen A, International Security, 17:3 (Winter, 1992), pp. 59-90.

Clausewitz on Strategy: Inspiration and Insight from a Master Strategist, von Ghyczy et al. A publication of The Strategy Institute of The Boston Consulting Group, Wiley Publishing (2001). ISBN 0-471-41513-8.

Coping with the bounds: A Neo-Clausewitzean Primer, Czerwinski T J, Institute for National Strategic Studies at the National Defence University (NDU) Publication (1998). ISBN 1-57906-009-9.

Game Theory, Second Edition, Hargreaves S P, Taylor & Francis (2007). ASIN B000PMG93A.

Learning to Lead: A Workbook on Becoming a Leader, Bennis W and Goldsmith D, Basic Books (2003). ISBN 978-0738209050.

Mastering The Art of War, Lui J, Zhuge L, translated and edited by Cleary T, Shambhala (2005). ISBN 978-1590302644.

Masters of War. Classical Strategic Thought, Handel M I, Routledge (2009). ISBN 978-0714681320.

MCDP 1 Warfighting, US Marine Corps, Distribution: 142 000006 00 (1997).

MCDP 1-1 Strategy, US Marine Corps, Distribution: 142 000007 00 (1997).

Military Methods of the Art of War, Sun P, translated with a historical introduction by Sawyer R D, Barnes & Noble (1998). ISBN 978-0760706503.

On Single Combat, Kernspecht K, Wu Shu Verlag Kernspecht (1997). ISBN 978-3927553071.

On War, von Clausewitz C, edited with an introduction by Rapoport A, Penguin Books (1968). ISBN 0-14-044427-0.

On War (indexed edition), von Clausewitz C, edited and translated by Howard M and Paret P, Princeton University Press (1989). ISBN 0-691-01854-5.

One Hundred Unorthodox Strategies, Battle and Tactics of Chinese Warfare, Sawyer R D and M L Sawyer, translated with a historical introduction and commentaries, Westview Press (1996). ISBN 978-0813328614.

Organic Design for Command and Control, Boyd J, Presentation (1987).

Organic Design for Command and Control, Boyd J, edited by Richards C and Spinney C, Presentation (2005).

Patterns of Conflict, Boyd J, Presentation (1986).

Patterns of Conflict, Boyd J, edited by Richards C and Spinney C, Presentation (2005).

The 33 Strategies of War, Greene R, Profile Books (2007). ISBN 978-0143112785.

Bibliography

The Art of War, Sun T, translated by Cleary T, Shambhala (1988). ISBN 978-0877734529.

The Art of War, Sun T, translated by Sawyer R D, Barnes & Noble (1994). ISBN 978-0813319513.

The Black Swan: The Impact of the Highly Improbable, Taleb N N, Random House (2007). ISBN 978-1400063512.

The Book of Five Rings, Musashi M, translated by Cleary T, Shambhala (1993). ISBN 0-87773-868-8.

The Concise 33 Strategies of War, Greene R, Profile Books (2008). ISBN 978-1-86197-998-8.

The Essence of Chaos, Lorenz E N, Taylor & Francis (2007). ASIN B000PUB6YO.

The Essence of War, Leadership and Strategy from the Chinese Military Classics, Sawyer R D, translated and edited, Westview Press (2004). ISBN 978-0813390499.

The Seven Military Classics of Ancient China, Sawyer R D and Sawyer M L, translation and commentary, Basic Books (2007). ISBN 978-0465003044.

The Strategic Game of ? And ?, Boyd J, edited by Richards C and Spinney C, Presentation (2006).

The Tao of Spycraft: Intelligence Theory and Practice in Traditional China, Sawyer R D, Basic Books (2004). ISBN 978-0813342405.

The Thirty-Six Strategies of Ancient China, Verstappen S H, China Books & Periodicals (1999). ISBN 978-0835126427.

Your Own Intelligence Service (Rus.), Ronin R, Harvest (1997).

ITG RESOURCES

IT Governance Ltd. sources, creates and delivers products and services to meet the real-world, evolving IT governance needs of today's organisations, directors, managers and practitioners. The ITG website (*www.itgovernance.co.uk*) is the international one-stop-shop for corporate and IT governance information, advice, guidance, books, tools, training and consultancy. *www.itgovernance.co.uk/iso27001.aspx* is the information page from our website for these resources.

Other Websites

Books and tools published by IT Governance Publishing (ITGP) are available from all business booksellers and are also immediately available from the following websites:

www.itgovernance.co.uk/catalog/355 provides information and online purchasing facilities for every currently available book published by ITGP.

www.itgovernanceusa.com is a US$-based website that delivers the full range of IT Governance products to North America, and ships from within the continental US.

www.itgovernanceasia.com provides a selected range of ITGP products specifically for customers in South Asia.

www.27001.com is the IT Governance Ltd. website that deals specifically with information security management, and ships from within the continental US.

Pocket Guides

For full details of the entire range of pocket guides, simply follow the links at *www.itgovernance.co.uk/publishing.aspx*.

Toolkits

ITG's unique range of toolkits includes the IT Governance Framework Toolkit, which contains all the tools and guidance that you will need in order to develop and implement an appropriate IT governance framework for your organisation. Full details can be found at: *www.itgovernance.co.uk/products/519*.

For a free paper on how to use the proprietary Calder-Moir IT Governance Framework, and for a free trial version of the toolkit, see *www.itgovernance.co.uk/calder_moir.aspx*.

There is also a wide range of toolkits to simplify implementation of management systems, such as an ISO/IEC 27001 ISMS or a BS25999 BCMS, and these can all be viewed and purchased online at: *www.itgovernance.co.uk/catalog/1*.

Best Practice Reports

ITG's range of Best Practice Reports is now at *www.itgovernance.co.uk/best-practice-reports.aspx*. These offer you essential, pertinent, expertly researched information on an increasing number of key issues including Web 2.0 and Green IT.

Training and Consultancy

IT Governance also offers training and consultancy services across the entire spectrum of disciplines in the information governance arena. Details of training courses can be accessed at *www.itgovernance.co.uk/training.aspx* and descriptions of our consultancy services can be found at *www.itgovernance.co.uk/consulting.aspx*.

Why not contact us to see how we could help you and your organisation?

Newsletter

IT governance is one of the hottest topics in business today, not least because it is also the fastest moving, so what better way to keep up than by subscribing to ITG's free monthly newsletter *Sentinel*? It provides monthly updates and resources across the whole spectrum of IT governance subject matter, including risk management, information security, ITIL and IT service management, project governance, compliance and so much more. Subscribe for your free copy at: *www.itgovernance.co.uk/newsletter.aspx*.

Lightning Source UK Ltd.
Milton Keynes UK
05 April 2011

170368UK00001B/70/P

9 781849 280358